DATA WAREHOUSING WITH ORACLE

An Administrator's Handbook

Sima Yazdani

Shirley S. Wong

To join a Prentice Hall PTR
Internet mailing list, point to
http://www.prenhall.com/mail_lists/

Prentice Hall PTR
Upper Saddle River, NJ 07458
http://www.prenhall.com

Library of Congress Cataloging-in-Publication Data

Yazdani, Sima
Data warehousing with Oracle: an administrator's handbook/Sima Yazdani, Shirley S. Wong
p. cm.
Includes index.
ISBN 0-13-570557-6
1. Database management. 2. Oracle (Computer file) 3. Relational databases. I. Wong, Shirley S., . II. Title.
QA73.9.D3Y39 1997
005.74'068—dc21 97-110661
CIP

Production Editor: *Kerry Reardon*
Acquisitions Editor: *Mark L. Taub*
Cover Designer: *Scott Weiss*
Cover Design Director: *Jerry Votta*
Marketing Manager: *Dan Rush*
Manufacturing Manager: *Alexis R. Heydt*

Prentice-Hall, Inc.
A Simon & Schuster Company
Upper Saddle River, New Jersey 07458

Prentice Hall books are widely used by corporations and government agencies for training, marketing, and resale. The publisher offers discounts on this book when ordered in bulk quantities.
For more information contact:
Corporate Sales Department
Phone: 800-382-3419 Fax: 201-236-7141
E-mail: corpsales@prenhall.com
or write: Prentice Hall PTR
One Lake Street
Upper Saddle River, NJ 07458

Printed in the United States of America

10 9 8 7 6 5 4 3 2 1

ISBN 0-13-570557-6

Prentice-Hall International (UK) Limited, *London*
Prentice-Hall of Australia Pty. Limited, *Sydney*
Prentice-Hall Canada Inc., *Toronto*
Prentice-Hall Hispanoamericana, S.A., *Mexico*
Prentice-Hall of India Private Limited, *New Delhi*
Prentice-Hall of Japan, *Tokyo*
Simon & Schuster Asia Pte. Ltd., *Singapore*
Editora Prentice-Hall do Brasil, Ltda., *Rio de Janeiro*

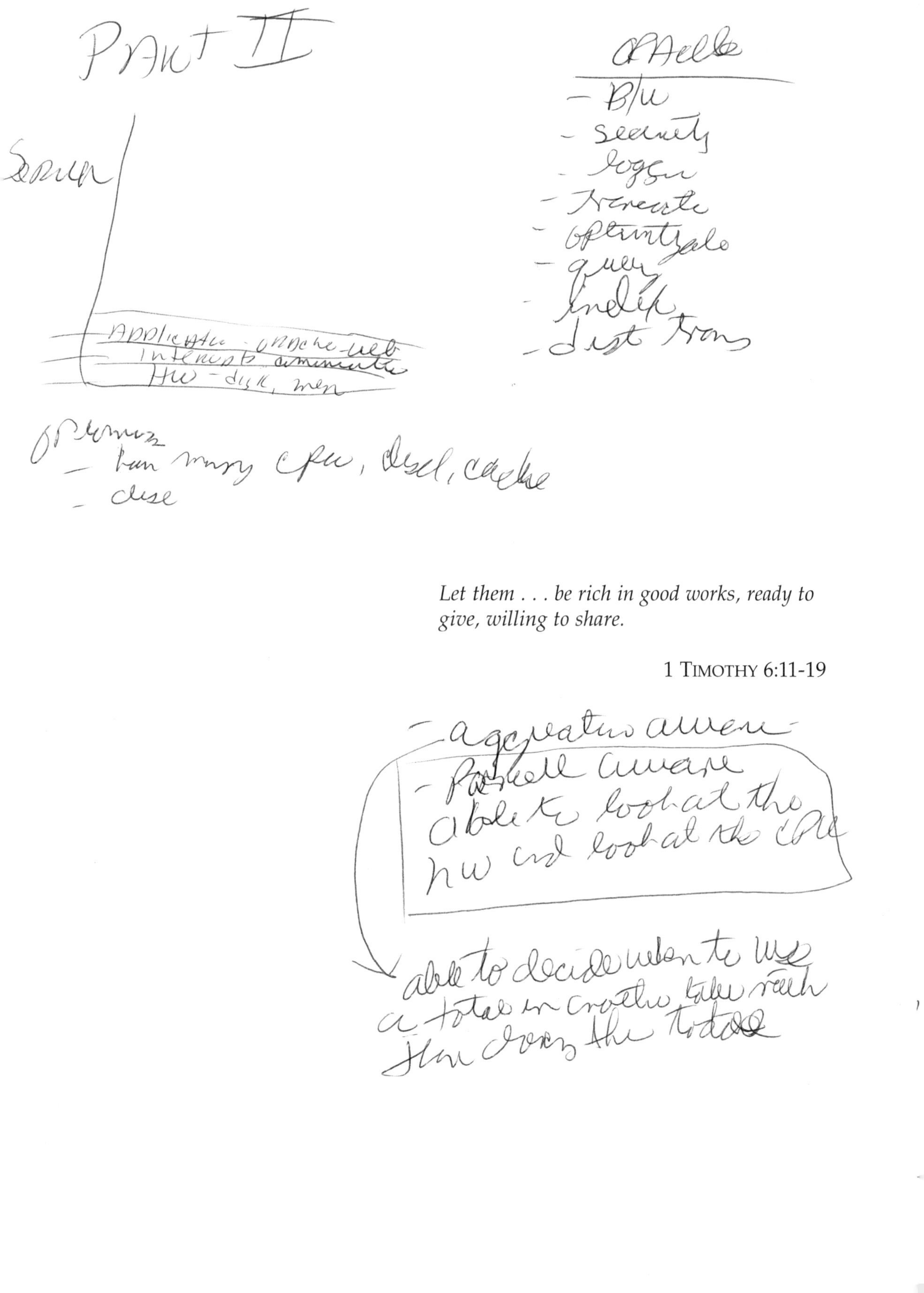

PART II

Let them . . . be rich in good works, ready to give, willing to share.

1 TIMOTHY 6:11-19

Client

Server

System Global area

Shared SGA

Database buffer

Redo logfile

SMON PMON DBWR LGWR

Index

tmp

Data

System

Redo log

Control

Init

- Crash loss transaction integrity

-

what is in the header of a data block?

BLOCK

- Header

- datafile

- table

- rows

- % free/used

- which rows trans

- committed

Loosely coupled system

oracle

oracle

DB

Oracle parallel system

Contents

Preface

Databases have become a critical and integral part of an enterprise, especially in the business world where performance related business indicators are monitored very closely. Relational databases have finally gained the acceptance they deserve and have come a long way since Dr. E.F. Codd's early proposal in 1969 in an article entitled *A Relational Model for Large Shared Data Banks*.[1] The advances in software systems engineering, database, and networking technologies are paving the way for powerful, strategic, and intelligent database applications. Information systems as the backbone of today's enterprise capture as much operational data as they can accommodate. Operational data are usually generated throughout the life cycle of a business process. They are simply the main objective record of transactions in an enterprise.

Some enterprises or organizations have to operate and react in a very fast paced, competitive, global market. In such environments, online tracking and the study of business indicators are crucial in making good and sound strategic decisions. The challenges and inefficiencies involved in the process of resolving these kinds of conclusive and complex inquiries have created major information technology opportunities. The data warehouse database application has emerged as the natural solution. Its charter is to meet the needs of proactive business analysts, planners, and executives for whom the concept of **time to market** and **smart planning** are essential. Despite the inherent customized and individualized nature of these applications, there are a lot

[1]E. F. Codd, A Rational Model for Large Shared Data Banks, CACM, 13:6, June 1970.

of commonalities in the optimization and management of their structure that can be modeled and from which much can be learned.

These applications are often very data intensive and voluminous. They generally consist of business-sensitive data, rely heavily on server and database technologies, must provide intelligent user interfaces, and must be distributed over multiple systems. This type of infrastructure requires planning and the implementation of solutions using the latest technologies with robust database engines, and tools. Oracle's relational database management system, Oracle Server, can be used as the back-end database server. In general, Oracle has been a popular choice when implementing database applications that require a powerful and robust database engine.

Presently, the number of data warehouse applications installed or under development is growing with considerable speed. According to a survey conducted by the Data Warehouse Institute in 1996, more than 50 percent of data warehouses are using Oracle. This large market share demands highly skilled information technologists who can build and optimize Oracle Data Warehouse applications. The inherent challenges in these types of applications are often hidden or discovered too late and consequently, become resource intensive and costly to resolve. It was common with network or hierarchical database applications for database administrators to get involved only after the application was designed and developed. This should not be the case for a data warehouse application that is based on a relational model. Relational database models by their very nature have already reduced the gap between the logical and physical views of the application compared to the two previous models, that is, the network and hierarchical models. With the extensions to the original SQL and the introduction of procedural capabilities to the database languages, a considerable portion of the application logic can now be stored in the database. This was illustrated in Kevin Owen's 1996 book titled *Building Intelligent Databases with Oracle PL/SQL Triggers & Stored Procedures*.[2] Therefore, database administrators can essentially be responsible for the integrity and quality of both the code and the data stored in the database. To stay on target and be able to meet the demands, database administrators must become familiar with not only the nature and usage of the database, but also the **end-users' goals** and **resource needs** of the database application. Inadequate

[2]Kevin Owens, *Building Intelligent Databases with Oracle PL/SQL Triggers & Stored Procedures*. Prentice Hall.

awareness of these critical factors and lack of familiarity with user needs can result in data warehouse applications that are not as effective as they are projected to be. The most common symptoms are limited availability, poor performance, limited scalability, inadequate data quality safeguards, and insufficient data security mechanisms. These symptoms end up becoming expensive for the Information Technology organization and its users, and also hours of painful, torturous, unproductive tactical firefighting on the part of database developers and administrators. Most of their highly skilled resources are spent on emergency fixes and enhancements rather than being spent on creating innovative methods to retrieve the hidden business-impacting knowledge from gigabytes and terabytes of data.

We have presented solutions in a proactive and strategic approach to the whole concept of data warehouse administration. The premise of this book is twofold. First, it promotes the **design-level solution** for these common problems so that they can be avoided. The Oracle 7 complex architecture and its extended SQL implementation provide the appropriate database server to meet these database administration objectives. Second, it promotes **engineering planning.** Based on our experiences and observations, inadequate in-depth understanding and sensitivity toward the end users' business coupled with oversight in addressing the performance, scalability, and security while the application is built will definitely increase the maintenance cost and impact the quality of the data warehouse.

This book provides sound and practical inputs to understand, plan, create, and administer an Oracle-based Data Warehouse application. It represents a subjective approach to Oracle-based Data Warehouse development and administration. It is based on an Oracle Database Administrator's view of the whole picture. This book also covers the concepts and fundamentals of an Oracle system architecture and demonstrates how to take advantage of specific features to achieve a high quality data warehouse application in a cost-effective manner. This book clearly describes the common infrastructure-related tasks involved in building a well-designed, scalable, properly managed, and secure data warehouse using Oracle. It provides approaches, plans, templates, and techniques that can facilitate monitoring and optimizing these kinds of applications while observing the reliability, security, performance, and storage capacity requirements. These approaches can be adapted to most data warehouse development projects. They are applicable throughout the analysis, design, and build stages of the project. The guidelines and solutions offered in this book can help avoid making costly mistakes and set the foundation for an extensible data warehouse application.

This book brings thousands of hours and dollars of experience to the reader and is a must for anyone considering architecting and administering a data warehouse application using Oracle server.

ORGANIZATION

Part I provides a big-picture definition of a data warehouse application from a Database Administrator's perspective. This part serves as the foundation for the rest of the book. It reviews the fundamental definitions and provides a frame of reference for data warehouse concepts. This part covers the major characteristics of a data warehouse. One crucial success factor that we emphasize is the definitions and clarifications of what a data warehouse mission and objectives should be from the business users' perspective. In this section, a distinction is made between the role of a relational database management system and a multidimensional storage system. Furthermore, a new responsibility referred to as data quality management is discussed. The target audiences for Part I are enterprise analysts, information systems executives, and anyone who is motivated to learn or is new to the data warehousing concepts. We did not make this part too technical; instead we focused on making it easy to follow so as to serve as a road map.

Part II examines the role of an Oracle database server in a data warehouse architecture. The role of a database is described along with the challenges and opportunities of having an Oracle-based Data Warehouse. To become familiar with the administration issues of an Oracle database in a data warehouse context, the system architecture is reviewed. Part II also outlines the strategies and types of system resources required for a data warehouse infrastructure. It provides guidelines for preparing input to the resource capacity planning process from the applications perspective. These inputs are derived from every stage of a data warehouse application life cycle. This part touches on topics such as file and memory structure, configuring, and tuning. It describes the steps involved in the design and physical creation of an Oracle database optimized for a data warehouse. It also covers the issues and challenges a system or database administrator may face and have to address. Part II provides a checklist of procedures that need to be in place to facilitate the ongoing support and administration of the Oracle database. The target audiences here are technologists, developers, DBAs, system administrators, and information systems managers.

Part III provides a synopsis of Oracle technology. We provide an introduction to basic database concepts, relational modeling, and SQL language. It also provides in-depth coverage of Oracle's Relational Database Management System (RDBMS) architecture, configuration, and Oracle's extension to SQL including PL/SQL. The target audience here is newcomers to Oracle, the data warehouse, or database technologies and concepts. This part serves as a quick reference to Oracle's technologies.

Below is a data warehouse functional road map.

Data Warehouse Topics	Relevant Chapters
Why Data Warehousing?	Chapters 1, 2, 3
Architectures	Chapters 6, 7
Data Modeling and Design	Chapters 2, 4
Infrastructure	Chapters 9, 10
Development Methodology	Chapter 2, 5, 7
Data Quality	Chapter 5
Meta Data	Chapters 4, 7
Tools	Chapters 4, 7
Performance Optomization	Chapters 8, 11
Database Administration Tips	Chapters 13, 15
Introduction to SQL, PL/SQL	Chapters 13, 15
Oracle Server Technology	Chapters 6, 8, 14

ACKNOWLEDGMENTS

Sima: First and foremost, I would like to thank my children, Setahrae, 9 years, and Hamid, 13 years, who often asked, "When are you going to be done with your book, Mom?" I thank them for being patient and for reminding me what life is all about. Also, thanks to my husband, Mansoor, who encouraged me when I first received the offer and has continued his support. Much gratitude to my parents, Dr. Ebrahim and Dr. Tayebeh Yazdani, for providing me with a loving, intellectual and stimulating environment in which to grow up. I often recall my father saying, "One can achieve anything one wishes as long as the desire is strong. . . ." Finally, I would like to thank Shirley for making this whole book a reality. Her invaluable attention to my personal and professional well-being, the book's content and direction, her penmanship, her affinity for detail, and the overall material organization. I feel extremely fortunate to have her as my role model, my mentor, and enjoy the opportunity to work with her.

Shirley: First, I would like to thank Sima, my co-author and friend, for her friendship, the opportunity to partner with her on this book, and her faith in me. Together, we have gone through long hours and numerous weekends in the trenches trying to meet the book timelines. Secondly, to my family, thanks for their continued support, understanding, and tolerance when I had to dedicate my time and energy to the book. Finally, I would like to dedicate this book to my beloved mother who has given me life, tremendous amounts of love and priceless advice. This book commemorates the immense sacrifices she has made for her children throughout her life.

Both of us would like to extend our special thanks to the following people and organizations:

- Cisco Systems, Inc., especially our CIO Pete Solvik, for extending his support and encouragement for this challenging project.
- Bert Bartow, who introduced the idea of writing a book on this subject, and Mark Taub, the editor who guided us along the complicated path of book publishing.
- Our proof readers and reviewers, Dr. Setrag Khoshafian, Kevin Owens, Clare Liu, Antoinette Hubbards, and Patrick Tse for their time and quality feedback.
- Our past and present managers and team mates in the Corporate Data Warehouse team, who spent countless hours making Cisco's Data Warehouse one of the most successful implementations in the industry.

Thanks to all the people who helped make this book project possible for us!

Sima Yazdani and Shirley S. Wong

About the Authors

SIMA YAZDANI

Ms. Yazdani Javanbakht is an information technology engineer with Cisco Systems of San Jose, California. Ms. Yazdani graduated with a Bachelor of Science in computer systems engineering from Western Michigan University and obtained a Master's degree in computer science from Southern Illinois University. She has worked as a software engineer and as a database administrator in several companies, using Oracle database server technology on various platforms and diverse applications since 1985. In 1994 she joined Cisco Systems data warehouse project as a database administrator and led the infrastructure efforts of the project life cycle from its inception. During the past year she has been responsible for the analysis and architecture of a business performance measurement tool for the data warehouse. On the academic side, she has been conducting research and developing courses on Oracle application development and database administration at the University of California, Berkeley and Santa Cruz Extensions since 1992. The challenges, experiences, and successes involved in Oracle database administration and the Data Warehouse project at Cisco Systems, along with the growing demands for more training materials on Oracle products have inspired Ms. Yazdani to write this book. She is currently conducting graduate level research in the area of information retrieval and multimedia database applications.

SHIRLEY S. WONG

Ms. Wong has had a distinguished career in systems development, management and consulting. She holds a Bachelor of Arts degree in English Literature and has pursued extensive technical and management training. Most of her professional career was with Bank of America Systems Engineering (BASE). She supported their payroll and personnel systems from an application developer capacity, was manager of several BankCard applications, and the last four years prior to her departure, was vice-president and systems director responsible for the bank's statewide retail office automation projects. Since leaving Bank of America, Ms. Wong has been working as an independent project consultant. She conceptualized and successfully implemented a multi-million dollar franchise project for a foreign investor and managed information technology projects for several domestic financial and investment institutions. She is currently a project manager for Cisco Systems' Corporate Data Warehouse team in San Jose, California. The complex challenges of an effective Decision Support System and its potential to positively impact an organization's financial performance have inspired her to co-author this book.

Part I

Data Warehousing Concept and Definition

If like the Creator, I had the whole under control,
Would dismantle firmament, component parts pole to pole
One universe anew, would create where with ease,
The free spirited could have access, to desired noble goal

TRUE TRANSLATION OF HAKIM OMAR KHAYYAM'S ROBAIYAT

Chapter 1

Data Warehouse from a Big Picture Perspective

It is often said, the age of the Industrial Revolution has finally been completed and the world has entered the age of the Information Technology revolution.[1] It is our belief that the need for data warehouse applications is one of the manifestations of this Information Technology age. A data warehouse is becoming more of a necessity than an accessory for a progressive, competitive, and focused organization. It provides the right foundation for building decision support and executive information system tools that are often built to measure and provide a feel for how well an organization is progressing toward its goals.

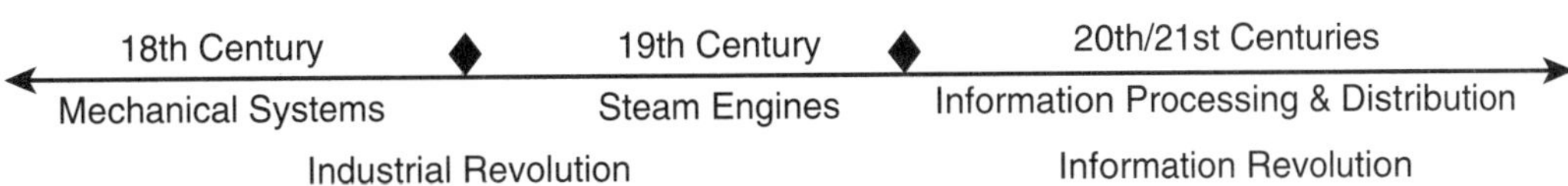

FIGURE 1.1 Information Technology Revolution.

[1]Andrew Tanenbaum, Computer Networks (Englewood Cliffs, N.J.: Prentice Hall), 1989, p. 1.

1.1 COLLECTING OPERATIONAL DATA

Advances in computer and networking technology have led to the introduction of very powerful hardware and software platforms that can collect, manage, and distribute large amounts of pertinent data. In the case of a business application, detailed transactions are often generated during product- or service-related interactions. These transactions are not limited to commercial sectors. They are also found in sectors such as, government, health care, insurance, manufacturing, finance, distribution, education, and so on. Any enterprise that has some computerized

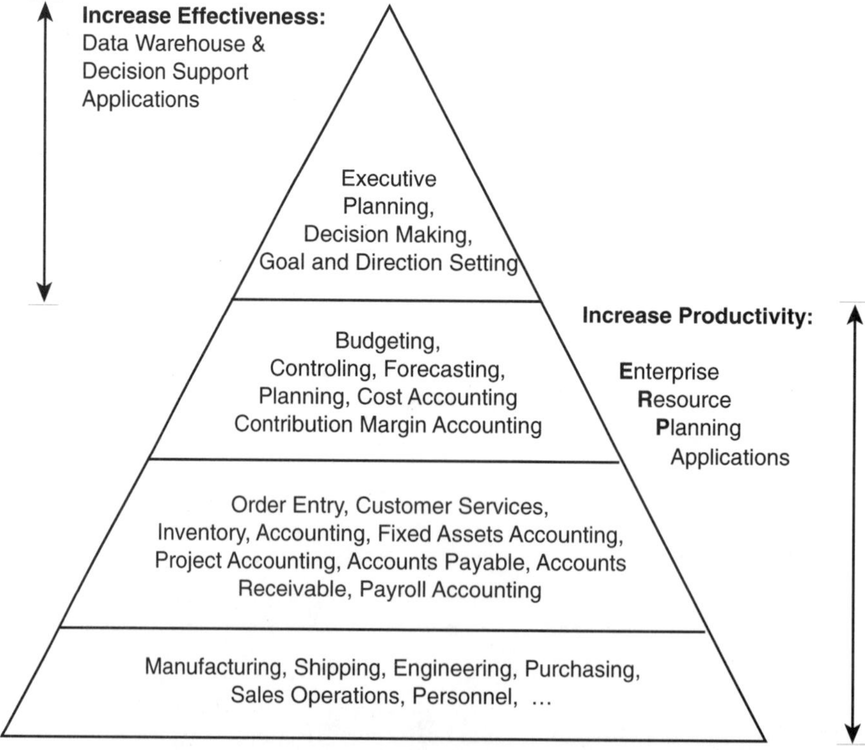

FIGURE 1.2 The goal of a Data Warehouse application in an enterprise is to increase the effectiveness of the enterprise decision-making and direction setting process.

record keeping systems and is interested in deducting or drawing logical conclusions from their voluminous, granular, and detailed information pool should consider building an enterprise-level data warehouse application. These enterprises will then be capable of improving their insights into the trends in their operations and eventually increase the accuracy of their forecasts and plans. The effectiveness of the data warehouse application intensifies especially when the operational data resides in distributed, nonhomogenous systems and replace manual data gathering and reconciliation procedures.

1.2 OPERATIONAL DATA AND ANALYTICAL INQUIRIES

Data is one of the most valuable assets of an organization or enterprise. Enterprises have always been using technology to track and record their organizational data. Below is a sample list of common information categories that are generated throughout the operation of a manufacturing company:

- Order entry
- Product manufacturing
- Financial accounts
- Sales leads
- Customer service
- Human resource
- Inventory

Operational data is the highly structured sets of information that support the ongoing and day-to-day operation of an organization. In case of a decentralized organization, operational data is generated at remote locations sometimes in nonhomogeneous distributed systems (see Figure 1.2). Distributed systems can span many different geographical locations and time zones. They are configured to provide scalability, visibility, and tracking capabilities of business processes. For instance, the order is entered by a customer representative in one site. The financial state of the order is verified at another site. Once approved, it is forwarded to manufacturing to be assembled. Finally, the shipping staff is alerted to fulfill the order that was booked at the remote site. Standard reports or ad hoc queries that inquire about the details of these events are typical examples of operational reports. They are generated on a regular basis. Any delay in their processing will have a significant disruption to the normal operation of that business. Examples of operational reports are

- All the orders and dollar amounts for a particular time period
- All the orders waiting to be fulfilled
- Levels of inventory for a series of product families

The inquiries of a business analyst are typically focused on the trends and patterns submerged in the operational reports. They generally have to generate numerous operational reports and manually correlate and aggregate them before they can see the integrated picture. Their inquiries or business problems are more philosophical than the inquiries of an operations manager. Let us use a simple example to see what are the usage of these inquiries. In a product manufacturing environment and sales operations scenario, operational data consist of:

- products shipped
- orders booked
- product configuration of an order

Product managers and sales managers need day-to-day operational data to monitor their progress toward their goals. The product managers run reports that show the volume of their products which were booked or shipped. The sales managers run reports that show the activities in their respective regions.

Business analysts, on the other hand, run the same reports for different time periods, sales regions, and certain other business criteria. They then extract the pertinent portions and enter them into a spreadsheet. The data is then manually summarized, labeled, categorized, and variances or deviations relationships are calculated. These steps may be repeated for every period or region before they start their research. Generally, they are looking for success or failure factors, patterns of growth, or the revenue changes in products. They will try to analyze to see if there are any clear cause-and-effect scenarios. The results of these types of research are then provided to product managers and sales managers as some sort of "business intelligence" to enable them to better focus their efforts and resources. The end result is better bottom-line performance for the whole enterprise.

As you can see from this example, all parties use the same data sets. The difference are the objective, scope, volume, and time factors of each party's need. The way the data is organized and presented is adequate for the product and sales managers but not enough for the business analysts (see Figure 1.2).

Of course, every organization and enterprise has its own mission, goals, and performance criteria. What is common to all is the difference of data usage and user perspective of the many groups of end users. While one group's need is day to day that is, operational, the second group's need is analytical and research oriented. Here are some examples of analytical questions that are typically considered in a business setting:

- Other than some totals and averages, what else can all these data tell me?
- What contributed to the decline of this trend?
- How can I find out which marketing strategy is more successful?
- How can I sense or gauge the onset of a decline or a surge in a particular market before it starts costing me?
- How can I improve my business forecast to manage my inventory effectively?
- Is there a correlation or common factor that drives these trends?
- What method of forecasting is historically more accurate?

These are the types of inquiries that business analysts are focusing on. They use very interesting algorithms and statistical models to generate business intelligence.

1.3 BUSINESS ANALYST'S DILEMMA

Now that we have become familiar with what some of our users do with the data, let's discuss the topic that is the basis for the existence of information technology (IT). Where exactly is the main problem? What are its characteristics? What can we do to help our users be more effective and innovative?

The problem that analysts are faced with, which we will refer to in this book as the **business analyst's dilemma,** is what we want to address here. We have seen that logistics factors as listed here can negatively impact and slow down efficiency and effectiveness of business analysts' analysis and research capabilities:

- growing volume of data
- data stored in many different systems and formats
- the criticality of quick decision making
- introduction of new products
- market dynamics
- change in organizational strategies

As a result, most business analysts' time are **not** spent in true data analysis but rather in the manual extraction and preparation of data for analysis. The manual process reduces the efficiency and effectiveness of the analysts' deductive processes and ultimately impacts the overall decision-making process. In the case of a fast-paced company and in a very competitive market, this inefficiency is not acceptable.

This problem can be aggravated by a decentralized enterprise model. If certain levels of forecasting and decision making are decentralized, acquisition of different applications may also become decentralized. As a result, the decision to select and build on appropriate Information Systems (IS) application falls into the end users' territory. Based on the deployment approach taken, this can provide the best solution to that department's business problem but potentially generate nonhomogeneous, questionable, poor quality, and inconsistent data to other systems. For instance, an enterprise customer list may be stored in a number of different systems with different formats and conventions. If the users of these data are the same as those who generate them, there may not be any problem. Problems arise when decision makers at the corporate level want to retrieve information to see the revenue generated by only the top ten customers.

In such an instance, more accurate forecasts and the patterns of all elements involved, such as customer behavior, product acceptance, strengths or weaknesses of discount programs, become essential for a good and on-target decision-making process (see Figure 1.3).

Business analysts, planners, and executives who are faced with a fast-paced market and tough competition often find it difficult to pose

FIGURE 1.3 Data in the Data Warehouse is preprocessed and presented such that it facilitates the cross functional monitoring and assessment of the overall enterprise direction. Whereas data in the other operational systems facilitates the management of the specific business functions only.

complex business questions to their existing information system databases. This deficiency eventually impacts their ability to respond to market trends instantaneously. Conventional corporate databases generally store transactional, departmental, and operational data that represent a cross section of an enterprise's day-to-day activities. Executives often feel they do not receive enough useful information from their information system (IS) resources. They are demanding a more flexible, on-line, and integrated system that stores and archives their daily business operation and adapts to their business perspectives and indicators, regardless of **how** data is being collected. This integrated system must be fast, flexible, extensible, and reliable to meet even minimum business requirements. **So, the focus of information technology should be in reflecting the decision makers' view of their business and not on a particular manufacturing or order entry system.** In fact, Dr. Codd, the father of relational model, has acknowledged these requirements and has proposed an extension to the original relational model—the delta model—that is especially designed to address business data specifications and management challenges.

1.4 CONVERGENCE OF MANY COMPUTER TECHNOLOGIES

The infrastructure that supports the data warehouse application relies on the same technologies that most other applications are dependent upon. The difference is in the variety and specialization at the product level that can greatly improve the quality of the data warehouse infrastructure.

Below are some technologies that have made their mark in the data warehouse marketplace. In order to produce a data warehouse that best meets users needs, these underlining technologies have to be evaluated as part of the periodic resource capacity planning. Depending upon the requirements and resources available, the best combination can be selected and configured.

- ❑ Server technology
- ❑ Client technology
- ❑ Database Management System (DBMS) technology
- ❑ Networking technology
- ❑ Mass storage technology
- ❑ Data presentation and publication requirements
- ❑ Software engineering methodology and tools

In addition to the data warehouse goals and user needs, the type of modules that will be built and the format and volume of data that has to be published through data warehouse tools also provide valuable criteria in the technology selection process.

1.5 COMMON CHARACTERISTICS OF A DATA WAREHOUSE

1. Data is divided into three categories:
   (a) Reference and Transaction Data
   - Includes lists, charts, and transaction data from source systems
   - Originally generated in the source systems
   - Can be kept in the data warehouse or an operational data store system
   - Is loaded into the data warehouse on a regular basis
   - Should never change once in the data warehouse (data correction and refresh are exceptions)
   - May be purged from the source
   - Is archived in the data warehouse if purged from the source

   (b) Derived Data
   - Is based on the reference data and certain business rules
   - Can always be re-created
   - Business rules must be approved by end-users

   (c) Denormalized Data
   - Is based on the detailed reference data
   - Is prepared periodically
   - Is the foundation for OLAP tools
2. Enhancements are done in an iterative approach.
3. Enhancements should be based on the overall architecture.
4. One end-user tool may not be adequate for all analytical needs. Depending on the amount of data and type of queries, different end-user tools must be selected.
5. Transaction-level database recovery is not necessary.
6. Data warehouse platform should be tuned for performance rather than quick recovery purposes.

A data warehouse serves as the decision makers' repository of subjectively selected and adapted operational data. It must be capable of handling ad hoc complex, statistical, and analytical queries. To better capture the special features in the business processes and map and integrate them with the operational data, the data solution and modeling of a data warehouse almost always have to be customized. The data requirements of the enterprise is terms of performance, success, and failure criteria are met. A data warehouse design and implementation is more of an art than a science (see Figure 1.4).

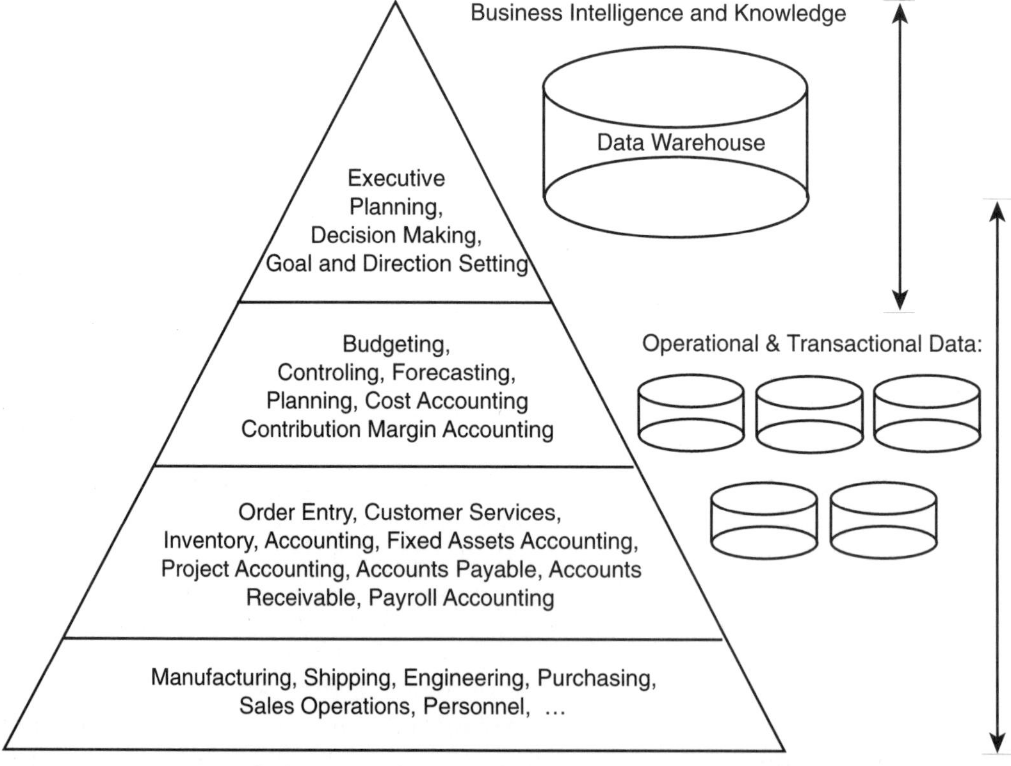

FIGURE 1.4 Data Warehouse provides an infrastructure to collect and process select data elements that are used in calculating enterprise performance indicators.

1.6 KNOWLEDGE DISCOVERY AND DECISION MAKING

1.6.1 DECISION MAKING BASED ON INFORMATION SYSTEM

The solution that information technology provides for the business analysts' dilemma is the concept of data warehousing. It is estimated that the size of a data warehousing market is at least $6 billion.[2] This is due to the fact that a data warehouse application is not something that can be bought. Every organization has its own unique heterogeneous environment and business rules. Therefore, a data warehouse has to be custom-built according to an organization's operational processes and rules. Fortunately, in the last couple of years research articles and guidelines have been published that provide a basic definition and architectural framework to be used as building blocks. Every implementation is different and yet is similar in some aspect. Depending on the architecture, a number of tools along with custom database design applications are employed to reach the desired objectives. One difficulty is the selection of appropriate tools. Keep in mind, not all the tools that are promoted as data warehouse tools are actually the best tools for complex analytical data exploration processing. By the same token, not all system integrators are experienced in implementing a data warehouse. These are issues that an Information Technology (IT) organization must effectively manage as part of the overall data warehouse administration.

As mentioned earlier, data is an asset and must be guarded as such. The implementation of a data warehouse requires a careful project plan that reflects the complexity of technologies, tools, environments, business processes, and most importantly, have the end users' expectations in mind. The scope of this IT opportunity to build a data warehouse does not end with the implementation. The postimplementation and continuous enhancement and extension of the data warehouse may be the most difficult challenge. As will be discussed in later chapters, this challenge can be handled with careful and proactive administration and infrastructure planning initiatives.

The following sequential list presents the decision-making process using a data warehouse. Steps 1 to 4 are done in the data warehouse and steps 5 to 7 are done by the business analysts.

[2]Gartner Group, SDM:R-SDM-101, June 9, 1995.

1. Load a subset of operation data into a data warehouse
2. Integrate new data with the existing data
3. Categorize those data sets into business-user-defined categories
4. Preprocess or calculate the following:
   (a) cross-reference data sets based on predefined criteria
   (b) summaries at different levels
   (c) calculate variances, deviations, and so on
5. Query based on certain factors, that is, products, regions, time periods, and so on
6. Do comparative analysis
7. Present to decision makers

1.6.2 KNOWLEDGE DISCOVERY AND DATA MINING

From an advanced database research perspective, data warehousing is a practical application that can directly contribute and benefit from the following research areas of computer science:

1. Knowledge Discovery in Databases and Data Mining (KDD)
2. Very large and distributed databases
3. Information retrieval
4. Parallel processing

Each of the above research areas has already started to address the challenges of data warehousing and is working hard to produce interesting solutions. The number of papers on data warehousing submitted to the database technology conferences has been unprecedented in recent years.

From a larger perspective, knowledge discovery and data mining has been defined to address the issues information technologists are facing today with mounds of data collected in corporate databases. The main challenge is what techniques can best facilitate the complex analysis and discovery of business intelligence and possibly predictive results from this vast amount of data. The charter for data mining is to provide the computational intelligence to extract targeted and possibly, interesting patterns from these mounds of data. It will help automate the process of presenting patterns, trends, and rules that are being referred to as knowledge hidden in gigabytes of data. The good news is that the topic of data mining is finally being clearly defined by scientists and this will set the foundation for more powerful data warehouse tools.

Data mining approaches and techniques have already proven very effective in two different data-intensive areas: medical information and astronomical surveys. One good example in this area is the research done by the California Institute of Technology published in December 1995.[3] Typically, astronomers collect sky survey information of the Northern Sky using a very powerful space telescope. The amount of information collected is astronomically large, that is, three terabytes of data containing information about two billion sky objects. Astronomers spend years analyzing these survey information in order to learn more about the origins of the universe. A team of scientists from the Jet Propulsion Laboratory (JPL) led by Dr. Usama Fayyad addressed this challenge by developing a powerful software system called the Sky Image Cataloging and Analysis Tool (SKICAT) to increase scientist efficiency by 40 times. By using a high-performance database application that automatically applies the classification rules and techniques, they were able to catalog billions of objects in the sky images in a very short period of time. Using artificial intelligence technology, decision tree techniques, and machine-assisted discovery, they were able to identify 16 new quasars that were formed in the early stages of our universe. This was considered a very important discovery for astronomers.

These types of results are very encouraging and fundamentally beneficial to data warehousing for business applications. The interest of academics in this field will continue to fuel advances for tools and technologies. Knowledge discovery and data mining pioneers have published a systematic process for knowledge discovery and proposed a number of successful application implementation methods. According to this research, data should be **prepared** before data mining and knowledge discovery techniques should be applied (see Figure 1.5). Data preparation in this context consists of

- ❑ Data selection and cleaning (outlier, inconsistency and noise removal)

[3]Usama M. Fayyad, Gregory Piatetsky-Shapiro, Padhraic Smyth, and Ramasamy Uthurusamy, *Advances in Knowledge Discovery and Data Mining*: Menlo Park, AAAI Press/MIT Press, 1996, p. 471.

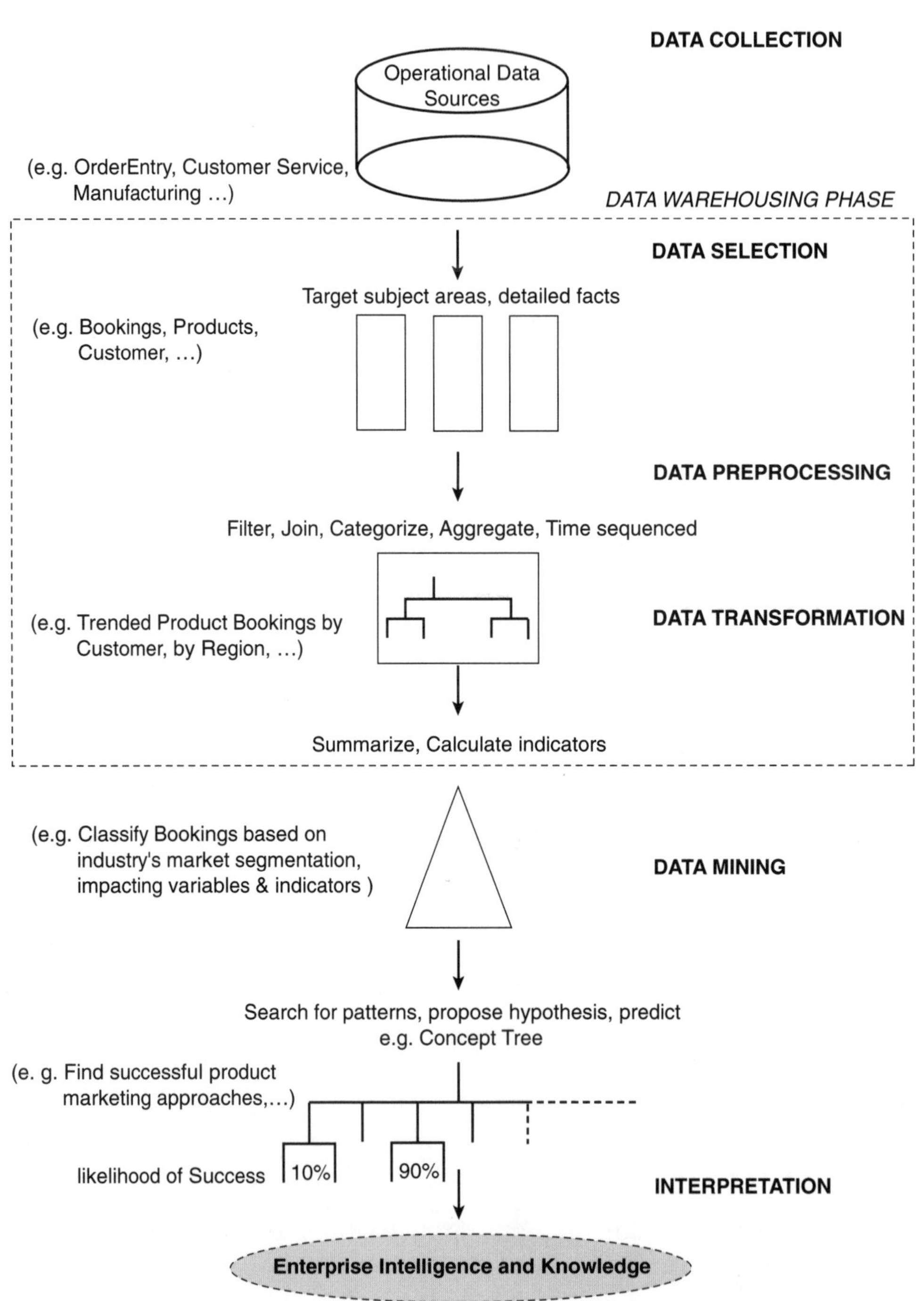

FIGURE 1.5 Data Warehousing in a more comprehensive context of Data Mining and Knowledge Discovery in databases.

- ❑ Categorizing and trending
- ❑ Scaling and calculating indicators
- ❑ Summarization

As we will see in Part II of this book, these steps will directly apply to the main stages of a data warehouse application.

1.7 THREE-TIER ARCHITECTURE

In Section 1.2 we discussed the difference between operational data versus analytical data. Here we will discuss that difference in terms of system architecture. One of the most important characteristics of a data warehouse application is its significant design and usage patterns. This is how it differs from the more prevailent systems that support operational processes, that is, On-Line Transaction Processing (OLTP) database applications. OLTP applications are developed to meet the day-to-day and operational data retrieval needs of the entire user community, whereas data warehouses along with On-Line Analytical Processing (OLAP) tools are being developed to meet the information exploration and historical trend analysis needs of upper management and executive user communities. OLTP transactions are short, high volume, provide concurrent on-line update/insert/delete, and many common procedures and queries. OLAP transactions are long, include infrequent updates but are more efficient in processing numerous ad hoc queries. Information in a data warehouse frequently comes from different operational source systems and is interpreted, filtered, mapped, summarized, and organized in an integrated fashion making it more suitable

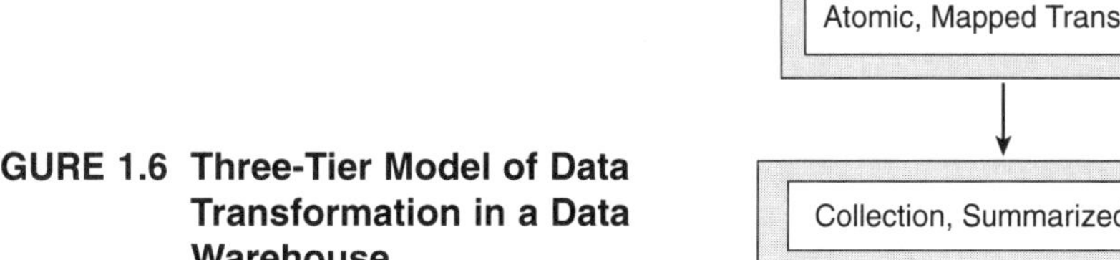

FIGURE 1.6 Three-Tier Model of Data Transformation in a Data Warehouse.

Table 1 OLTP versus OLAP

OLTP	OLAP
current data	current and historical data
short database transactions	long database transactions
online update/insert/delete	batch update/insert/delete
normalization is promoted	denormalization is promoted
high volume transactions	low volume transactions
transaction recovery is necessary	transaction recovery is not necessary
low number of concurrent users	low number of concurrent users
various ad hoc queries	more predefined queries
	requires numerous indexing (apprx 50% data)

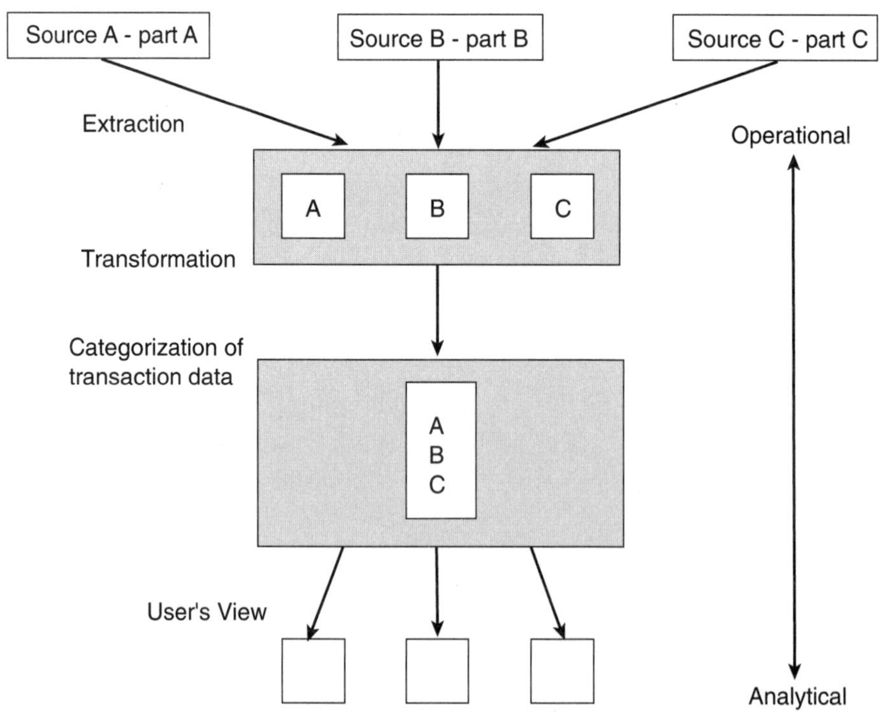

FIGURE 1.7 Three-Tier Architecture.

for trend analysis and decision support data retrieval (see Figure 1.6). Table 1 depicts the major differences between OLTP and OLAP.

One approach that has been recommended by the pioneers of data warehouse design is called a star or collection model. In this approach, based on the common denominator of the user requirements, a small number of cross-referenced or joined data sets are generated from the detailed data sets (see Figure 1.7). As shown in Figure 1.8 the data sets detailing parts, customers, orders, and regions are all denormalized and stored in a star or collection table that is more in line with the users' understanding of the data.

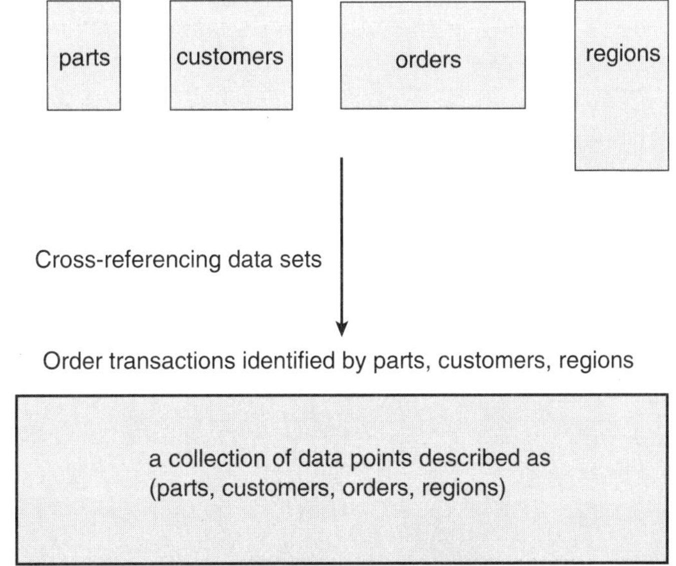

FIGURE 1.8 Implementing the "Star Schema" approach through prejoining of Tables.

Chapter 2

What Makes a Data Warehouse Application Successful?

The previous chapter painted the picture of the decision-making process in an enterprise with lots of operational data. We also discussed the data warehouse application's contribution to the success of an enterprise. Hopefully, that will increase the understanding of our users' challenge in the search for business information and intelligence. It is this empathy along with our interest in applying computing technology that will result in a productive synergy between the technologists and the data warehouse users. This strong synergy will also resolve the business analyst's dilemma issue in regards to an effective data warehouse application. As the saying goes, "necessity is the mother of invention." Imagining the problems of your end users and fully understanding their business processes are the best ingredients for setting the goals of your data warehouse. There is always a general definition and goal for a data warehouse that can be applied to all domains. The important success factor is the adaptation of this high-level goal to the analytical information needs of your particular user community.

One of the simpler definitions of a data warehouse application used in the industry is: **A subject-oriented information store**

designed specifically for decision support.[1] A data warehouse implementation should minimally meet the following goals:

- Reflect the business users' perception of operational data
- Incorporate business-specific classification and indicators
- Allow iterative search and inquiry
- Provide rapid response time
- Render tools and facilities that simplify the recognition of patterns and trends
- Provide appropriate security
- Handle data quality at the load, preprocess, and presentation levels
- Architect a data warehouse that is scalable and extensible

To better define the scope of the goals intended for a data warehouse, define the team's vision and mission statement early on in the project initiation.

2.1 MISSION STATEMENT AS A GUIDING LIGHT THROUGH THE LIFE CYCLE

A clear organizational mission statement is essential in defining the purpose and the direction of all other related action items. Since the data warehouse application is going to be servicing many different groups of users and will constantly go through enhancements, situations may arise where, without this guiding light, members of the project team or users will have a difficult time keeping deliverables within the scope. The mission statement will help project objectives stay within the limit. It should be concise, straightforward, and representative of the essential and identifying benefits of the project and its deliverables.

[1]W.H. Inmon, Using the Data Warehouse, John Wiley and Sons, New York, 1994.

2.2 ROLE OF THE INFORMATION TECHNOLOGY ORGANIZATION

The strategic role of managers of an information technology organization in the development and deployment of a data warehouse application has many aspects. The following are some critical aspects that we have experienced:

1. In partnership with user communities, define and update the mission statement.
2. Facilitate the cross-functional efforts that will be required to identify source systems and reference data.
3. Provide a strategic plan to control the integrity of reference data across different systems.
4. Help define the scope and priority of the deliverables.
5. Provide appropriate development and test tool environments.
6. Identify and nurture creativity among the technical staff.
7. Facilitate and enforce staying up to date with revelant new technologies and tools.
8. Help evaluate the appropriate processing tool and plan for its user support, training, installation, and upgrades.

The first three are especially important. One of the major challenges of a production data warehouse is the proper treatment of reference data. It is not uncommon to see, for example, the **customer name** or **customer ID** of a particular customer represented differently in each of the source systems. Though it is the role of a data warehouse to integrate all these different representations of the same concept, that is, customer, it is also important to develop a strategic plan to proactively treat and standardize reference data at all sources.

2.3 DATA WAREHOUSE APPLICATION AS AN IN-HOUSE SOFTWARE PRODUCT

This topic deserves special attention from the standpoint of quality control. In fact, it is not limited to only a data warehouse application, it should also be applied to any software development effort in an IS department. The reason it is mentioned here is to draw a distinction between the way a data warehouse project is treated compared to other IS project implementations. Treating this application like a software product will automatically raise the quality standards that surround it. The following characteristics should be kept in mind when designing a data warehouse application:

1. Development should follow a specific methodology and life cycle suited for a data warehouse. The principles of software engineering techniques must be reflected in the life cycle.
2. Development tools such as CASE and source code control are essential. Time and resource requirements should be included in the project plan.
3. The cost and benefit of every new enhancement should be thoroughly evaluated and agreed upon.
4. The application should be architected and implemented such that it is easily extensible and maintainable. It is very likely that the technical staff who helped develop the application will be gone by the time the application is in full production.
5. End users should have access to regular training schedules.
6. The monitoring of batch jobs must be straightforward. It should be packaged so it is possible to delegate the monitoring to a totally different IS operation group or a batch scheduling system.
7. Releases and enhancements must be planned like a software upgrade. Conversion of the existing data must be clearly addressed.
8. Integrated testing and standard testing scripts should be formally included in the project plans.
9. A trained customer service person/team needs to be formed to provide assistance to users.
10. All bugs and corresponding fixes must be tracked and archived.

2.4 SOFTWARE ENGINEERING PRINCIPLES

2.4.1 SOFTWARE DEVELOPMENT METHODOLOGY: BLUEPRINT-BASED CONSTRUCTION

Large system software development requires a high degree of discipline and skill sets. The skills used in the architectural design are the

most critical and generally least well developed. Often, the design just happens, with not much consideration for the capabilities or limitations of the components involved. It is one of the goals of this book to enrich the architectural design stage of an Oracle based data warehouse application by providing the database administration perspective to the entire analysis, design, and build phases of the life cycle.
Here are some practical pointers promoting the goodness of software:

1. Be familiar with the Oracle Server architecture and how a transaction is resolved.
2. Be familiar with support challenges so they can be planned.
3. Use traceable and trackable database design and on-going enhancements.
4. Optimize the (application and ad hoc) queries based on Oracle's optimizer.
5. Take advantage of parallel processing at hardware and software levels.
6. Plan and design to have testable, reliable, and quality results.
7. Use object-oriented database design methodology that fits in naturally and ensures a quality implementation.

Despite a lot of research and a large number of proposals and methodologies published in this area, unfortunately, few software development projects in information systems departments deliver high-level architectural specifications. The architectural descriptions that do not contain technical details look more like a work breakdown structure that is not taking advantage of the recent advances in the software engineering arena. One good way to properly address this problem is to have the technical architect and the project manager agree on the development process life cycle and support it throughout the life of the project. One other important issue to consider is in which order different parts of the software system will be implemented, integrated, and tested especially when there are cross-functional concurrent development efforts going on. The coordination and synchronization of these phenomena should be one of the major infrastructure projects supporting the development process.[2]

[2]DCI, Data Warehousing Conference, Chicago, August 1995 and Data Warehousing Institutes Conference, San Diego, January 1997, p. 30.

The information systems management buy-in, support, and encouragement can fundamentally improve the quality of an application's development. In actuality, this concept may seem like an overkill and unnecessary for information system projects, but what we really found is data warehouse applications are too data and process intensive as such, the more reason why one cannot afford to ignore these principles while expecting high quality with a low maintenance cost.

CASE and workflow tools are particularly built to address this problem by facilitating the user requirements, analysis, design, and build stages. Although they are not very easy to use, they present a road map and encourage, remind, and help validate different levels of a development process. They are a necessary infrastructure component.

2.5 CAPITALIZING ON EXPERIENCE, DESIGN, AND ADMINISTRATION TECHNIQUES

Now that we have examined different types of requirements, the concept of **software goodness**, and the overall concept of software quality assurance, it is time to discuss how we can plan and prepare for these challenges in the context of Oracle data warehouse administration. Traditionally, database administrators are called in to rescue during the physicalization of the logical schema, namely, at the end of the development phase and in crisis modes during maintenance. This is not sufficient when we are also focusing on the measurable quality characteristics of the data warehouse. Adding a DBA perspective to the development process will not only address the data and process quality issue but also will enhance it.

In Chapter 14 we will look into the components of a typical Database Management System (DBMS) software. One of the components of such a complex system is the performance monitoring utility. This utility provides statistical information of the system that can help the DBA diagnose and locate the contentions to decide the best optimized approach. In fact, most complex system software comes with such a facility. The size, criticality, sensitivity, nature, and usage patterns of a data warehouse application have often posed as difficult challenges for the administrators (data, database, project, and system administrators). A few of these challenges are:

1. Performance optimization
2. Flexibility
3. Scalability
4. Cost of maintenance
5. Data quality
6. Synchronized data distribution
7. Usage patterns
8. High availability
9. Reliability
10. Security
11. Structural and semantic data integrity

We have found that the best way to address and be prepared for these challenges is to add **data warehouse audits and monitoring systems** to the list of application requirements and consider them like any other user requirements. They must be scoped, analyzed, designed, documented, developed, and released along with other deliverables. Based on the principle of **necessity is the mother of invention**, such systems have been added to medium or large data warehouses only after the fact and after painful drops in quality and user satisfaction ratings.

Furthermore, as with other project requirements, there is no single design solution that is suitable for all data warehouse projects. The good news is we will give you a list of requirements in the subsequent chapters to use as a template that can be adapted to your environment.

2.5.1 PROFILING SOURCES OF DATA

Operational data are continuously generated and support the day-to-day operations of the enterprise. These source systems represent the automated portion of the existing business process. The relationship and the mechanics involved among the modules of the source system with the enterprise business process must be understood and briefly modeled as part of the data warehouse requirements gathering. The entities, attributes, relationships, size, volatility, growth, and constraints of data in source systems are often analyzed at the beginning of the data warehouse project. Once the data warehouse is designed, built, and released, subtle but impacting changes to the source system go unnoticed. The challenge is to manage changes to the data and structures **proactively** based on a plan and process. Another challenge is to avoid constant data **shocks** and **surprises**. These surprises have often contributed to **data quality** issues, which are cited as one of the most common causes of data warehouse project failures. Typically, during the transportation and transformation of the data these changes get discovered. At this stage in the game, solutions are more **reactive** than **proactive**.

To manage these changes proactively, we propose the **system profiling** approach which tracks and monitors data as part of an ongoing analysis. The method proposed here is to build a data warehouse utility module that is responsible for continuous auditing and monitoring of data transportation, transformation, and performance. For the same reasons an enterprise executive can conceptually use the data warehouse to monitor performance, patterns, and trends. A data warehouse administrator requires tools and utilities that automatically collect and monitor the data warehouse usage, capacity, quality, and performance. Administrators of the data warehouse application will eventually need a more extensive application-level monitoring system. They generally monitor quality through manual analysis of the databases' and systems' statistical information. This can be time consuming and, as a result, does not take place as often as it should. For an administrator to be more effective in meeting the quality requirements of the overall application, data warehouse applications must be designed with auditing and monitoring capabilities in mind. From that perspective, we need to start learning more about the source data that might have been collected and buried in user documentation during user project interviews. Administrators will need this information to identify clues that might shed more light on characteristics such as entities, attributes, relationships, size, volatility, growth, and constraints of data in source systems.

They may have to either participate in the Joint Application Development (JAD), Rapid Application Development (RAD), and user interview sessions, or through cross-functional initiatives to ensure that source system information is trickled down to the data warehouse.

Record the following facts in the database for auditing, monitoring, trend analysis, and diagnostic purposes over a period of time:

1. Collect statistics on data volume and demographics as they travel through different stages.
2. Collect the starting, ending, and aborting times of individual functions.
3. Record all database errors and the methods used to resolve them.
4. Audit database access using Oracle's auditing facility.
5. Record the data warehouse uptimes.
6. On an ongoing basis survey end users on their most used queries and criteria.
7. Capture the text of SQL statements from the Oracle Server data dictionary, the shared pool area in the System Global Area (SGA).
8. Encourage modularization by providing module and code templates.
9. Develop a set of test cases and monitor system throughput on a continuous basis.
10. Be sensitive to large surges in volume and number of changes to the source data.
11. Develop management reports and chart report results.

Chapter 3

Understanding Business Users' Views and Definitions of Data

Data collected from different source systems and integrated together in the data warehouse are not useable unless modeled and organized based on the end-users' perspective of the data. The effectiveness of the data warehouse application is a function of IT's understanding of their users' perspective. The following thinking is pretty common in IT departments: "Oh, users don't know what they want. If only they could make up their minds and not change the specs on us, the IT staff, it would have been done by now…." The problem with this kind of attitude is the IS staff is expecting their end users to be like system developers. They totally forget the IS department's role as solution providers to the rest of the enterprise and their own roles in "understanding what users want." After all, it is the IS staff's role to go and enter their users' world, observe their processes, identify their road blocks, and propose effective solutions with their business partner.

The outcome of our understanding the users' perspectives should be thoroughly captured in the data and process modeling efforts and deliverables. These models are basically the **blueprint** or map of whatever projects we are about to build. It will be the place where users and IS come to an agreement prior to starting any build process. In general, during the scoping and high-level analysis phases of the project the following subsections should be considered.

3.1 DATA OWNER

Those users who determine the validity and scope of the reference data, that is, customers, products, forecast data of an enterprise, must be identified as the data owners. They will be the ones who can help define the security and integrity model of the data and will be responsible for data entry and maintenance. If the reference data is a business concept, data ownership is transferred to the user community and if the reference data is specific to a data warehouse system, then the data ownership remains in the IS data warehouse team.

3.2 IDENTIFYING BUSINESS PROCESSES: HOW DATA IS USED

Data collection and business process identification can be done through face-to-face meetings and site visits. IT's role is to introduce information technology solutions and observe the actual usage and manipulation of data, that is, presentations, statistical calculations, and the overall data analysis process. There are numerous terminology concepts, algorithms, calculations, assumptions, and eye balling that are done by the end users that need to be captured. Systems personnel have to put themselves in the users' place to be able to see their viewpoints. Depending on the methodology followed, there are techniques that can be used. An effective and useful technique is to observe how the data from the data warehouse will flow through the organization, what kinds of interpretations or decisions will be made using the data, and how the data is packaged and presented to other people in the organization. Throughout these observations you can begin identifying and classifying those automated analytical processes that will enrich the data warehouse design.

3.3 DEFINING THE DELIVERABLES

Deliverables of the data warehouse project are defined as part of the initial evaluation and scoping of the project. The following aspects of the deliverables should be determined as early in the life cycle as possible in order to reduce the risk of encountering unforeseen issues during rollout:

- time line
- front-end tools
- frequency of update and refresh
- look and feel of the final front-end interfaces
- data sets and attributes in each data set
- cross-reference mapping
- capacity planning
- data administration ownership and utilities

Deliverables should be listed using terminology that is familiar to the users. These deliverables reflect the interest of all the data warehouse user community. The challenge is to find the commonalties and be able to categorize them so that transformation and aggregation of common data sets can be grouped and analyzed together. It is possible that two seemingly different deliverables are based on the same sets of data and criteria of presentation may be the only difference.

3.4 PRIORITIZING THE DELIVERABLES

Depending on the time and resources available, end users along with project managers should provide guidelines as to what and when deliverables will be delivered. Conflict in prioritizing deliverables can be resolved through:

- relationship management
- a steering committee
- a conflict resolution team
- enterprise strategy and mission

3.5 INFORMATION SECURITY POLICIES

Security policy criteria can be discussed and clarified by the owners of the data. It is common for the developers not to be as sensitive as the data owners. The granularity of the security level of database management systems is usually at the database object level, namely...user, table, column, and so on. Whereas, the information security requirements of a data warehouse are often deeper and more data content related. The difference has to be mapped programmatically as part of the information security model of the data warehouse application. Thus, the end users' role in defining the scope of the security model is extremely essential and should minimally include the following:

- identify security layers internal or external to an enterprise
- define sensitive data scope for each layer
- policies to extend or revoke data security privileges
- steering committees and business departments policies

3.6. LEVERAGING THE EXISTING TECHNOLOGY INVESTMENTS

In Section 1.4, we talked about the convergence of many different computer technologies. One of those areas is the DBMS technology. Since the ultimate goal is to produce a solution that meets the decision support requirements of your particular organization, it is possible that the initial releases of the data warehouse will be based on the existing DBMS. The appropriate staffing and skill sets required to support all aspects of a new DBMS should be carefully considered. It is more important to engineer your customized solution and deliver the functionality in order to move forward than spend excessive time in trying to encompass and cover every aspect of new available technologies. The data warehouse should be able to read its raw data from any source. The source systems may be as simple as flat files and as sophisticated as a relational Database Management System (DBMS). The DBMS used as the central repository of the data warehouse can be whatever the IT organization is prepared to support in the following areas:

- database administration
- system administration
- networking configuration
- hardware configuration
- development tools
- technical training

Chapter 4

End-User Data Access Tools

4.1 DATA WAREHOUSE QUERY TOOLS

In recent years, the data warehouse marketplace has seen an explosive growth in the number and varieties of front-end data access tools. They are generally positioned as client/server tools that provide an intuitive Graphical User Interface (GUI) to the unfriendly back-end database server. Also as a means of providing an easy to use point-and-click model that allows the user to identify the data sets and form joins at will without having to write any syntax-rich SQL, they are easy to use. The challenge is to identify a tool that handles the following characteristics:

- Submission of a more optimized query to the database
- Ease of installation, configuration and deployment
- Number of platforms it can support
- Ability to run in the background on the client
- Price per seat

- How simple is it to integrate with other tools, that is, metadata repositories
- Vendor's potential
- A Web interface
- Flexibility of client-level modeling
- Range of statistical, time series, and user-defined functions
- Charting and graphing capability
- Seamless integration with business office tools such as Excel
- User-defined agents that trend the data
- How much data it can handle without impacting performance
- Time it takes to prepare data, making them readable by these tools

To further clarify the specialties of data warehouse tools in comparison with other database application tools used for reporting, it is important to briefly explain the star and snowflake schema.

4.2 DATA MODELING STRATEGY

4.2.1 STAR SCHEMA

The star schema is the outcome of dimensional modeling. This modeling technique starts with the users' intuitive perception of the information collected, rather than the normalized (removing redundancy) relationship existing between data sets. This schema is developed to address the data navigation difficulty and performance issues of highly normalized data models. Dimensions are those categories by which the analyst would like to organize, aggregate, or view data. For instance, a sales business analyst may want to look at the sales information by market segments, periods, products, and geographical regions. Figure 4.1 is a simplified data model representing the sales transaction data, also referred to as Sales Facts, aggregated by corresponding fiscal periods, market segments, products, and region dimensions. In a relational database system, dimensions and fact data sets can be designed using relational tables.

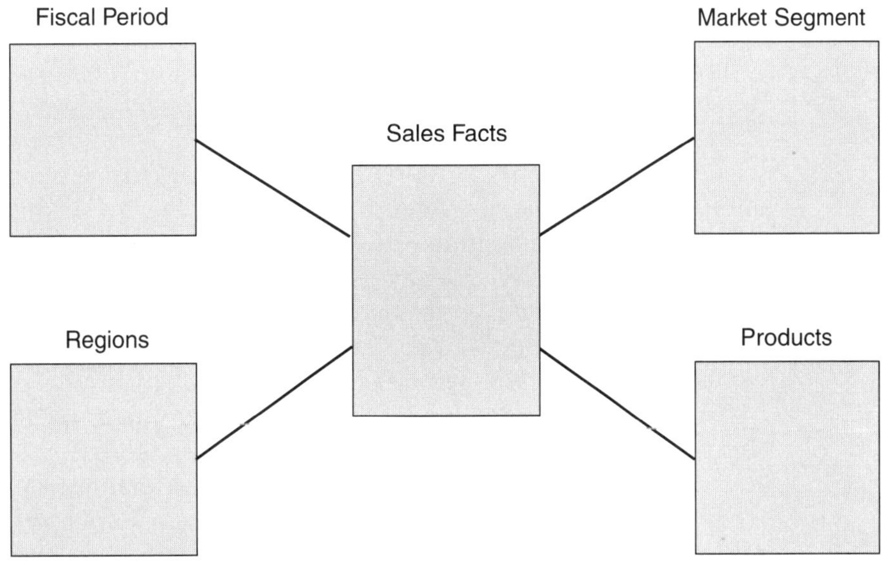

FIGURE 4.1 Star Schema.

4.2.2 SNOWFLAKE OR MULTIFACT TABLE STAR SCHEMA

As the diversity of subjects covered in the data warehouse continues to grow, more opportunities are created to measure and track the enterprise performance and trends from different perspectives. In such situations, the original simple star schema with a single fact table will not be adequate; it must evolve to meet new requirements. One approach is to increase the scope of attributes in the star schema central fact table and increase the number of dimensions. This approach, as time goes by, can gradually turn the **fact** table into a real **fat table**. As more dimensions are added, the level of aggregation decreases, but the level of granularity increases. Even though it seems simpler to model, it will eventually cause serious performance and scalability issues in a large and fast-growing data warehouse. Due to the volume of records in the fact tables and some of the deep hierarchical dimensions, the data selectivity of desired Decision Support System (DSS) gets reduced over time.

In general, aggregation of a large volume of detailed fact data into certain levels of hierarchy, the summarization modules and the ad hoc queries are overburdened with the load, thus impacting performance. For instance, as long as the sales order data is aggregated at the sales theater level, for example, North, South, East, West, the selectivity of a theater is high and the performance is good. Once the sales order data is aggregated by sales manager, for example, if there are hundreds of managers, the selectivity of order data will be much lower. To aid in a situation such as this, a star schema is modified into a snowflake schema to provide more data partitioning. The preferred strategy is to evolve the star schema into a snowflake, also known as the multifact table star schema (see Figure 4.2).

The goal of a snowflake schema is to provide aggregation at different levels of hierarchies in a dimension. This goal is achieved by normalizing those hierarchical dimensions into more detailed data sets to facilitate the aggregation of fact data. It is possible to model data warehouse data into separate groups where each group addresses specific performance and trend analysis objectives of a specific DSS

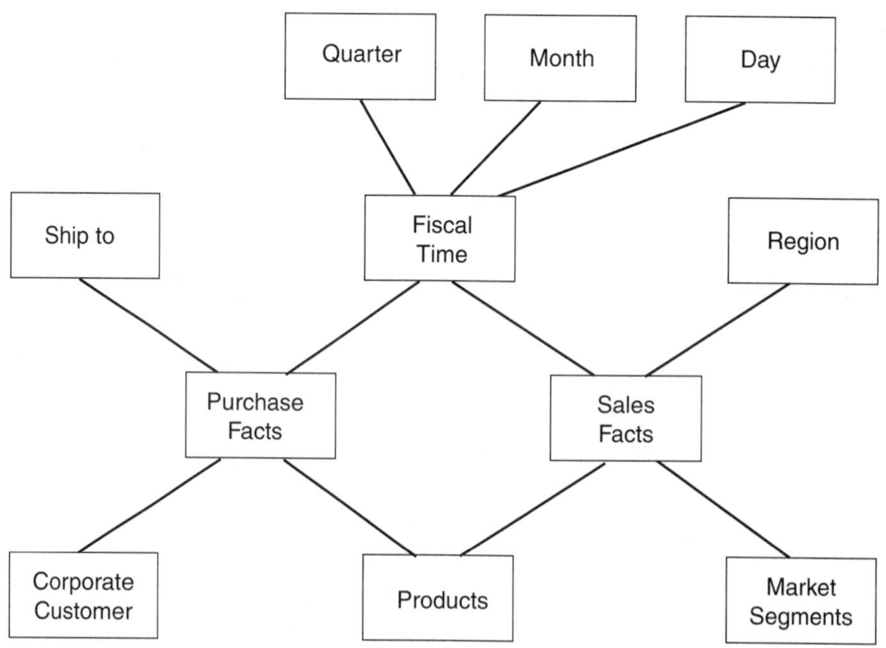

FIGURE 4.2 Snowflake Schema.

user. Each group of fact data can be modeled using a separate star schema. It is possible to have a number of star schemas that have one or more dimensions in common.

Of course, there are other proposed models addressing the more advanced challenges of a large multisubject data warehouse that have not been covered here. A book titled *Data Warehouse Tool Kit*[1] provides an in-depth survey of domain-specific data modeling challenges and the corresponding solutions. The common and central component in most architectures is the database management system, and most probably a relational database management system. We have found that the root cause of some of the costly mistakes in strategic decisions during a database application project life cycle, and more specifically, the difficulties in administering a data warehouse application, has been the lack of attention to the fundamentals of database concepts and software engineering principles. There are numerous other resources that cover these topics in detail. For reference, an introduction to definitions and capabilities of database servers in general and Oracle7 specifically is provided in Part 4.

4.3 AN EXAMPLE OF DERIVING DIMENSIONAL MODELING FROM ER MODELING

As discussed in Section 4.2, multidimensional modeling based on expected special usage is the Entity Relationship (ER) view of data that have been augmented with additional entities, redundant and derived attributes, and relationships. It represents a collective view of interesting data. In Figure 4.3, a few entities are added to the original ER model to represent the business concepts of fiscal calendar, geographical, and product category hierarchies.

4.3.1 START WITH THE ORIGINAL ENTITY RELATIONSHIP MODEL

At a very high level, the source operational system might have all types of system of records and they may not always be based on a relational model. Even if they are based on a relational model, the base Entity

[1]Ralph Kimbal, *Data Warehouse Tool Kit*, John Wiley and Sons, 1996.

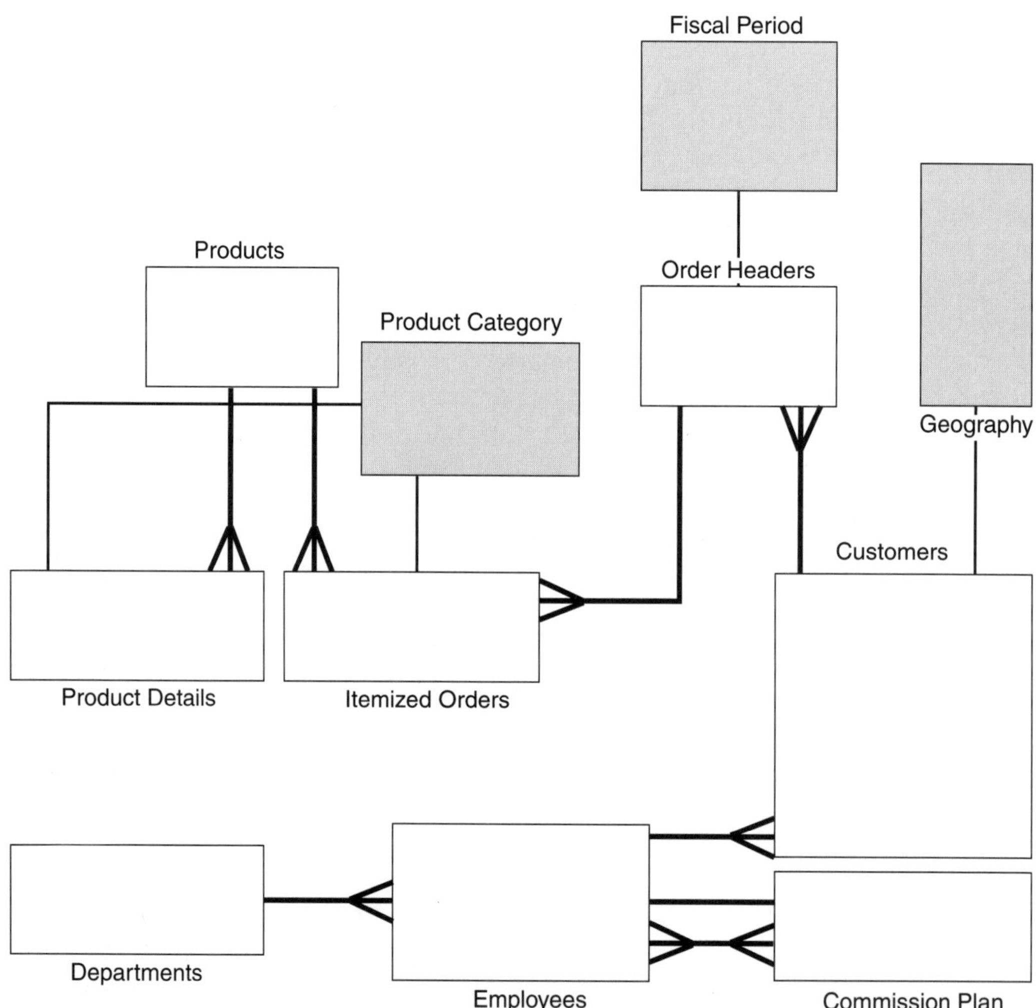

FIGURE 4.3 Simple Entity Relationship Model of a Product Ordering Process.

Relationship (ER) model may not always be published or available. The following process can help in getting the modeling started in a data warehouse so that not only the inherent integrity of the source data continues to be preserved, but it is also conditioned to perform at its best when an aggregated and cross-referenced ad hoc query is submitted.

In most application development methodologies, data modeling is the end result of the analysis and requirements gathering process. In the same context, when modeling a data warehouse repository, the source systems involved along with their system of records need to be thoroughly understood. This will in turn help conceptualize a simpler ER model representing each of the source systems. This exercise also underscores the importance of identifying the following information about each data set:

- Interesting data sets, that is, data sets worth bringing over into the data warehouse
- Interesting data elements and attributes
- The role and purpose of each data set, that is, are they transactional, referencial, or mapping data
- Domain, that is, data type or range characteristics of each attribute
- In the case of attributes referring to a state of a process, understanding the meaning of each status value
- Security requirements of each attribute
- Attributes that compose the primary key for each entity
- Referential integrity among attributes
- The business definition explaining those attributes with meaningless, flexible labels

Example: Assume that by studying a particular product ordering database module of an accounting system, as shown in Figure 4.3, the following tables can be derived. These tables can form the basis of the ATOMIC tables in the data warehouse.

TABLE: **Products**
Contains: **Reference Data**

Product ID	Description
X386	Desktop computer with 80386 chip
X486	Desktop computer with 80486 chip
X586	Desktop computer with 80586 chip

TABLE: Product Details
Contains: Reference Data

Product ID	Standard Price	Start Date	End Date
X386	$2,000.00	10/1/81	1/1/91
X486	$3,000.00	7/7/87	7/7/95
X586	$4,000.00	9/1/89	1/1/97

TABLE: Itemized Orders
Contains: Transaction Data

Item ID	Item Price	Item Total	Order Header	Product ID	Quantity
1	$2,000.00	$8,000.00	PO3444-1	X386	4
2	$3,000.00	$15,000.00	PO3444-2	X486	5
3	$4,000.00	$36,000.00	PO3445-1	X586	8

TABLE: Order Headers
Contains: Transaction Data

Header ID	Customer ID	Order Date	Ship Date	Commission Plan
PO3444-1	ATT-123	7/9/96	8/1/96	Plan A
PO3444-2	BAC-111	6/1/95	7/7/95	Plan B
PO3445-1	MCI-222	5/15/96	6/5/96	Plan A

TABLE: Customer Information
Contains: Transaction Data

Customer ID	Name	Address	City	State	Zip	Phone
ATT-123	AT&T	101 Front St	SF	CA	94105	396-1121
BAC-111	BofA	110 Calif. St	SF	CA	94106	356-2222
MCI-222	MCI	202 Eddy St	SSF	CA	94015	878-5007

TABLE: Employee Information
Contains: Transaction Data

Employee #	Name	Hire Date	Salary	Job Title	Dept.	Commission Plan
323	Mary Doe	4/1/90	50K	Sys Analyst	173	2
271	Harry Win	2/1/88	45K	Admin Asst.	400	3
381	Judy Horn	5/15/94	68K	Manager	459	4
300	Salil Yusoof	8/15/93	80K	Consultant	347	3

TABLE: Departments
Contains: Reference/Mapping Data

Dept. #	Dept. Name	Manager	Location	Part of
347	Cost Accounting	Jeff Shaffer	San Mateo County	173
459	Finance Division	Jannet Lew	Santa Clara	500
172	Network Operation	Gina Skully	San Jose	600
173	Manufacturing	Greg Smith	San Jose	600
500	Administration	Tom Peters	San Jose	500
600	Production	Tom Peters	San Jose	600

TABLE: Commission Plan
Contains: Reference Data

Plan ID	Plan Name	Percent
3	Global Discount	30
2	National Discount	25
4	Regional Discount	40
3	Local Discount	30

TABLE: Product Category
Contains: Reference/Mapping Data

Category ID	Product ID	Category Parent ID
P0000	All_products	P0000
P1001	X386	P0000
P1001X	X386-SW	P1001
P1002X	X586	P0000
P4000-1	X486	P0000

TABLE: Regions
Contains: Reference/Mapping Data

Region ID	Region Name	Region Parent ID
1	EASTCOAST	5
2	WESTCOAST	5
3	MIDWEST	5
5	N.AMERICA	6
6	AMERICA	7
7	WORLDWIDE	
8	EUROPE	7
9	ASIA-AFRICA	7
10	AUSTRALIA	8

TABLE: Market Segment
Contains: Reference/Mapping Data

Segment ID	Segment Name	Customer ID
1	HEALTHCARE	1010101
2	TECHNOLOGY	2020220
3	GOVERNMENT	2020202
4	RETAIL	1010100

4.3.2 MOVE TOWARD A DIMENSIONAL MODEL

The data warehouse should first start with the entities of the conceptual model of the source system. This section illustrates how the data warehouse dimensional database model is an augmentation and a denormalized version, that is, the reverse process of functional decomposition[2] of the original source system conceptual and logical ER model. This augmentation occurs at the physical modeling phase when entities are translated into tables, and referential and domain constraints are translated into database level constraints.

To ensure the preservation of the data integrity, the starting point of the data warehouse dimensional model includes all the tables, as listed in the previous section, as the ATOMIC layer. Surely, when data is imported from multiple and heterogeneous source systems, the translation and integration of data types and domains will add to the complexity of the modeling process. Nevertheless, the solution is in the logical modeling of the ATOMIC tables so that domains are compatible with the merged data coming from multiple source systems. Once the conflicting data types, status codes, classifications, and so on, are resolved at the ATOMIC layer, the remaining dimensional modeling effort is very simple. This topic, resolving the data integration and cleaning issue in the data warehouse, deserves more in-depth discussion, which is not within the scope of this book. For further reference, please refer to a very good reference book.[3]

It is important to emphasize the difference between data modeling for an OLTP database application versus an OLAP database application. This is an area that is new and is often overlooked by even experienced database administrators, application developers, and data modeling professionals. As mentioned earlier, the goal of having a data warehouse should be to represent massive mounds of detailed operational transactions that end users visualize and use for further interpretation or simply for reporting. Thus, the purpose of the data warehouse data modeling effort is not to optimize and ensure the integrity of **create**, **update**, and **delete** database operations. In OLTP type environments, the data model must be optimized to ensure fast

[2]C.J. Date, *An Introduction to Database Systems*, Vol. 1, 5th ed. Reading, MA: Addison-Wesley, 1990.
[3]Ralph Kimball, *The Data Warehouse Toolkit*, Wiley, N.Y., 1996.

update, delete, and create transactions with minimum reference data redundancy. In OLAP type environments the objective is to keep reliable, dependable, and well referenced data organized and categorized in a way so the search, query, and aggregation of the data is highly optimized. Maintaining the referential integrity at the ATOMIC layer ensures records that violate the inherent and intended data integrity and quality are prevented from entering into the data warehouse. In order to ensure the end user's intuitive and relevant data relationships, mappings are represented appropriately and additional entities are allowed to increase data redundancy to the logical model. In summary, the following two basic techniques are used to help move toward the desired dimensional model:

- Introduce new mapping entities illustrating end-user classifications
- Compile highly normalized tables together into COLLECTION tables.

The time dimension is one of the fundemental business classification concepts. Time trending is expressed through dates and calendars. Generally, businesses evaluate their performance based on their fiscal calendars. It is therefore important to model the fiscal calendar in the data warehouse logical model using a time hierarchy. In addition to the time period, there may be many other concepts that are relevant to a particular end-user domain but are not represented in the source system logical model. This may also be a good time to model those concepts and further expand the original logical model.

Time is a simple and common concept and is a good example for illustrating the dimensional concepts of **rollup** and **drilldown**. Figure 4.4 represents this hierarchical relationship.

We can make effective use of a hierarchy model to see the aggregation of certain values or counts at any level of the hierarchy. For instance, product ordering transactions can be aggregated into the following scenarios:

1. Total **daily** order dollars for every product ordered since the beginning of the month.
2. Total **weekly** order dollars for every product ordered since the beginning of the month.

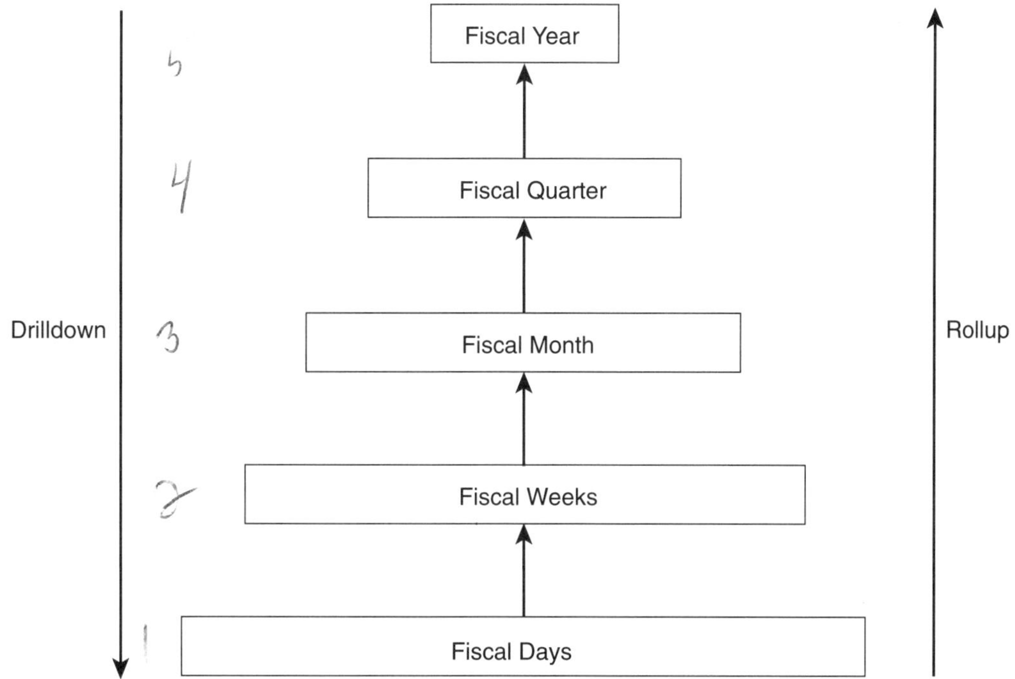

FIGURE 4.4 Time Dimension Hierarchy with Five Levels.

3. Total **monthly** order dollars for every product ordered since the beginning of the year.
4. Total **quarterly** order dollars for every product ordered since the beginning of the year.
5. Total **yearly** order dollars for every product ordered in the past five years.

Moving down from items 1 to 5, the granularity gets more coarse. This is referred to as a **rollup** of order dollars across the time dimension. Moving up from items 5 to 1 is referred to as a **drilldown** of order dollars across the time dimension.

The tables that follow are physical representation of the time hierarchy as described above.

TABLE: **Fiscal Years**
Contains: **Reference Data**

Fiscal Year	Begin Date	End Date
FY96	8/1/95	7/31/96
FY97	8/1/96	7/31/97

TABLE: **Fiscal Quarter**
Contains: **Reference Data**

Fiscal Quarter	Begin Date	End Date	Fiscal Year
Q1FY96	8/1/95	10/31/95	FY96
Q1FY97	8/1/96	10/31/96	FY97

TABLE: **Fiscal Month**
Contains: **Reference Data**

Fiscal Month	Begin Date	End Date	Fiscal Quarter
199601	8/1/95	8/31/95	Q1FY96
1996012	7/1/96	7/31/96	Q4FY96

TABLE: **Fiscal Week**
Contains: **Reference Data**

Fiscal Week	Begin Date	End Date	Fiscal Month
19960101	8/1/95	8/7/95	199601
19961201	7/1/96	7/7/96	1996012

TABLE: Fiscal Holidays
Contains: Reference Data

Fiscal Holiday	Date	Fiscal Week
1996H1	9/2/95	19960201
1996H2	11/28/95	19960404

Once we have identified each of the levels of the time dimension, we can move on and represent a **collective** and **flat** view of the levels of the time hierarchy.

TABLE: Fiscal Month Period
Contains: Time Hierarchy Data

Period ID	Start	End	Days Duration	Period	Fiscal Quarter	Fiscal Year
199701	7/31/96	8/31/96	31	August 96	Q1FY97	FY97
199702	8/31/96	9/30/96	30	September96	Q1FY97	FY97
199704	11/1/96	11/30/96	30	November96	Q2FY97	FY97
199707	2/1/97	2/28/97	28	February 97	Q3FY97	FY97
199601	8/1/95	8/31/95	31	August 96	Q1FY96	FY96

The same process can be adapted to the ATOMIC tables that contain reference data with mapping information. Depending on the data model, the hierarchy can be simple (one parent for every level) or complex (more than one parent level for every level).

The following tables illustrate dimensional modeling of the product category. Let's assume there are only two levels in this hierarchy.

The first table represents just the product family groups that are added.

TABLE: **Product Families**
Contains: **Categories That Include Some Other Products**

Category ID	Category Parent ID
P0000	P0000
P1001	P0000

The second product table is denormalized into a COLLECTION table. It has absorbed the relevant attributes of the other tables (product details and the product category).

TABLE: **Product Hierarchies**
Contains: **Products and Their Extended Attributes**

Product ID	Standard Price	Start Date	End Date	Description	Category ID
X386	$2,000.00	10/1/81	1/1/91	Desktop w/ 80386 chip	P0000
X486	$3,000.00	7/7/87	7/7/95	Desktop w/ 80486 chip	P0000
X586	$4,000.00	9/1/89	1/1/97	Desktop w/ 80586 chip	P1001
X386-SW	$100.00	10/1/89	1/1/99	Software Pak 386	P0000

The above denormalization will help avoid unnecessary joining of tables whenever a search or query operation is requested.

These COLLECTION tables are larger in terms of volume and wider than the individual normalized tables. It is crucial to research and analyze before adding any new attributes. As much as the denormalization and composition can improve performance by avoiding the actual table joins, a blind addition of attributes and widening of each row in a table can decrease the overall effectiveness. Hence, include only the interesting attributes that are explicitly needed for end-user access. As needed, some additional derived values such as classification, indicators, ratios, and so on, are also precalculated and added to every record. One major downside of the COLLECTION table is if the levels of a particular hierarchy increase or decrease, it can require a massive recomposition of the COLLECTION table which can be very time consuming.

One final note in regard to handling dimensions and hierarchies is worth mentioning here. In the above example, the time dimension is called a simple hierarchy because every level has only one parent level. The aggregation and the so called **rollup** of values in lower levels of the tree into the higher levels of the tree are simple to conceptualize and calculate. As a result, most OLAP tools require that the dimensional model include only simple hierarchies. However, in the real world there are many cases where an item has more than one parent item in which case it is referred to as a complex or overlapping hierarchy. For instance, consider the scenario of two employees of the same company who are also the parents in the same family with two children. The program that rolls up the number of employees' children should consider this overlap; otherwise a double counting can occur which is incorrect.

One practical workaround in simplifying the complexity of the overlapping hierarchies is to first learn more about the hierarchy. Often, when it comes to usage, end users tend to focus on a simple portion of the complex hierarchy or tree at a time. Here are some pointers:

- ❏ Identify user requirements and reporting needs that involve simple views of the tree
- ❏ Identify from which level the overlap starts occurring
- ❏ Clarify the assumptions, definitions, and members of each level
- ❏ Identify what establishes the parent relationship at the database level

The next step is to physically partition the complex hierarchy into simple hierarchies or tables suited for each of the end-user perspectives and data access. This creates a complex model which can overburden the data load cycle of the data warehouse. In such a case, the frequency of the refresh process should be weighted against the benefit.

4.3.3 THE STAR SCHEMA

As mentioned in Section 4.2, the beauty of the dimensional modeling is when we start introducing the **fact** tables referencing the members of the dimensions. It is from the combination of fact tables and their corresponding dimensions that the so called **star schema** is evolved. By referencing the fact table in database queries, the following data and I/O intensive tasks that can impact the on-line performance can be avoided:

- Joining multiple tables (usually it becomes resource-intensive if it is more than 4 tables)
- Calculations on the fly
- Aggregation and grouping based on certain attributes

The star schema is just another physical modeling approach following the original conceptual model. The driving factor is how it can produce an optimum performance result for certain frequently used queries. As covered in Chapter 1, the fact tables represent the end users' collective view of mounds of transaction records. The granularity of the fact table depends on the requirements.

For instance, daily product sales is much more granular than the monthly product sales. The mapping information that helps link an attribute in the original source system model to another attribute in the star schema is of utmost importance. This information at best should be included in an on-line metadata infrastructure. At a minimum, the following mapping information should be recorded:

- Conceptual model of the source transaction system
- Derivation of the dimensional physical model
- Derivation of the fact tables supporting the star schema

Preferably, a data modeling tool can be used to record the above models. Oracle Designer 2000 is an acceptable and appropriate tool that can facilitate and expedite the modeling and prototyping process. The following example represents the monthly product sales fact table.

SALES FACTS

Total Sales	Total Units	Avg. Selling Price	Market Segment ID	Product ID	Region ID	Period ID
56505	4342	13.01	1	P1001	2	August 92
43434	3333	13.03	1	P4000-1	3	September 92
32424	344	94.25	3	P1001X	4	November 92
56500	4300	13.13	1	P1001	2	August 93
43400	3300	13.15	4	P4000-1	3	September 93
65456	944	69.34	3	P1001X	4	November 93
87505	442	197.98	2	P1001	2	August 94
43434	35333	1.23	1	P4000-1	3	September 94
324	4	81.00	3	P1001X	4	November 94
56444	42	1343.09	1	P1001	2	August 95
99453	133	747.77	2	P4000-1	3	September 95
12121	244	49.68	6	P1001X	4	November 95

4.4 ON-LINE ANALYTICAL PROCESSING

4.4.1 OLAP (ON-LINE ANALYTICAL PROCESSING)

The term OLAP became a new decision support buzzword back in 1992 with an article published in *Computerworld* by Dr. E.F. Codd. In that article, Dr. Codd evaluated a number of products in the market and found Arbor Essbase as the only one that complied with all the 12 rules. There are reports that the study was commissioned by Arbor Software, but nevertheless, Dr. Codd, as the father of the relational database, added a great deal of credibility to this field of information technology. It magnified the challenges and charted the course for DSS software vendors to focus and deliver.[4]

Dr. E.F. Codd's initial 12 rules of OLAP-capable tools are as follows:

[4] Roman Borguin and Herb Edelstein, *Planning and Designing the Data Warehouse,* (Prentice Hall, Upper Saddle River, NJ), 1997, p. 203.

1. Multidimensional conceptual view
2. Transparency
3. Accessibility
4. Consistent reporting performance
5. Client/server architecture
6. Generic dimensionality
7. Dynamic sparse matrix handling
8. Multi-user support
9. Unrestricted cross-dimensional operations
10. Intuitive data manipulation
11. Flexible reporting
12. Unlimited dimensions and aggregation level

The main objective of OLAP, as seen by Dr. Codd, is the ease of interactive querying followed by a stream of successive queries where the current query is based on the previous ones. The performance should be such that it will aid the end user in their heuristic search for knowledge. If the response time is longer than what an active analytical mind in the midst of a stream of thoughts expects, the tool is not adequate for OLAP. For example, an executive who is focused on finding trends and possible causes for success and failure of their enterprise may need to issue about five successive queries before reaching an interesting view of the data. The response time for resolving each query should be comparable to the speed with which our brain cells process information. If the executive or the business analyst has to wait five minutes for **one** query to come back, this tool would not be sufficiently analytical or friendly. For instance, the user may start with a high-level summary of total sales in all regions and as the area of interest narrows, select one region and drill down to territories in that region. As the train of thought continues, the analyst may decide to isolate the area of search to one product for a particular quarter to see the trend of sales. To reach such a performance the data access layer should be architected, designed, and built so that it utilizes every opportunity to produce fast, heuristic, scalable, and friendly access to the data. The emphasis is on access and not minimizing the update, insert, and delete data anomalies as explained earlier in Section 4.3. To reach these objectives, OLAP software vendors have begun looking for a data storage and query implementation that is more appropriate for data-intensive queries, indexing, compression, and calculations. The result of this approach has led to the birth of the multidimensional database structure sometimes referred to as the multidimensional database (MDD or MDB). They are condensed, indexed data structures that consist of cells of data. Only relevant data across all possible dimensions are stored in each cell. It takes a good dimensional modeling effort targeted to solve the most pressing business questions to make the best use of this special indexing and storing scheme.

The data warehouse query and OLAP tools can be divided into two categories:

1. Low end—limited in terms of volume of data(in megabytes), cost, and OLAP features
   - GQL (www.andyne.com)
   - PABLO (www.andyne.com)
   - Cross Target (www.dimins.com)
   - Business Object (www.businessobjects.com)
   - Cognos Impromptu (www.cognos.com)
2. High end—rich in terms of scalability (in gigabytes) and OLAP features
   - Red Brick (www.redbrick.com)
   - Oracle Express (www.oracle.com)
   - Gentium (www.pmp.co.uk)
   - SAS (www.sas.com)
   - Holos (www.holossys.com)
   - Arbor Essbase (www.arborsoft.com)
   - Kenan (www.kenan.com)

4.4.2 RELATIONAL OLAP—ROLAP

With the expansion of the capabilities of relational database management systems into the true executive information system type application, and OLAP as opposed to OLTP, the concept of a relational-database OLAP (ROLAP) tool has been developed. These tools are definitely a better choice when dealing with hundreds of gigabyte scale volumes of data that can take advantage of multiprocessor servers and large cache memory. They can also understand and interface with a SQL-based relational database. But the cost of deploying ROLAP is much greater than that of an OLAP tool, though currently its the only avenue to meet the scalability and relational database integration challenge. A desired set of characteristics for a ROLAP tool can be:[5]

- Provides a SQL interface
- Generates and submits complex SQL optimized for the RDBMS
- Has a metadata interface
- Monitors usage and can provide input for possible useful aggregated fact tables
- Aggregate interface that suggests to user which aggregate tables to use
- Supports client/server architecture
- Can handle large database with many users

Tools that somewhat fit in this category are:

- Information Advantage (www.infoadvan.com)
- Microstrategy (www.microstrategy.com)
- Informix MetaCube (www.informix.com)
- Oracle Express (www.oracle.com)
- Red Brick (www.redbrick.com)
- Platinum InfoBeacon (www.platinum.com)

4.5 MULTIDIMENSIONAL DATABASE TOOLS SELECTION CRITERIA

The overall selection of the best data warehouse tools is not an easy task, especially when the functionality of these tools is changing rapidly. Therefore, one should not invest too much in one tool and with more functionality showing up with the advances in intranet application architecture, standardization efforts, Java-enabled OLAP tools, 3D visual queries expect more interesting tools to be introduced that may be worth evaluating. The key areas of evaluation criteria to be considered are:

[5]Ibid, p. 215.

1. Functionality
   - Supports desk top platform requirements that is the standard for your IT organization
   - Multidimensional access, view, and analysis capabilities
   - Interface with metadata repository or data dictionary
   - Highly visual, robust, and flexible front end
   - Direct access to the data warehouse database server that is, drill through trending, charting capabilities
2. Scalability
   - Scalability of a number of dimensions
   - Levels in dimensions
   - Total rows in a dimension
   - Number of users
   - Ability to take advantage of SMP and VLM
   - Ability to load data incrementally as opposed to all or none (a total rebuild)
   - Allows users to create custom calculations and groupings in a model and save it
3. Fit with the organization and computing environment
   - Supports IT desktop platform requirements
   - Provides multiuser, shared, and secured access to data across organizational levels
4. Future
   - How adaptive is it to new trends in technology and in coming up with new releases?
5. Application Programming Interface (API)
   - Provides API for popular front-end tools like Microsoft tools and Web browsers
6. Web interface

According to the META group,[6] in addition to the ad hoc query tools that now exist, a new breed of data warehousing tools called **decision groupware** that is independent of the existing OLAP tools will emerge. This new breed can have the following features:

[6]Oracle Corporation, *Oracle Magazine*, March/April 1996, p. 120.

- ❑ Workflow enabled
- ❑ Distributed heterogeneous database access
- ❑ Distributed Object Linking and Embedding (OLE)
- ❑ World Wide Web front end
- ❑ New multimedia
- ❑ Mobile multidimensional analytical querying

Thus, it is vital to plan for evaluating data warehouse tools to be evaluated at least once a year.

4.6 THE DATA CUBE PRESENTATION OF FACT TABLES

Once the fact tables are prepared, depending on the OLAP tools and services selected in the architecture, data cubes may be constructed outside the database server using the information prepared in the fact table. The visualization of more than three dimensions is generally difficult, so only three dimensions of fiscal period, product, and market segment are represented here. Accessing through these data cubes is the focal point of OLAP-ready data warehouse architecture.

Scenario: A market research firm likes to analyze the AMOUNT OF DOLLARS spent for computer upgrades by different segments of the market. Every data point in this space consists of three dimensions namely; product, market segment, and time, known as a "triple" or "data cell."

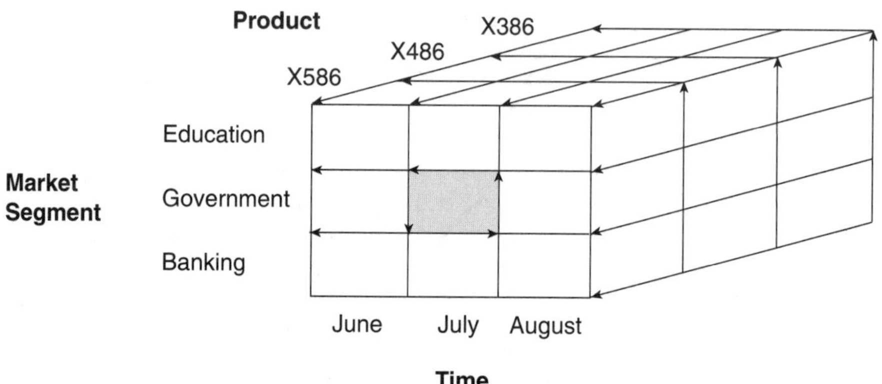

Business executive

What was the total $ spent on X586 upgrades in **July** by **government** agencies?

How does that compare with the forecast $ spent?

Should the future forecast be changed?

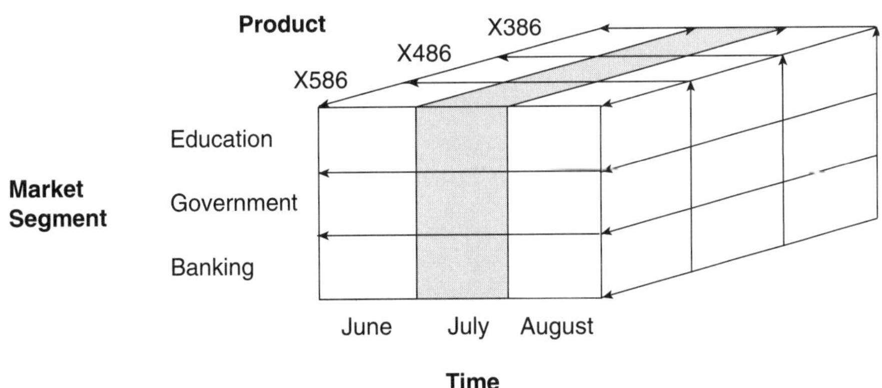

Financial analyst

What was the total $ spent in the month of **July**?

How does that compare with the forecast $ spent?

Should the future forecast be changed?

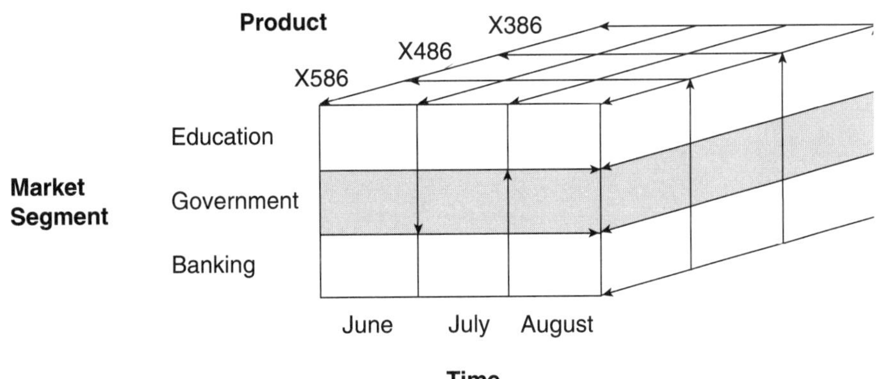

Marketing analyst

What was the total $ spent by **government** agencies?
How does that compare with the forecast $ spent?
Should the future forecast be changed?

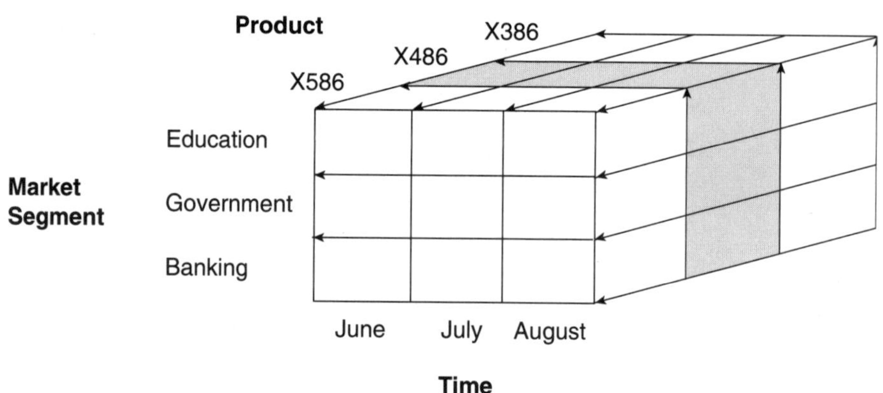

Product analyst

What was the total $ spent on **X486 upgrades**?
How does that compare with the forecast $ spent?
Should the future forecast be changed?

The physical implementation of data cubes are generally done through the use of complex object data storage models and special indexing schemes that are optimized for fast access and retrieval. It is therefore important to plan and perform the incremental updates to the fact table at the database level prior to building the data cubes.

Chapter 5

Data Quality Management: A New Responsibility

5.1 QUALITY ENGINEERING

We would like to start this topic with a quote from Aristotle: "Quality is not an act it is a habit." Almost everyone agrees on the concept of quality and its benefits. It is a self-explanatory discussion. Our intention in this chapter is to provide visibility to this important and actually an essential characteristic of a data warehouse. **Essential** because without it none of the other features of a data warehouse are usable. In fact, all the topics we discussed in the previous chapter have a direct link to the concept of ensuring a quality data warehouse. All the topics and techniques discussed are practical and realistic. What we would like to discuss in this chapter is the question of how to systematically implement quality in the context of a data warehouse application. What method is realistic, practical, effective, and long lasting? What can we do to ensure high-quality data and process in our data warehouse application? Of course, there are many correct answers to these questions.

Unless an explicit attempt is made on the part of a data warehouse manager and administrator to have **quality** visible in every level, the requirements for implementing a quality data warehouse are usually underestimated. As a result, when the time comes to expect quality results or enforcements, we will notice that there are not enough time or resources to improve quality—at which point compromises and last minute decisions are made trying to do the job that should have been done throughout the life cycle of the data warehouse.

The good news is that ensuring quality in the data warehouse is not an impossible or unrealistic commitment. There has been much research with good implementation done in this area. The elements that can guarantee the quality are the strong belief and support from management and the belief and technical training of the staff. The support of management ensures that enough time and resources are set aside to implement the tools and techniques that can assist delivery of high-quality data warehouse products. Below are some suggested measures for quality and data warehouse administration that can be customized for any given environment.

Measures of Quality

- ❑ Customer service
- ❑ Business and technical content
- ❑ Continuous tangible deliveries
- ❑ Alignment with business needs

Data Warehouse Administration Focus

- ❑ Data warehouse as a component of the enterprise's overall information architecture
- ❑ Establish procedures and checkpoints
- ❑ Testing criteria, procedures, and models
- ❑ Auditing criteria, procedures, and models
- ❑ Use of automated monitoring of the database to support proactive administration

5.2 SOME LESSONS FROM ISO 9001 STANDARDS

Data warehouse development can use many of the lessons used in other branches of engineering. Some of our favorite ones are the guidelines published by the International Standards Organization (ISO) called ISO 9001. They are simple, clear, and practical. The following characteristics of a data warehouse application make it a good candidate for applying ISO 9001 quality standards:

1. Intensive use of computer resources
2. The ongoing and iterative data warehouse development
3. High rate of turnover among the data warehouse developers
4. Dynamic nature of source systems, business rules, and views

ISO 9001 guidelines have proven very effective in many engineering fields, especially software engineering. Implementing quality control on software is not an easy task. As will be discussed in Part II, data warehouse application development can become a much less painful process if it is treated like a software product that is to be developed and released to the end customers, especially from the aspect of ease of maintainability. The four following guidelines are the basic pillars of ISO 9001:

1. Document the procedure
2. Follow the procedure
3. Document what was supposed to be done and was done
4. Document what was supposed to be done but was not done

They are simple to remember and simple to apply at any stage. Naturally, every stage has to be translated into special processes and deliverables. At this point, the challenge is how to apply these steps to a data warehouse development process. In our opinion, the actual method can be different in various environments and can be a function of the team members' creativity. The end result is the ensurability of quality.

5.3 DATA QUALITY IS A DISTRIBUTED RESPONSIBILITY

In Part I we discussed the topic of the "data owner" in a data warehouse. Data owners provide the definition and the business process surrounding the birth and use of those data. Once data is defined and brought into the data warehouse, ensuring its quality becomes a "shared" responsibility between data warehouse implementors, that is, the IS group, and the data warehouse sponsors, that is, business user groups.

This shared responsibility fuels the cooperation of these two groups. The generation of the business requirements serves as the implementation of the first step of the ISO 9001 guidelines. **Document the procedure** irrespective of the methodology used. The design and development phases are equivalent to the implementation of the second guideline; **follow the procedure**. Most IT application development projects are similar up to this point only but fall short where the two last guidelines are concerned. Last minute and undocumented changes to the data structure, data definition, processes, and infrastructure can strategically and potentially lower the quality of the data warehouse. This is one of the major challenges of all IS applications, especially for a data warehouse. Most quality issues in IS applications that we have observed generally resulted from not following these last two guidelines. We therefore emphasize the importance of being aware of and focusing on implementing the last two ISO 9001 guidelines: **Document what was supposed to be done and was done** and **document what was supposed to be done but was not done**.

Poor data quality of a data warehouse may be the result of an undisciplined practice which does not consider internal software applications having a critical impact on the business. As a result, enhancements and changes, such as updates to data models, application code versioning, testing, application code review, design review, are all downplayed and overlooked. As a result, the commitment to follow a methodology which serves as a road map along with the quality of the end result falls through the cracks.

To avoid this unpleasant dilemma for our data warehouse, we need to ensure that everyone who is involved in the project—end users, managers, developers, and administrators—minimally follow these four basic guidelines of the ISO 9001 or its equivalent.

If following these guidelines requires more resources, make that very clear to the project sponsors from the beginning. It is much better to plan and set expectations at the beginning rather than later. As long as the procedures are well documented, the resources allocated will be used effectively. Otherwise, often the organization has to add more expensive resources to manage a poorly planned application if implementation of quality is compromised and overlooked in the early stages. By following these basic guidelines, it is possible to reach the famous quality concept of a **zero defect** product. You would be surprised how willing end users are to spend money to get the appropriate resources to ensure data quality and a well-managed data warehouse.

5.4 APPLYING ISO 9001 TO DATABASE APPLICATION DEVELOPMENT[1]

Figure 5.1 identifies the deliverables involved in every major milestone of a database application development process regardless of the tool set used. At every one of these milestones, we have the opportunity to review ISO 9001 guidelines, namely,

1. Document the findings and model.
2. Implement the model.
3. Document what was implemented.
4. Document what was in the model but was not implemented.

5.4.1 QUALIFYING AND QUANTIFYING SYSTEM REQUIREMENTS

At a very high level, Figure 5.1 portrays the logical description (that is, the functional model, conceptual model, and logical data model), the physical description (that is, application model, database physical design, and application) and database object implementation that are required when implementing a database application. A data warehouse application is not an exception and can greatly benefit from this methodology. The object is to isolate opportunities that can help to identify boundaries of what **data quality** translates into in the data warehouse implementation.

As we saw in Chapter 1, the data warehouse application is that layer of custom code that further processes the raw operational data and provides more usable, timely, and comprehensive information to data analysts and strategists within an organization. In general, as with any software system development, it is important that the data warehouse be implemented within the scope of the **mission statement** and have

[1]John A. McDermid, *Software Engineer's Reference Book*, Butterworth Heinemann, Oxford 1991. p. 17/4.

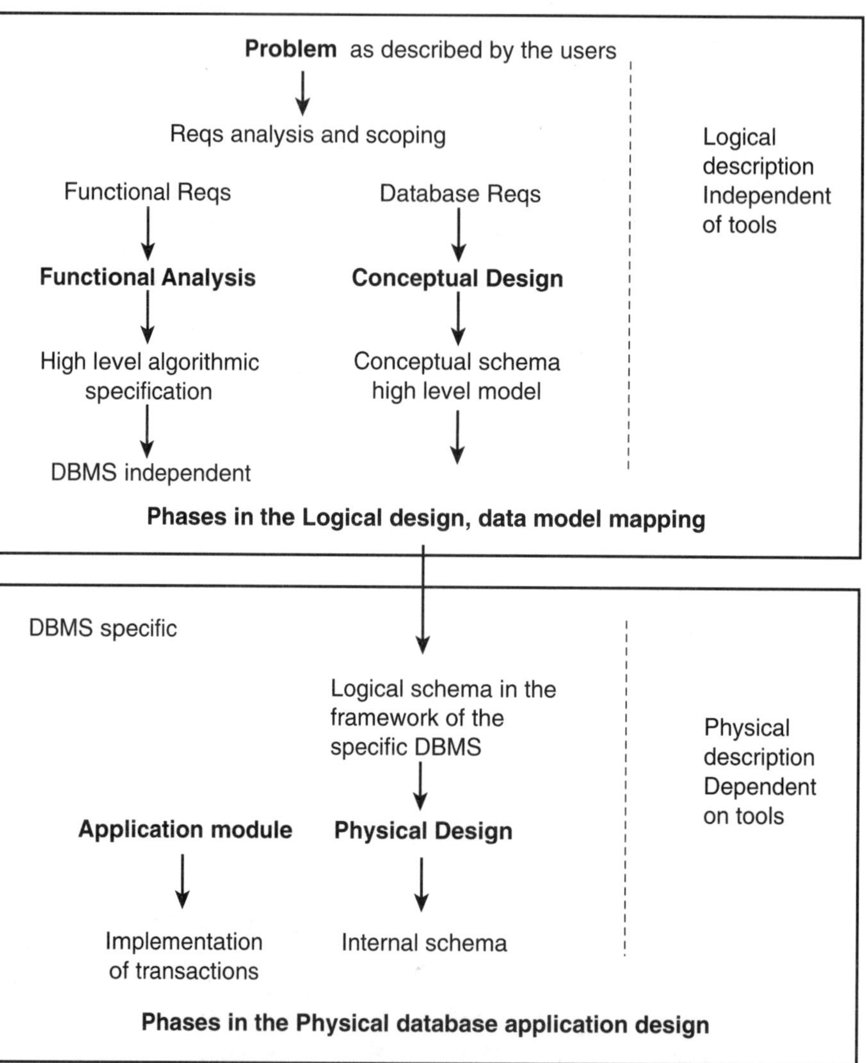

FIGURE 5.1 Documentation Milestones of a Database Application.

clear goals addressing the requirements. Complying with software engineering principles automatically guides the development process and provides techniques to assure that the goals and objectives are met. Unfortunately, with the advances in application development tools, developing software with no or minimal compliance is not only possible but also very attractive for those who are focused on delivering just **something**. This approach is reinforced by the fact that the lack of compliance in software development, unlike other material product development, may not initially be apparent. How many systems do you know of that were put together and were deployed successfully initially but started requiring enhancements from day 1?

Over time the issues of changes in the business process, scalability, and data diversity challenge the constraints built into the system, the weaknesses of the design, and installation. The question is what can best be done to avoid, at worst minimize, this costly and predictable occurrence? Here is an approach that can lead the data warehouse application toward being a **well-designed and solid system** that will also fulfill an organization's overall mission. In a business context, the data warehouse application should eventually help generate revenue, automate and simplify data analysis efforts, and enable data analysts to apply their intellectual power toward more sophisticated data mining and creative ways of interpreting their data.

Generally, the requirements of a system can be divided into three categories:

1. Functional requirements
2. Direct quantifiable requirements
3. Unquantifiable requirements

5.4.2 FUNCTIONAL REQUIREMENTS

The high-level functional requirements are generally captured during the specification gathering sessions and are recorded in the form of text documents. When describing requirements, it is important to relate the concept of each requirement to a measurable property. These requirements are often complemented with diagrams. It represents a contract between the developer and the client and must be agreed upon. One approach is to have one function for every output data item.

5.4.3 DIRECT QUANTIFIABLE REQUIREMENTS

Performance, throughput, and uptime requirements have to be scoped and the acceptable range has to be defined during the requirements specification phase. Quantifiable requirements that are based on certain functionalities are implemented through a set of software modules. The quality and the **goodness** of the entire system start from each of these modules. A number of development standards have been proposed to help evaluate and quantify the goodness of software modules. The table below is an abstract guide derived from *Evaluation Criteria for Goodness of Software Design*[1] proposed by the Software Engineering Institute. It can be used to measure the quality of the software modules developed.

The objective is to have a good level of coherence inside a module and coupling between modules in order to achieve maintainable, modifiable, reusable, and extensible software.

Coherence within a Module	Coupling between Modules
Abstract Object oriented Related to and encapsulating a single class of objects or abstract data type	***Abstract*** Check procedure calls by type on services between modules
Functional Related to a single function	***Networked*** With export/import interface between modules
Temporal All initialization	***Block Structured*** Nested blocks
Logical All input functions	***Common*** Via common data access
Coincidental Contents of the module there by chance	***Direct*** Unrestricted references to code and data between modules

5.4.4 UNQUANTIFIABLE REQUIREMENTS

Often user requirements that are not quantifiable are given as desirable properties.[2] They are generally divided in two categories:

[1]Software Engineering Institute, Capability Maturity Model for Software, 1993.

[2]John A. McDermid, *Software Engineer's Reference Book*, Butterworth Heinemann, Oxford 1991, p. 17/5.

1. User interfaces and quality attributes
   - User friendliness
   - Robustness
   - Reliability
2. Long-term behavior related
   - Maintainability
   - Modifiability
   - Extensibility
   - Reusability

Part II

Data Warehouse Architecture and Optimization

Though nights are tranquil, restless is my searching soul
Deluged in tear drops, towards virtue I crawl
This bony bowl named head, never is sated from wants
Evidently will not fill, since upside down is the bowl!

TRUE TRANSLATION OF HAKIM OMAR KHAYYAM'S ROBAIYAT

Chapter 6

Role of the Oracle Server in the Architecture

6.1 COMPONENTS OF DATA WAREHOUSE ARCHITECTURE

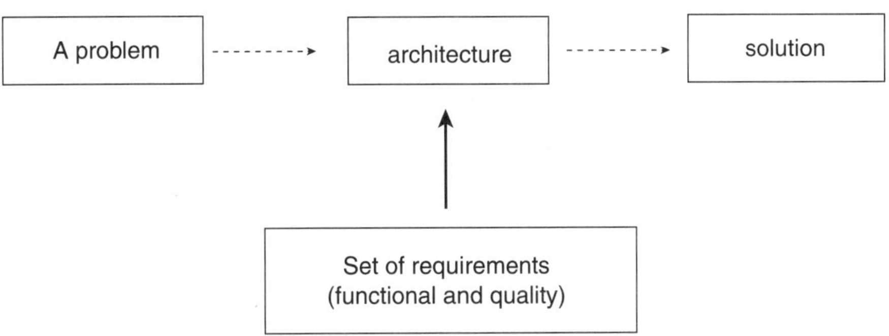

Conceptually, the principal motivation in having an architecture is to design a system that when implemented meets the specific set of requirements and delivers the functionalities to the end users of the system.[1] Requirements include both functional and nonfunctional constraints.

[1]W.H. Inmon, *Using the Data Warehouse*, John Wiley and Sons, N.Y., 1994.

A high-level architecture is a big picture of a developer's perspective of how a problem is going to be solved. The architecture defines the roles, responsibilities, and relationships of the primary components within the system. In the last ten years a number of different data warehouse architectures have been proposed. The best data warehouse architecture is the one that provides the best framework for a particular data warehouse project. Thus, there is no one formula or cure-all. The best data warehouse architectures are those that can be adapted to a particular set of requirements. The two architectures proposed here are two of many which seemed to be used in a majority of data warehouse implementations. They are relatively adaptable to most medium- or large-size data warehouse requirements.

It is very natural for a value-added data warehouse application to grow[2] very rapidly.[3] Data warehouses are generally required to provide access to historical data. Of course, it all depends on how the subject areas are managed in the data warehouse. Generally, in a financial data warehouse, historical data is kept on-line up to seven years because of financial liability laws and regulations. As source systems go through periodic data archiving and purging activities, the historical data in the data warehouse become more and more important and essential to end users for trend and forecast analysis. Therefore, the architecture should allow for the rapid growth of data content and complexity of data access requirements. The high-level criteria of scalability, optimized performance, robustness, flexibility, sustainability and openness, data volume, refresh cycles, availability and uptime, complexity in business rules and data presentation should help determine how a data warehouse architecture should be implemented. The components of the data warehouse can be implemented through a pool of off-the-shelf products, technologies, and customized codes. The challenge is in making the most appropriate decisions and selections of the components for the architecture without producing unnecessary complexity.[4] Any level of complexity that does not support the system deliverables will result in a high cost of maintenance and operation overhead. Case studies have shown how much of the unjustified cost of maintenance and operation of a data warehouse was directly

[2]In popularity, diversity of subjective data, data volume, data models, and so on.

[3]In some cases three-hundred percent per year.

[4]That is, matching the best IT solutions to the most pressing problems.

proportionate to the degree of code complexity and customization. The larger the amount of customized code, the more resources are needed to manage it. These are resources which could otherwise be used to work on additional mission-critical deliverables.

Two high-level data warehouse architectures are presented here; the Oracle Warehouse and the Classical data warehouse as described by William Inmon[5]. Although there are some commonalities in both architectures, the differences are primarily in the component types and perspectives. The Oracle Warehouse emphasizes the physical components and the infrastructure while the Classical data warehouse emphasizes the phases of data transformation as the data process through the various tiers of the data warehouse architecture. A comprehensive architecture can benefit from both perspectives.

6.1.1 ORACLE WAREHOUSE

This architecture emphasizes the role of hardware, database server, and other off-the-shelf tools available in the market that can be integrated to form the infrastructure. It is a good guideline when dealing with high data volume, scalability, performance, and rapid growth in a variety of data subject areas.

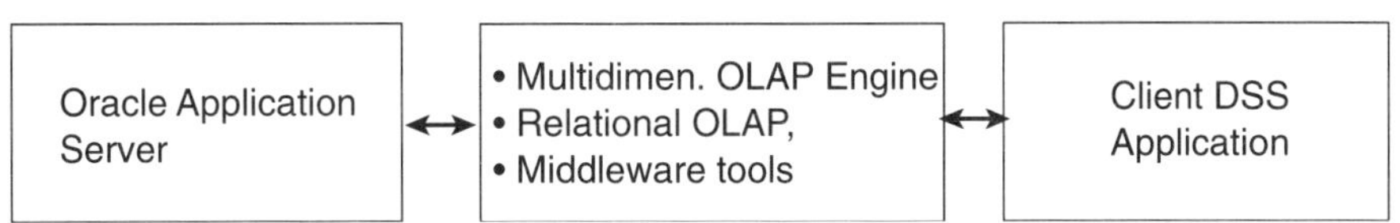

FIGURE 6.1 Three-Tier Architecture of an Oracle data warehouse.

A warehouse database is organized by subject rather than by application because it contains only the information necessary for decision support processing. Productivity and operational databases are updated continuously by data entry professionals and OLTP-type applications. A warehouse database is refreshed from operational systems on a periodic basis, usually during off-hours when network and CPU utilization is lower. A data warehouse in its simplest form

[5]William Inmon, *Using the Data Warehouse*, John Wiley and Sons, New York City.

involves a two-tiered homogeneous architecture in which a single-server tier hosts the warehouse database and a client tier hosts the front-end decision support and analysis tools. A more complex data warehouse is based on a three-tiered architecture that uses a separate layer for data access and presentation. As shown in Figure 6.1, the first tier is the server tier, the second is a multidimensional OLAP engine or relational OLAP tools, and the third tier is the client tier that consists of decision support application interfaces like ad hoc query and Web intranet applications. Building an effective data warehouse involves much more than simply copying data and making mounds of data available to users through some ad hoc DSS tools. Data must be restructured hierarchically and redefined based on business definitions and not on application vendors' definitions. Data must be transformed through cleansing data errors and anomolies, new derived and calculated fields, and flags to sort, group, and summarize. Multidimensional warehouse layers often include precomputed summaries, aggregated totals, and predefined views that improve data rollup and query performance.

The primary components of an Oracle data warehouse[6] are:

- ❑ A data model
- ❑ A warehouse server
- ❑ A data warehouse application server
- ❑ A middleware layer
- ❑ Data scrubbing utilities
- ❑ Data transport utilities
- ❑ Data replication engines
- ❑ Meta data repositories
- ❑ Client analysis tool set

The following sections provide detailed descriptions of the above components.

A Data Model: The data model describes the warehouse data contents. Using classic entity relationship modeling and the newly emerged dimensional modeling techniques (covered in Section 4.2), it

[6]As described in the March/April 1996 issue of *Oracle Magazine*, p. 39.

represents subject areas of interest and data measures that need to be tracked. The goal of this data modeling effort is to facilitate decision support type access. To reach this goal, two modeling strategies, called the star and snowflake schemas have been proposed by the pioneers of data warehouse applications. The data model is developed during the early stages of the design. It will be referred to during implementation analysis, extract plans, and on an ongoing basis during the evolution of the data warehouse. Use of data modeling tools and techniques and the use of CASE tools are most essential in managing the definition changes in this area.

A Warehouse Server: The warehouse server is a highly powerful machine suited and tuned for this type of application and supports process and task parallelism at the Central Processing Unit (CPU), Disk Input/Output (I/O), and memory level capabilities of these servers. A typical configuration includes SMP (Symmetric Multiprocessor), MPP (Massively Parallel Processing) machine with RAID (Redundant Array of Independent Disks), very large memory (VLM), and a very large supply of disk and memory cache.

A Data Warehouse Application Server: The application server contains custom codes responsible for periodic refresh, aggregation, and summarization. In addition to business rules, the data population method impacts the level of complexity in this layer of custom code. Data population can be a bulk download or a change-based replication. The implementation of the latter is more complex but results in better performance when dealing with highly volatile operational data. The complexity and adaptability to change can be optimized and better managed with the use of a metadata tool.

A Middleware Layer: This layer contains infrastructure support software, such as:

- ❑ Scheduling jobs and events utilities
- ❑ Oracle SQL*Net Client/Server program interface
- ❑ Data administration auditing and monitoring tools
- ❑ Source code and release control utilities
- ❑ Backup and recovery utilities
- ❑ Performance monitoring tools

Data Scrubbing Utilities: These utilities are used for validating, filtering, categorizing, integrating, consolidating data and other functions. They can be both customized or built using off-the-shelf components.

Data Transport Utilities: These utilities extract and load programs. Third-party off-the-shelf products, Oracle 7 Replication SQL*Loader, export/import, COPY command, and embedded SQL procedural program modules can all be utilized in implementing data transport. The following tools are suggested for this purpose:

- Information PowerMart
- Carleton Passport
- Intellidex Systems
- Prism Warehouse Manager

Data Replication Engines: Database-level support for replicating changes of the source data to a remote database can be utilized in implementing this layer. Oracle 7 support for asymmetric (snapshot) replication, symmetric replication, and standby databases can all be utilized to implement a more complex data replication engine.

Metadata Repositories: These repositories are a house of knowledge in regard to nature and usage of the subject areas in the data warehouse. This repository is a superset of a developer's view of the application: the data model on the one hand and the end user's perspective and interpretation of the decision support fact data and functions on the other. It can be as simple as a spreadsheet or as complex as a small database application managed by modeling tools such as Oracle Designer/2000 CASE tool, LogicWorks' Universal Directory, Prism Solutions' Prism Directory Manager, and HP's Intelligent Warehouse tools. By utilizing these modeling and directory tools, design decisions, usage standards, module descriptions, module data dependencies, and user information can be maintained and accessed on-line by developers as well as end users.

Client Analysis Tool Sets: These tools are end-user interfaces to access data in the warehouse. These tool sets can include client/server ad hoc query tools, OLAP client software, and intranet Web interfaces. This last component can be implemented by using custom code or using Oracle Express and family of Web products. Other tools suggested for this purpose are

- ❑ Brio Technologies' Brio Query
- ❑ Business Objects
- ❑ Andyne's GQL
- ❑ Cognos' PowerPlay
- ❑ Information Advantage
- ❑ Microstrategy's DSS Agent
- ❑ Pilot Software's Lightship

Figure 6.2 illustrates an implementation approach to an oracle-centric data warehouse architecture.

Key benefits of an Oracle data warehouse architecture

- ❑ Provides a list of required components
- ❑ Supports a short development cycle

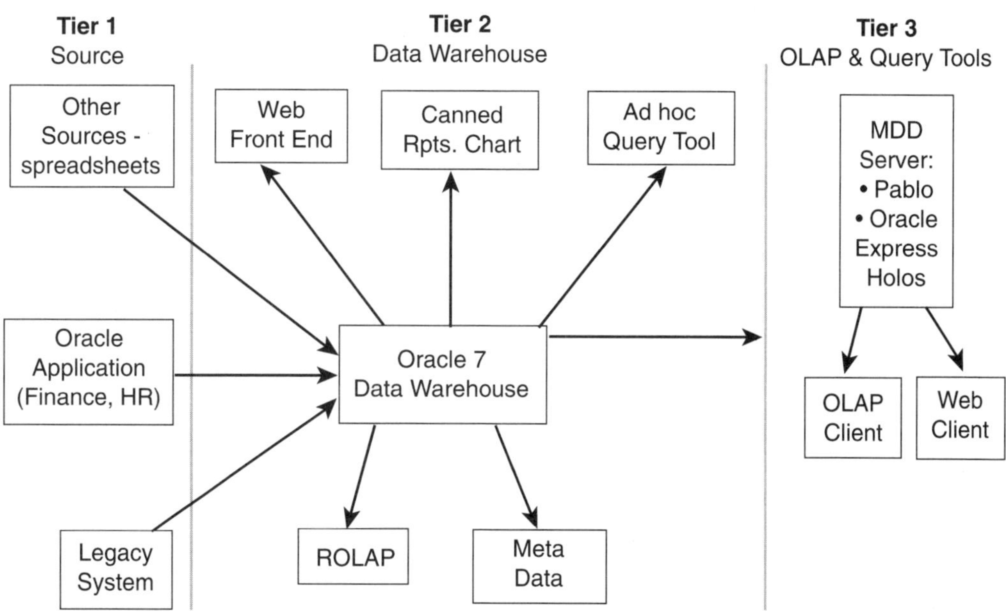

FIGURE 6.2 Three-Tier Architecture of an Oracle data warehouse.

- Can be an integrated Oracle solution
- Emphasizes an implementation approach

6.1.2 CLASSICAL DATA WAREHOUSE

Figure 6.3 illustrates a conceptual view of a classical data warehouse architecture.

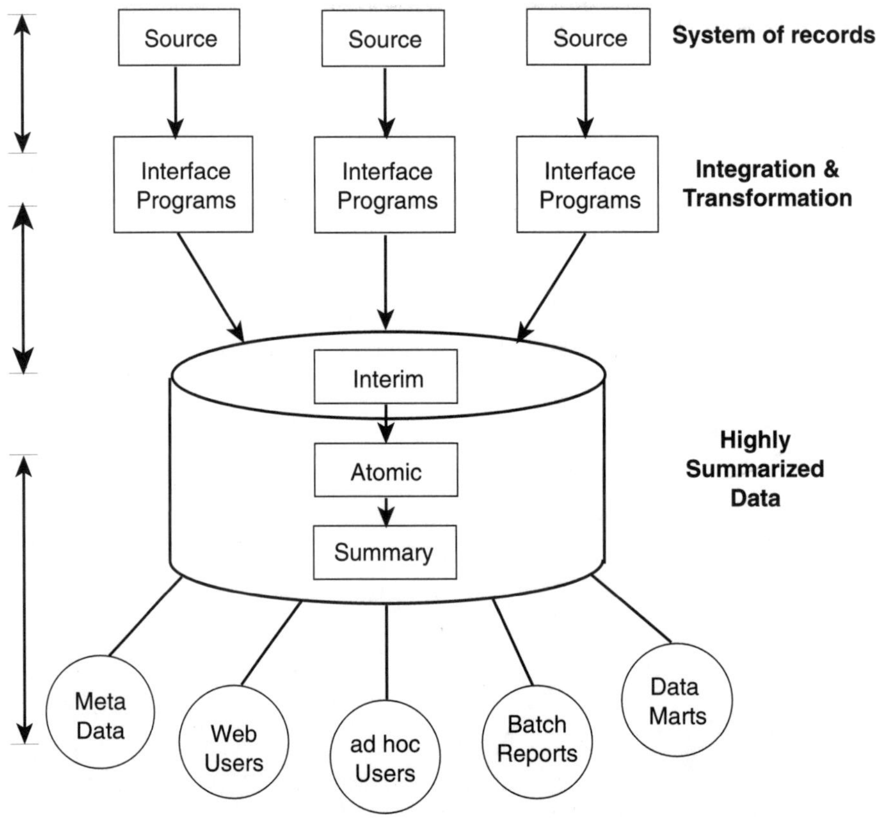

FIGURE 6.3 Classical Data Warehouse.

Key benefits of a Classical data warehouse

- Emphasizes the roles of each tier, is a more extensible architecture that allows heterogeneous database models, technologies, and tools interface (see Figure 6.4)
- Focuses on the results rather than technology type
- Is an open approach and is independent from the source systems
- Enables continuous availability and flexibility in implementation and modification of business data definition
- Supports exploratory ad hoc analysis
- Emphasizes analysis and design approach

A data warehouse usually includes all or some of the following components:

- System of records, that is, order entry, manufacturing, and operational systems.
- Current detailed data , that is, last six months' orders and shipment information.
- Old detailed data, that is, five years of order and shipment information that was purged from the operational system.
- Central repository of data, that is, the data warehouse database.
- Replication of summarized data at the departmental level, that is, preselects a subset of relevant and preprocessed data.
- Highly summarized data trended against time at the corporate level, that is, preprocessed monthly, quarterly, and yearly product orders.

Tiers	Source	Users
Tier 1 users/mgrs.	Data from legacy systems	Operations
Tier 2	Integration/transformation modules	Product managers, program managers, business planners
Tier 3	Highly summarized data	High-level executives,

FIGURE 6.4 Three-Tier Classical Data Warehouse Architecture.

- Data warehouse metadata, that is, information about data content and the processing performed on the data in the data warehouse.
- Integration and transformation program modules.

The following sections provide a more detailed description of each of the above components.

System of Records: The systems and methods an organization uses to record its transactions. It can be manual or automated. It may record data via notes, books, spreadsheets, or databases. In the case of database applications, transactions are automatically traced and recorded in a fashion that represents detailed characteristics of the transaction in a system of records known as source application systems. Transaction records may come from different departments where data is generated as current operational data. As data comes into the data warehouse and goes through the transformation, they may again be replicated in the data warehouse as an interim or staging state of the data. These represent a subset of the data that a corporation has in its applications. They are not necessarily perfect and must be mapped, cross-referenced, and cleansed as they go through the data warehouse.

Current Detailed Data: A subset of data from a system of records that has the information which the data warehouse users are interested in. Data is imported and integrated with data coming from other source application systems as the ATOMIC state. These data are organized by subject, not by the application source system types, for instance, all orders, all products, all customers, and so on, of a retail shop.

Old Detailed Data: Data that is generally archived off the source systems and is not needed for the current operation of the organization. They are stored in the data warehouse as historical in their ATOMIC state. They are massive and are rarely accessed.

The Central Repository of Data: Data in a data warehouse is a full-featured database and is managed by a database server. This is where a subset of data generated in an organization is reorganized and maintained. It is reorganized into subject-oriented categories, hierarchies, integrated, and mapped to abstract and qualifying concepts. Denormalization and data redundancy is very common. The database server is system-level software that is responsible for the management of the physical data through its numerous services. End-user access is provided through user interfaces that provide direct or indirect access to a subset of these data. Data in this repository is generally transformed and collected at departmental and highly summarized levels using dimensional modeling. For instance, all products are categorized as low-end, mid-range, and high-end.

Replication of Summarized Data at the Departmental Level: A subset of data in the data warehouse that is suited for a particular business user organization. For instance, sales, finance, and customer service organizations of a corporation may all need product order information but might not all show the same security, aggregation, and data definitions. Systems using this data are also called Data Marts.

Highly Summarized Data Trended against Time at the Corporate Level: These data are stored in the data warehouse and are much smaller in size compared to the departmental summary of current detailed data. They are primarily prepared for the use of executive management who would like to get the bottom-line figures at a glance.

Data Warehouse Metadata: At times simply referred to as metadata, these datasets are key to the transformation of data from state to state in the data warehouse. Metadata can be equated to a data warehouse's information map or directory, dictionary, or card catalog.

Integration and Transformation Program Modules: As current detailed data pass through the data warehouse, these programs or modules work on the system of records and turn them into corporate data.[7] Once completely transformed they can be used for complex analytical querying. Functions and queries performed after this state can be both ad hoc or premodeled and packaged in a client desktop module that is generally initiated by the end users. It is important that the data warehouse development team have visibility into the type, frequency, format, and style of queries requested by the end users on an ongoing basis. By further studying these ad hoc queries, the data warehouse team can identify the commonalities. These commonalities can be the foundation for further data warehouse enhancements and optimization. As mentioned in Chapter 3, the more we know

[7]A Journey from INTERIM to ATOMIC to SUMMARY states.

about the end-user goals, business processes, or analytical methods, the more we can provide directly effective, optimized, and quality products. The logic and system development methodology used in the integration and transformation module should be modular, flexible, and extensible to allow for continuous enhancements.

The DBMS server provides services as the central repository. Due to the volume and extent of data transformation, it is important that the DBMS server can be configured to take advantage of scalability features of the server platform such as,

- Very Large Memory (VLM),
- Symmetric Multiprocessor (SMP),
- Massively Parallel Processor (MPP) architecture, and
- Redundant Array of Independent Disks (RAID).

6.2 ADVANTAGES OF USING AN ORACLE SERVER

Oracle Server has the following characteristics that are very useful in building a robust data warehouse application:

- Enterprise-scale relational database server
- Adapts well with SMP (Symmetrical Multiprocessing) and MPP (Massively Parallel processing) hardware architectures
- Oracle VLM (Very Large Memory) option on 64-bit processors—up to 4 gigabytes of data can be cached
- Oracle Express—a server-based OLAP solution
- Extensive distributed database capabilities
- Synchronous and asynchronous data replication
- Highly tunable server
- Gradual support for Standard Systems
- Network Management Protocols (SNMP)
- Support for cost optimizer
- Efficient data loading utilities
- Optional fast indexing creation
- Support for flexible database file I/O distribution

- Support for implementing complex security model
- Support for parallel processing at the server and application levels
- Support for multinational languages
- Portable across many platforms
- Extensive object storage definitions
- Support for database audit facility
- Read-only table spaces
- Debugging facilities
- Performance diagnostic tool, such as EXPLAIN PLAN and TKPROF utilities
- Support for database level statistics
- Stored procedures, triggers, and packages
- Support for 3GL embedded SQL
- Informative data dictionary
- Native CASE tools and methodology to manage metadata
- Row-level concurrency facility
- Scalable user process support through multithreaded server architecture
- Table-level caching
- User profile facility

6.3 CHALLENGES OF USING AN ORACLE SERVER

The following major challenges have been identified for a medium- to large-scale Oracle database application. They are not at all insurmountable; they are merely listed to prepare the reader for the complex nature of administering an Oracle Data Warehouse. We will discuss later in this book how all of the following challenges can be resolved with appropriate measures. The key to resolving the following challenges is the competency of the technical staff, preparation, planning, and the application of sound software engineering principles:

- Resource-intensive database backup and recovery procedures
- Lack of implementation guidelines and standards

- Limited database administration tools and utilities
- Default installation and functionalities often not optimized
- Requiring extensive application testing before Oracle upgrades
- Inadequate documentation details of new features and capabilities
- Need for capacity planning and dynamic growth management
- Scarcity of Oracle database administrator resources
- Oracle SQL Optimizer
- A comprehensive meta data tool

Chapter 7

Role of a Data Warehouse Application in the Architecture

7.1 TRANSPORTATION OF DATA INTO THE DATA WAREHOUSE

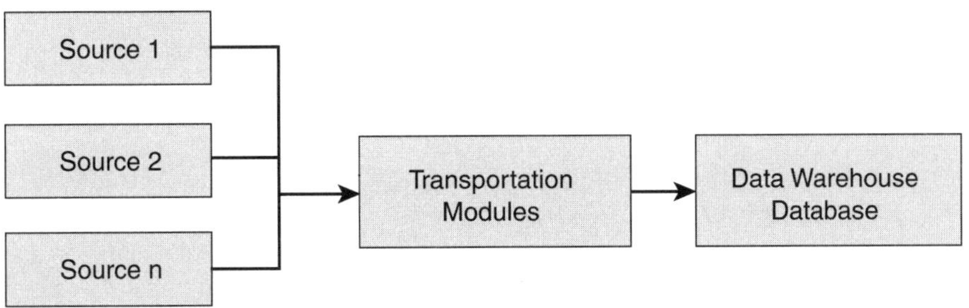

The transportation of real-time operational data into the data warehouse can be implemented using a number of different technologies. Depending on the data delivery requirements, transportation of data from the system of records can be modeled using one or a hybrid of technologies. We have included here a set of basic questions and criteria that can determine which technologies are more suited for a particular environment. The level of flexibility dictates the complexity of the transportation mechanisms. The best approach is to consider all the realities involved in the business process and the real-time source systems when developing the requirements. In the data warehouse market, there are a number of products that can satisfy these roles. The technologies used in those products should be technically analyzed to determine if they meet the requirements of the data warehouse architecture. Most of them are appropriate for the small- to medium-sized data warehouses. Of course, research and development in this area is continuing. We should look forward to more robust, flexible, extensible, and scalable products in the not too distant future.

In Chapter 8 we will focus on the features that are available in Oracle7 and describe their functionalities. This information can be utilized to explore the possibilities in terms of implementing an in-house customized solution playing the role of the transportation module in the architecture. The transportation module can then be designed to meet those criteria.

The following questions need to be considered when designing the transportation module:

- How different is the data management technology used in the source system compared to the data warehouse?
- What are the time windows available for the source systems to extract data?
- How constant or volatile are the data structures?
- What process is used in changing the structure or domain of the data in the source system?
- Should the changes in the data set structure remain transparent to the transport modules?

Below are some important considerations pertaining to the format and structure of data in the system of records:

- Are they ASCII flat files, indexed files, relational database, or flat files?
- What is the volume of data and how frequently is it changed?
- What is the relationship, especially referential integrity, among the source data sets?

- What criteria should be used to ensure that the data sets extracted have data integrity?
- Is there a specific business process milestone that has to be reached before the extract starts?
- How frequently does data need to be resummarized in the data warehouse?
- What are the domain characteristics of the source data sets, that is, the data type, width, maximum, minimum, valid state, invalid state, and so on?
- What other processes in the system of records read and write into these data sets?
- Which data sets have to be extracted on an incremental basis?
- Which data sets have to be extracted on a full load basis?
- What is the bandwidth of the networking infrastructure?
- Should the data sets be loaded in a specific sequence?
- Which ones can be extracted in parallel?

7.2 DATA CREATED IN THE DATA WAREHOUSE

In a data warehouse application it is typical to have requirements categorizing the detailed transactions into category types that are not necessarily known to the source systems. These category types can be represented as a set of data elements representing some business concepts that are not maintained systematically in the source system. These data elements can be performance indicators, productivity measures, business sectors, products, and transaction classifications that can be assigned to or derived from the detailed transaction data based on certain business definitions and criteria. Traditionally, deriving these performance indicators and transaction categories takes days and hours of manual or desktop processing. The calculation or maintenance of these data elements is one of the main benefits of a data warehouse application. These data elements and their definitions must be clearly defined by representatives of the data warehouse and the data owner. In the analysis phase of the life cycle, they are identified, defined, approved, and used in the data and process model. Later in the design phase, they are represented in the entities and functions.

The important factors for these new data elements are their quality and administration. Data quality starts with the data definition. Any obscurity or misinterpretation at the definition level will result in an enormous data quality problem with large-scale repercussions. Often, the definition and the calculation used to derive the data are acceptable to one group of users, but not acceptable to another. Allowing time and resources in the project plan to facilitate and resolve these differences to bring consensus among user groups early on in the project life cycle is definitely worth the investment. It may even require that the information technology team responsible for building the data warehouse take ownership and ensure that this takes place.

Techniques used to facilitate this process are JAD (Joint Application Development), RAD (Rapid Application Development), and prototyping. They are effective in terms of staying focused and progressing through the various phases. To support these types of data elements, additional modules may have to be implemented to facilitate maintenance. Modules such as data entry interfaces, consistency and exception reporting tools can help data owners be self-sufficient in terms of maintaining and monitoring the data.

The correlation of real-time operational data and some of these data warehouse inherent data elements sometimes becomes so meaningful and relevant to business users and their performance analysis that it actually generates further improvement in the business process and decision makers' effectiveness. The change in the business process may even surface data elements for inclusion in the upstream source systems as opposed to the downstream data warehouse applications. Certainly, any changes to the data sets in the source system should be handled by the data warehouse, which may at times generate enhancements and modifications to the transportation and transformation modules. This should not be viewed as an unwelcome change. Afterall, one of the objectives of a data warehouse application is to contribute to the effectiveness of strategic decision-making processes. From a technical perspective, the less reference data maintenance that takes place in the data warehouse, the better.

The transportation modules also provide an opportunity to contribute to some level of data integration. To end users of the data warehouse who analyze the market presence through customer profiling, information on all customers is vital. It is irrelevant where the customer list is coming from, even if it is from different source systems. It is not uncommon for customer data to come through different business channels and partners. Also, it is very natural to see customer data stored in heterogeneous platforms, data files, technologies, and possibly, languages. In the final analysis, they are all customers of an enterprise and must be integrated. The transportation modules provide the first opportunity to unify different data sets for the same subject area.

7.3 PRESENTATION OF DATA TO END USERS

An extremely effective way to present data is to transform data into star schema and prepare for access through user interfaces.

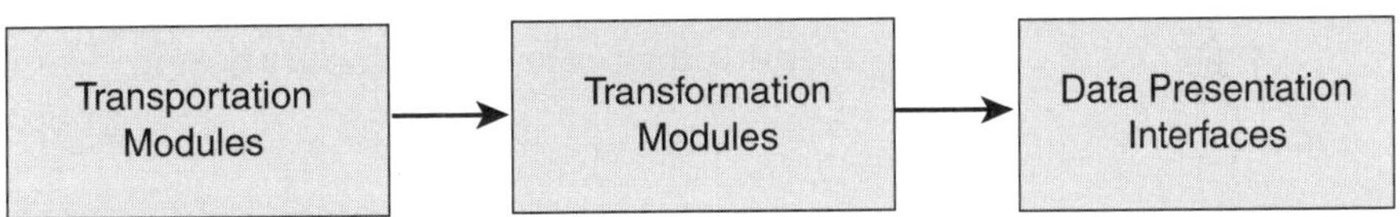

Transformation modules are composed of functions that are responsible for taking in transported data sets for every subject area and process and store them in the data warehouse repository. It is at this level of processing that data is transformed based on business rules documented during analysis. The more fine-tuned the modeling effort is, the more specific and accurate the functions involved will be. These modules are sequenced and parallelized depending on the data integrity and relationships among the subject areas. Data integrity, state, and process modeling techniques and the time and resource investments made using CASE and modeling tools will yield a hefty payoff in this phase. The modularity, code reusability, loose coupling among modules, and high internal cohesiveness of each module are important software engineering techniques. Additionally, they help ensure flexibility, smaller critical path, extensibility, and performance monitoring, which are all factors that increase the reliability and low cost of maintenance for these software modules. Since this type of data warehouse development relies on internal development, undocumented assumptions, nonstandard coding, cutting corners on the application development standards, lack of adequate design, and code reviews will definitely render a high cost of maintenance for the information system's organization responsible for the data warehouse application.

The ease of data manipulation using SQL can produce an illusion that oversimplifies the challenges involved in producing a database application as critical as a data warehouse. These challenges should not be underestimated. This is where believers in disciplined software development at all levels of IT, from developers to managers, should contribute to the enforcement of the techniques and standards. This approach must be encouraged by lead architects as 50 percent or more of the project's annual budget is spent on areas that could have initially been avoided. With the advances made in object orientation, object-oriented development tools, and the multifacet modeling techniques, it is extremely beneficial to use all the methodology that object-oriented methodologies are able to provide.

The transformation of data can include different levels of data preparation in the batch processing mode. Depending on the condition of the data and the requirements of the data warehouse deliverables, a number of functions may have to be implemented in the transformation module.

7.3.1 DATA TRANSFORMATION FUNCTIONS

Some of the most common functions used in a data warehouse load and transformation module are defined below.

Cleaning	Remove "invalid" data from the data sets
Scrubbing	Remove complex inconsistencies in the data
Integrating	Unify different data sets of the same subject area coming from different sources
Categorizing	Organize data into more natural categories
Aggregating and rolling up	Group the detailed transactions in a hierarchy

Pivoting	Analyze data from different perspective
Summarizing	Adding up detailed transaction from a specific perspective
Identifying elements of dimension	In short, a domain of variables. From the domain perspective, they are rules based on which transaction (raw or real-time data) is measured. For instance, when analyzing the dollar amount spent on a computer upgrade, one can analyze the total dollars spent based on product type, market segment type, and financial periods. From an object-oriented perspective, it is a class of objects.
Identifying members of a dimension	Different distinct values in a particular dimension. They are the unique key values of an entity. Cardinality of a dimension is the number of unique values in the dimension. From an object-oriented perspective, it is the object part of a class. Good candidates for a dimension usually have a low cardinality or member.
Calculating measures	A particular value recorded in a transaction record, that is, total dollars spent.
Identifying attributes of a dimension	Characteristics that describe a member of a dimension, for example, product entity is a dimension. "X386" is a member of that dimension. "Clock rate" can be an attribute in this dimension that is interesting to business executives.
Populating fact data	A set of all the interesting facts about a measure or a transaction with associated dimensions explicitly identified. For instance, a survey response record that determines what kind of computer received upgrades, how much was spent on that upgrade, in which month, and the category of the market segment being surveyed.
Building data cube	A multidimensional data structure that categorizes variable and raw transactional data into array-like structures. It is easy to visualize a physical object with three dimensions: height,

	length, and width. A particular abstract object can have more than three dimensions. The set theory and Cartesian product set theory help represent the multidimensional aspects of some abstract concepts like "business forecasting," which can be based on many factors, aspects, angles, or dimensions. In the field of data warehousing, the term dimension is used to represent this concept.
Calculating derived data field	The additional natural attributes that can be calculated using the values available in the raw data and a programmed function. The function can be mathematical, statistical, financial, heuristic, or logical.

7.3.2 SUMMARY OF DATA ARCHITECTURE

The example covered in Chapter 1, Section 4.2 illustrates the steps involved in the data modeling efforts. The steps can be summarized as follows:

Step 1. Study the groups of end users, their job functions, and job goals. What are the questions and queries that these end users would like from the data warehouse? Here are some questions to consider:

- What is the total of *X* aggregated by *Y* and *Z* aggregated by *U*?
- How does that compare with my forecast of *X*?
- Should I change my future forecast ? What is the trend?

Step 2. Prepare the normalized view of data into subject areas. Remember that these data may be coming from different source systems. They may or may not originally be in normalized form. (Data normalization is described in Part III). This data normalization describes the relationship among entities. In Part I, this tier of the model is referred to as the ATOMIC layer.

Step 3. Based on end users' queries, identify domains or dimensions for measurement purposes. The relationship among entities in a database design reveals the associations among them. These associations are good candidates for dimensions. In the above example, product, customer, and employee are likely dimensions since they are being referred to in other tables. They become the reference entities. Members of these dimensions must be part of the measures in the fact table to be accessed by multidimentional tools.

In addition to the reference tables, we may also want to create new mapping tables that help categorize and classify data. These new classes will become additional dimensions in the final schema. Typically, business analysts prefer to categorize products at a high level and in a manner that is consistent with the rest of the business and the industry. This kind of classification makes it easier to perform executive-level sales and product marketing analysis. Often these classifications are irrelevant or unnecessary to the manufacturing and engineering divisions of the company where the products originated. In some cases, manufacturing and engineering may use product codes and symbols that make it difficult to categorize along the business executive's view of the company's market potential.

Step 4. Organize dimensions into hierarchies that represent end-users views.

Generally, concepts like time, geography, sales organization, and product families are natural candidates to be turned into a hierarchy. These hierarchical relationships are necessary to facilitate the aggregation and rollup at the end-user access level. Modeling data into hierarchical relationships is not common in relational databases due to the update and insert anomalies that it can cause. In a data warehouse optimizing for the end-user's read access, this is not a constraint anymore (see Figure 7.1).

Step 5. Identify attributes of dimensions that describe important and measurable facts about dimension members.

This could be those characteristics that are common in the industry and help identify the classification of an element in a dimension. Thus, these attributes are usually dimension-specific. Depending on the end-users questions, we can determine which attributes should be included and which ones should be avoided. Of course, the objective of a data warehouse does not include the creation of everything cross-referenced with everything else. Actually, this is one of the critical parts of data modeling for a data warehouse database. Underestimating the research and investigation in this process results in fact tables that are unnecessarily large, resulting in unnecessary batch processing overhead. The overhead usually has enough of an impact that it is not overkill to rejustify them every six months. As part of a regular performance evaluation of the data model, survey the end users and document why each and every attribute should be carried into the fact table.

Step 6. Identify measures and attributes that are not represented in other tables.

Denormalize entities into a fact table that includes all those attributes that are interesting to end users including derived and calculated values. The set of fact tables represents the COLLECTION layer as mentioned in Chapter 4.

Step 7. Define functions that perform, calculate, evaluate, and simulate the manual analytical processing.

The schema generated with this effort is called a star schema. It is possible in a complex data warehouse to have a number of fact tables in which case, the schema becomes a snowflake schema.

7.4 DATA WAREHOUSE AS AN EXTENSIBLE SOFTWARE SYSTEM

As mentioned in Section 2.4, object-oriented database design rules lend themselves nicely to the parameters and constraints of a data warehouse application architecture. In the previous chapters we discussed a number of characteristics for a data warehouse application. Here is a summary review.

1. Data intensive and a fast-growing application.
2. Convergence of heterogeneous, multivendor, multigeneration computer technologies.
3. Complex abstraction of entities and attributes into more natural business concepts.
4. Exploits the aggregation, inheritance, and grouping relationships among entities to facilitate, slice, dice, drill down, and drill through queries.
5. Client/server architecture and dynamic computing environment.

6. Strong data-slice-level security requirement that goes beyond data structures.
7. Due to the sizable in-house development involved and the incremental development nature of a data warehouse, modules of a fine-grain architecture must be very well defined.
8. Scalability, reliability, predictability, performance optimization, flexibility, code reusability, parallelizing batch processing, and complex data presentation are all desirable features of a data warehouse implementation and are natural object-orientation objectives.
9. Ability to cope with an ever-increasing demand from executive and decision makers to have access to systematically analyzed and trended data accessible at all times and from all geographical locations.
10. Continuous release of powerful OLAP tools.
11. Increase in popularity and consequently increase user demand in expanding the diversity of subject areas, dimensions, and measures.
12. To have good data quality monitoring facilities, the dynamic nature of data in transformation modules must be traceable.
13. The importance of a rich data dictionary, metadata, and semantic synchronization among developers, end users, and administrators.
14. Ability to do data mining and data visualizing as an advanced level of OLAP requires a more intelligent batch and event processing. A type of intelligent processing that can infer trends and patterns in data.

In Section 7.3.2, the relational data modeling and storage aspect of a data warehouse application architecture was discussed. Here we would now like to focus on the functional modeling part of the architecture.

As mentioned earlier, the role of a data warehouse application in the architecture primarily consists of data transportation and transformation components. Some of these components can be implemented using off-the-shelf products, but a considerable amount of software level control and coordination is needed for translation into relatively large custom codes. The design and implementation of these components will be very similar to the design of a common batch transformation system where a given input is processed with a spe-

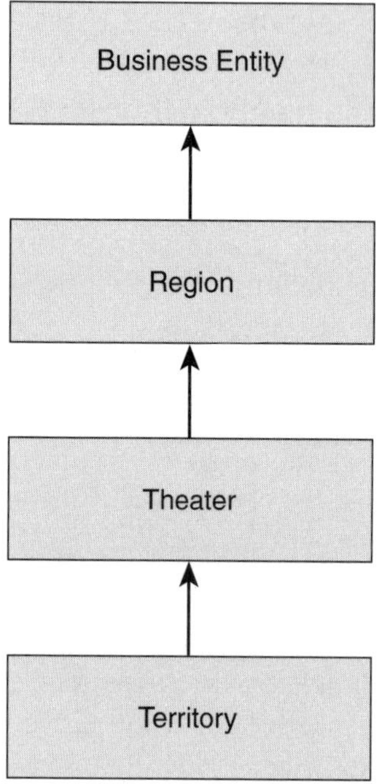

FIGURE 7.1 Inheritance Hierarchy of a Sales Organization.

cific function to calculate or produce an output. The challenge in the design of such systems is in the detailed modeling of the functional parts. A well-designed set of transportation and transformation modules certainly provide an invaluable advantage when it comes to enhancing and extending the capabilities and data diversity of an existing data warehouse application.

$$\text{Maintenance productivity} = \frac{\text{Added functionality}}{\text{Cost of development}}$$

The cost of such maintenance can easily skyrocket if the functional parts of the data warehouse application are not designed to be easily extensible. Consequently, everytime a new data set is to be added to the list of data warehouse information offerings, a comprehensive development effort needs to take place. It is not uncommon to see these new enhancements account for more than half of the operating cost of a data warehouse. In reality, most systems are developed only to meet the current project objectives and requirements. From a project management perspective, however, it is often necessary to phase the data warehouse deliverables to maintain the scope of the project. In which case, it becomes inevitable to have scheduled enhancements as often as every four months.

The high cost of enhancements is not a desirable result from both management and technical perspectives. Questions that should be asked of the development team are:

- ❑ Why is this data warehouse application not scalable and the cost of maintenance high?
- ❑ How can a system be flexibly designed and architected to allow for ongoing enhancements?
- ❑ What can be done strategically from the inception of the project to ease and optimize this unavoidable challenge?

We would like to answer these questions with a **methodological** approach. These challenges can be easily addressed when an object-orientation approach is used minimally at the systems analysis and design phases of the data warehouse application.

Object orientation is an advanced software engineering methodology that fundamentally addresses the above common questions. One of its default benefits is to lower the cost of maintenance and improve the maintenance productivity when the application requirements are continuously changing. It is the goal of object orientation to model the real-world concepts and the interactions between processes as directly and dynamically as possible.[1] It acknowledges the diversity in the data representations and entity classifications in system analysis and design approaches. This closed and well-defined modeling approach, by nature, helps produce dynamic, adaptable, and reusable components. In the next section we will look at the basics of object orientation in system design which provides a framework that can be used to represent the architecture of a data warehouse application. The object modeling technique is a very common object oriented methodology. *Object Oriented Modeling and Design* by Raumbaugh and Lorensen is a good reference book pertaining to this topic.[2] (See Figure 7.2.)

[1]Setrag Khoshafian, *Object Oriented Database Design*, Wiley and Sons, 1993, p. 145.

[2]Rambaugh and Lorensen, *Object Oriented Modeling and Design*, Prentice Hall, New Jersey, 1991, p. 201.

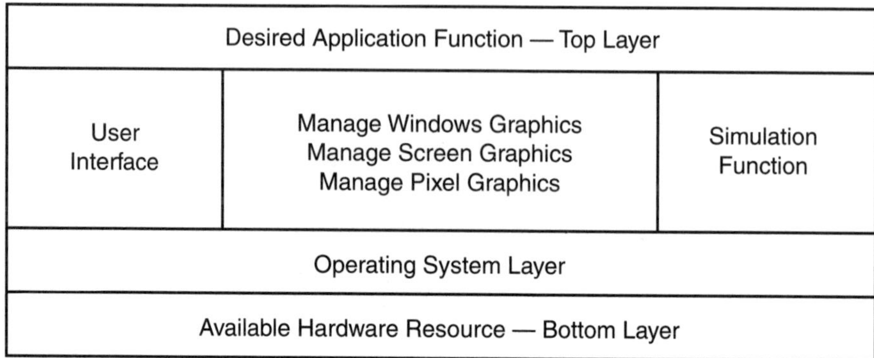

FIGURE 7.2 Block Diagram Architecture of a Graphical User Interface Application.

7.4.1 OBJECT-ORIENTED SYSTEM ARCHITECTURE DEFINITIONS

The OO system architecture and design consists of high-level specifications of major components called subsystems or functions. The relationship between the subsystems is handled through interfaces. The explanation of the services of these subsystems and the relationships among them is the system design specification which should describe the software control and data storage approaches and strategies. In short, the system design and the architecture of an application system is composed of all of the following components:

- Layer
- Partition
- Subsystem
- Interface
- Software control
- Data storage
- Boundary conditions

The main challenge is to produce a simple architecture for the data warehouse application that can produce the required functionalities with the least interaction among its subsystems. The basic definitions of the key concepts in a system architecture are listed in the following table.

Layer	A subsystem at a high level of abstraction is a layer. Generally, the lowest and highest layers are responsible for interfacing with the outside world.
Partition	A partition divides a layer into more subsystems.
Subsystem	A subsystem is distinguishable through its specific services. It is composed of objects that collaborate and are responsible for providing certain services. These services are defined in terms of functions. Each of these functions can be further broken down into more specific functions.
Software Control	The description of the relationship and the interaction from most layers of a system with the outside world is the software control. Depending on how the process is initiated, software control can be divided into three styles; procedure-driven, event-driven, and concurrent.
Procedure-Driven Control	It is implemented through a very specific and optimized algorithm in which the sequence of events is preselected and coded in a program module.
Event-Driven Control	It is implemented through an "event loop" and a "callback" function. The interesting aspect of an event-driven control is that a user can select an event from a list of possible events. The event loop that has been waiting to receive these requests receives this selection and forwards the control to the appropriate operating function by calling it. Once the operation is completed, the event loop receives the control back from the function and returns the result to the user. The event loop subsystem is also referred to as a "dispatcher" or "monitor."
Concurrent Control	It is implemented by designing objects and modules that are assumed to be executed in parallel. This allows the ability to perform more operations at the same time. This feature is especially important when the hardware resource provides multiple processors.
Boundary Conditions	It describes how different conditions and states of the system should be handled when it is not in its normal and expected steady state. It addresses system initialization, system termination, and system failure.
Data Store	Represents data structures, files, and databases.

Batch Transformation Processing	One of the common architectural frameworks that best fits a data warehouse application. In such systems data transformation functions on an entire set of input data sets are systematically executed.

7.4.2 OBJECT MODELING TECHNIQUES

This methodology encourages the system designer to describe a system from three different perspectives:

Dynamic model	The dynamic model defines the sequence and control of events, states, and operations. The dynamic state of a system is illustrated using a state diagram.
Object model	The object model defines the objects and different types of associations that can exist among them. The object components of a system and their associations are illustrated using object models.
Functional model	The functional model defines the processes and the flow of data among them. The data flow diagram is used to illustrate the details.

The back-end data transformation process portion of a data warehouse application can be implemented using the batch transformation system framework. In such a case, the most important and complex model is the functional model. The other models, dynamic and object, are either extremely trivial or simple. At a minimum, the system design should include a data flow diagram.

Figure 7.3 illustrates the main functional milestones involved in a data warehouse batch refresh process. Data stores are shown using parallel lines. Functions are shown as oval shapes. A directed line shows how data subsets are processed and moved through the functional modules. By combining these models, subsystems, and software controls, characteristics of a well-defined system design can be generated using this system design. The data warehouse data transformation functions can be implemented such that it is easily extensible and scalable. The object-oriented analysis and design techniques produce a number of design specification deliverables that prioritize and guide code developers throughout the implementation phase.

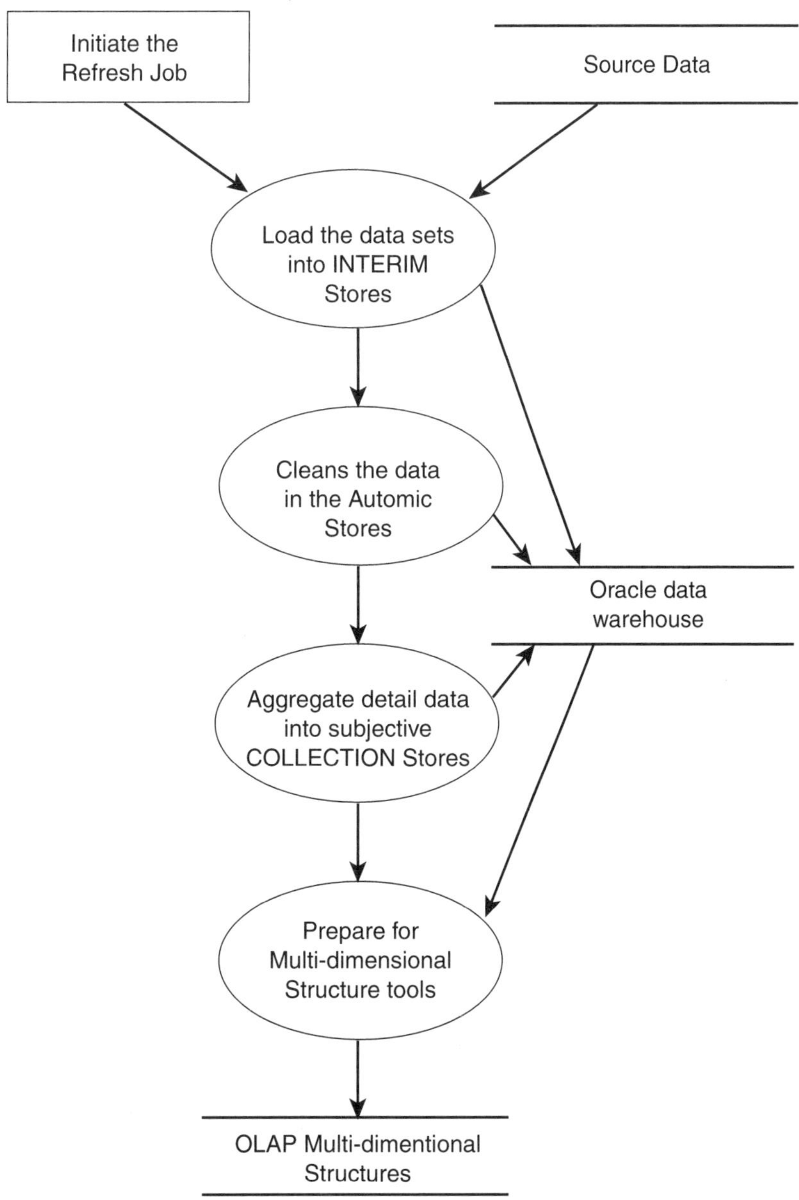

FIGURE 7.3 Data Flow Diagram of a Data Warehouse Application.

The more algorithmic decisions are performed at the design level; the less difficulty will be faced during the maintenance phase. This OO method simplifies the functional points and reduces the guesswork and inconsistent state handling at the coding level. We have found the following matrices very useful and practical in conveying the results of analysis and design efforts.

Dynamic States of Data Matrix

	State 1	State 2	State 3
Event 1	YES	NO	NO
Event 2	NO	NO	YES
Event 3	YES	YES	NO

Process-Data Dependency Matrix

	Process 1	Process 2	Process3
Data set 1	YES	NO	YES
Data set 2	NO	NO	YES
Data set 3	YES	YES	NO

Function Responsibility Matrix

	Function 1	Function 2	Function 3
Responsibility 1	YES	NO	NO
Responsibility 2	NO	YES	YES
Responsibility 3	NO	NO	YES

For in-depth and comprehensive coverage of object-oriented database application and design, you can refer to *Object Oriented Databases*[3] by Dr. Setrag Khoshafian. His book presents a comprehen-

[3]Setrag Khoshafian, *Object Oriented Database,* New York, John Wiley & Sons.

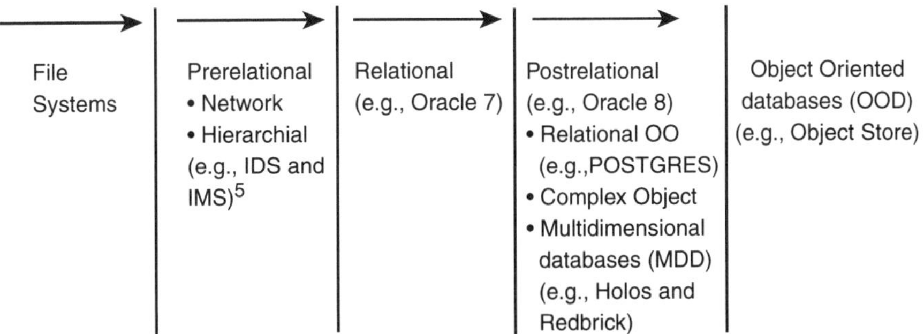

FIGURE 7.4 Evolution of Database Models.[4]

sive definition and discussion of Object-Oriented Analysis (OOA) and Object-Oriented Design (OOD) of database applications. The rich notation and diagramming techniques of OOA and OOD guide application designers through a better and stronger system specification. Dr. Khoshafian, in another book titled *Multimedia and Imaging Database Design*, discusses the evolutionary process of database models. (See Figure 7.4.) Multidimensional data models are one form of complex data models. He defines extended and object-relational models as relational systems that have incorporated object-oriented features as incremental extensions. Since the focus of this book is on an Oracle data warehouse and is an administrator's handbook, we will see in the next chapter how Oracle servers are evolving as object relational database servers. We are continuing to see object-oriented and OLAP features being added to Oracle servers, as such, bringing them closer to the long desired object-oriented database management system.

Object orientation is a natural and evolutionary step in the field of software development from which data warehousing can greatly benefit. The most important benefits are the increase in data quality, transformation traceability, and reduced cost of ongoing IT maintenance.

[4]Setrag Khoshafian and A. Brad Baker, *Multimedia and Imaging Databases*, Morgan Kaufman Publishers, San Francisco, 1996, p. 16.
[5]IDS, *Integrated Data Store*, General Electric, 1970s.
IMS, Information Management System, IBM, 1960s.

Chapter 8

ORACLE FEATURES SUITABLE FOR DATA WAREHOUSING APPLICATIONS

The purpose of this chapter is to draw your attention to the relevant data warehousing aspects of Oracle server technology. The assumption is that the audience is familiar with the basic architecture of the Oracle7 Server. Oracle server documentation sets provide the best reference information. For your convenience, we have included an overview of Oracle Server technology in Part III.[1]

8.1 ORACLE 7.3

Oracle 7.3 was released as the relational component of Oracle Universal Server. It includes a number of new and enhanced features suitable for data warehousing applications. In many ways, database servers are like cars. They are first presented to the market with a set of basic functions that are preset and defined by their manufacturers. Every additional feature set is considered an option. Options like air conditioning are nice but they are likely to add overhead to the engine as well as the price.

[1]*Oracle 7 Server Concepts Manual*, 1996. *Oracle Corporation Oracle 7 Adminisrator's Guide*, 1996 Oracle Corporation.

Generally, options are not needed by every customer but may be very necessary for some other customers. In the same manner, Oracle 7.3 has some new features as listed below that can be very useful to data- and query-intensive database applications such as data warehousing.

- Improvements in performance and scalability
- PL/SQL 2.3
- Oracle Enterprise Manager
- Enterprise Replication Server

The list of enhancements can be divided into at least two categories, performance enhancement and storage management.

Performance Enhancement

- PL/SQL improvements
- Stored triggers
- Hash joins
- Optimizer histograms
- Direct-write sorts
- Query optimization
- I/O optimization
- Stored procedures
- Complex security
- Job-queue facility
- SNMP-compliant replication MIB (Managing Information Base)

Storage Management

- Unlimited extents/dynamic data file growth
- De-allocation of unused spaces
- Dedicated temporary table spaces
- Fast index rebuild
- De-fragmentation
- Free space management
- Resizable data files
- Read-only table spaces
- Support for hierarchical storage management

8.2 ENTERPRISE DATA WAREHOUSE OPTIONS

As we stated in Chapter 6, the database server has a very central role in the data warehouse architecture. In that context, there are at least three criteria that can make or break a data warehouse database application: **performance**, **data quality**, and **security**. We are going to look into Oracle 7.3 features and identify the ones that will have performance benefits. To achieve the desired performance in a data warehouse application, the entire application architecture should be defined around this concept. The architecture focuses on defining the roles and capabilities of every layer, platform, network, database server, process model, and application code. Every layer should be designed with this goal in mind. The database server as the centerpiece should primarily address the topics of performance and scalability. In other words, the core of data warehouse operation and performance requirements challenges database servers with respect to efficient use of I/O, memory, and CPU resources. Oracle has intended to meet these challenges in Oracle 7.3 by utilizing the following approaches in its algorithms. The architecture is still the same as in previous versions of Oracle 7.

- ❑ Parallel processing techniques
- ❑ Lower cost of data transfer from memory to disk and vice versa
- ❑ Intelligent distribution of the workload among available system resources, CPU, and disk
- ❑ Increased "reuse" and "sharing" of objects

The inclusion of these enhancements indicates a strategic commitment on the part of Oracle as a leading player in addressing data warehousing requirements. This by itself is encouraging and extremely good news for mainstream customers. In Part I of this book we attempted to demonstrate how different OLAP and OLTP applications are. It is important to note that Oracle 7.3 performance improvements are minimal and only at the algorithm level. Hopefully, more fundamental improvement will follow. In the meantime, the best approach is to benchmark, evaluate, and test every relevant feature before including it in the production data warehouse server. Many factors such as platform configuration, network, system, load, and capacity should be taken into consideration.

8.2.1 ENHANCING SORT OPERATION

Oracle 7.3 has improved the sort operations throughput by using dedicated temporary table spaces. Sort operations can occur implicitly as part of a SQL statement that involves at least one of the following operations:

- ❑ CREATE INDEX
- ❑ ORDER BY
- ❑ SELECT DISTINCT
- ❑ GROUP BY
- ❑ UNION
- ❑ Unindexed joins
- ❑ Correlated subqueries

These operations involve sorting intermediate results sets. Oracle's implementation of sort operations involve the use of a work space area called the TEMP segment. Release 7.3 has enhanced the management of this work space area. The conceptual differences between the default functionality and the new functionality are presented here.

Default Functionality: Use TEMP Segments. A process that is responsible for the resolution of the SQL request will use its memory area, Process Global Area (PGA), to perform the sort. If PGA sort structure (SORT_AREA_SIZE) is large enough to hold the intermediate join results, sort will take place in PGA. If the intermediate join results end up being larger than the sort area in PGA, Oracle allocates a new TEMP segment first in the block buffer area in SGA and later in a table space. The table space selected is the previously identified and designated TEMPORARY table space for that user.

Once the sorting is done, these TEMP segments are dropped. The benefit of this approach is in the implicit acquisition of the TEMP space. A user process does not have to wait in line to acquire one. The downside is the dynamic space management of TEMP segments. The allocation and de-allocation occur for every concurrent sort activity. It requires a lot of I/O at the disk level, database locks in SGA, and internal function calls at the database server level. This algorithm can potentially cause a slowdown and bottleneck for query-intensive applications.

Enhanced Functionality: Use SORT Segments. In Oracle 7.3, a special SORT segment is created per instance and per table space to support the sort operations directed for that table space.[2] This SORT segment is created by the first sort operation and then reused and extended if necessary to support other operations. Each sort segment is managed by a new structure in SGA called SORT_EXTENT_POOL (SEP). SEP maintains the status of each sort segment by assigning "FREE" or "IN USE" states in memory. The benefit is that there is no dynamic allocation of space with I/O level cost. The downside is relatively more administration and monitoring is required, especially if the SORT segments are created in the same table space as the permanent objects. To address this issue, Oracle recommends creating dedicated temporary table space and configuring the right number of SORT segments.

SORT Segments Activation

1. Create a dedicated temporary table space:
   ```
   CREATE TABLESPACE appl_x_temp TEMPORARY
   ```
2. Configure end user's Oracle account to use this dedicated table space:
   ```
   ALTER USER appl_x_user TEMPORARY TABLESPACE appl_x_temp
   ```
3. Monitor data dictionary V$SORT_SEGMENT to see if more segments are needed.

8.2.2 OPTIMIZER IMPROVEMENTS

In Chapter 11 we will look into the role of Oracle Optimizer in the server architecture and the two **rule** and **cost** modes or algorithms. From a forward looking perspective, the idea of cost-based query optimization is very sound and promising, but when it comes to applying it to any query, it has not been as predictable as the rule-based optimizer. Oracle 7.3 includes significant enhancements to feature sets of a cost-based optimizer. Here is a summary of the ones worth investigating.

[2]Eyal Aronoff, Kevin Loney, Noorali Sonawallen, *Avanced Oracle Tuning and Administration*, Osborne McGraw Hill, Berkeley, 1997.

Parallel execution of aggregation	The SQL operations, UNION, UNION ALL, NOT IN, and GROUP BY, are set-based operations that require full table scan to achieve the desired aggregation. The query execution plan may include multiple merge and comparison operations. Prior to Oracle 7.3, the Oracle Server engine used to read the entire content of underlying tables to aggregate them sequentially. Oracle7.3 automatically recognizes this scenario and calls for the parallel execution of intermediate result sets.
Parallel aware query optimization	It considers parallel processing when planning the execution path for a query. It identifies the number of disks used to store the data and the number of available processors on the systems to determine default parameters for parallel query processing. These parameters determine how many parallel sort and merge processors should be invoked to complete the tasks. The following entries in the initialization parameter file help manage this feature: Parallel_default_max_instances = 0 Parallel_max_servers = 8 Parallel_min_percent = 0 Parallel_min_servers = 2 Parallel_server_idle_time = 5 Recovery_parallelism = 0
Optimizer histogram	This feature improves the query performance of a special data distribution scenario. When data distribution of a column value is not uniform, the use of an index in search for the data records is not necessarily beneficial. If the selectivity is low, using the index does not improve the performance. Using this feature,

	the optimizer first evaluates the distribution of data in a column specified in the WHERE clause. It estimates how many rows are likely to be returned and uses this information to make better **guesses** in regard to the use of index. In order to activate this feature, the table whose column is used in the WHERE clause must be explicitly profiled in the data dictionary using the ANALYZE command prior to query execution: ANALYZE TABLE emp COMPUTE STATISTICS FOR ALL INDEXED COLUMNS SIZE 10 In this example, the histogram size 10 is used as an example. It is best to use a number that equals or is close to the number of distinct values in the column with low selectivity.
Hash join hint	Whenever there is an equi-join (a two-table join where records with matching attributes are desired), the optimizer normally sorts each table and then merges the result (sort-merge). Using the hash join optimizer hint, a hash table on the smaller table is used to determine which data blocks contain the record. This is done dynamically and in memory (SGA). The following conditions must exist before it can be effective: • Four new INIT.ORA parameters; hash_area_size = 655,360 hash_join_enabled = TRUE hash_multiblock_io_count = 8 sequence_cache_hash_buckets = 10 • Cost-based optimizer goal for the session • Table has to have been recently ANALYZED

The impact of the above features can be monitored through the new additions to the Oracle data dictionary. Here is an example of the results of histogram analysis:

```
SELECT   ENDPOINT_NUMBER
FROM     USER_HISTOGRAMS
WHERE    TABLE_NAME = 'EMP';
```

8.2.3 ASYNCHRONOUS READ-AHEAD

The concept of asynchronous I/O is not new. It has been used at the operating system level before. Using this technique at the database server level is new and is an effective way to improve overall system throughput. It achieves high throughput by overlapping I/O and data processing operations. While the current set of data is being processed, additional data blocks are read from or written to disk. This Oracle 7 feature is available only on certain platforms. Oracle 7.2 first delivered asynchronous write-ahead. With this feature, every time a batch of blocks is submitted to disk, database writer (DBWR) does not " block" or wait for the completion acknowledgment signal that should come back from the write operation. DBWR is now free to execute other tasks, which eventually results in a very busy and productive DBWR. Similarly, the synchronous read-ahead feature overlaps the database block read operation with other processing tasks. It benefits queries involving large tables. The initialization parameters, ASYNC_WRITE and ASYNC_READ (or USE_ASYNC_IO), must be used to activate this feature. In case of ASYNC_WRITE, only one DBWR background processor should be configured to run as opposed to multiple DBWR.

8.2.4 REDUCED INTERNODE DATA TRANSFER DURING PARALLEL QUERY ON PARALLEL SERVER NODES

In case of a distributed database query, using the parallel query option, Oracle 7.3 improves the query performance using the concept of data locality. Data are sorted on their local nodes provided that they determine the data sets coming from each node. It distributes the tasks of launching the appropriate query processors on the nodes that house the data sets. As a result, the unnecessary network traffic is avoided.

8.2.5 PARTITION VIEWS

Often a data warehouse application as the keeper of the historical data may face enormous growth in the number of records and size of its fact tables. In such a case, one can split the table into multiple smaller tables or so-called partitions. The entire entity is the result of the UNION ALL of the two tables. A number of activities such as the following will benefit from this splitting:

- Data load and purge
- Index creation
- Query processing
- Export/import
- Administration

8.2.6 STORAGE MANAGEMENT

Oracle 7.3 has made a number of improvements in regards to efficient use of disk and I/O.

Table and Index Creation	Tables and indexes can be created using the "UNRECOVERABLE" option. This option avoids the use of buffer cache and rollback segments, for example; CREATE TABLE EMP(...) UNRECOVERABLE.
Storage Clause's Maximum Extents	The STORAGE clause provides an opportunity to determine the space allocation pattern. One of those elements is MAXIMUM EXTENTS. In reality EXTENTS produce fragmentation and should be monitored and controlled. The limit used to be platform-specific but once the table or index reached that limit, it could not get extended. To alleviate this problem, Oracle 7.3 imposes no maximum limit on this value.
De-allocating Unused Space	A table can grow and shrink in the course of its life. The space database level blocks once used and then freed continue to remain allocated to the object. This can be problematic when there is a shortage of available space.

Coalescing Free Space	Contiguous free space used to be coalesced automatically by SMON which was quite intensive and a performance overhead. Oracle 7.3 provides this flexibility to the DBA on demand, for example, ALTER TABLESPACE workspace COALESCE.
Resuable Temporary Segments	Temporary segments are created to provide an environment where large sort operations can take place. By default, once the sorting is done these temporary sort segments had to be dropped. Up until Oracle 7.3 these segments were created like tables and with all the associated overhead. With Oracle 7.3, a special temporary table space with a more efficient file format was created. Any operation that uses sort—CREATE INDEX, ORDER BY, SELECT DISTINCT, GROUP BY, UNION, unindexed joins, and correlated subqueries—can benefit from this enhancement: CREATE TABLESPACE temp TEMPORARY I PERMANENT These segments can then be reused by the next sort operation. As a result, the system does not have to query from DBA_FREE_SPACE and try to find a contiguous segment. Use the V$SORT_SEGMENTS data dictionary to see their status. This feature can be configured using the SORT_EXTENT_POOL (SEP latch) parameter.

8.2.7 PL/SQL 2.3

The PL/SQL 2.3 engine has improved in a number of different ways. Using PL/SQL to implement the load and transformation modules of a data warehouse application is beneficial from the following aspects.

- ❑ Increase Developer's Productivity: Using object orientation features of PL/SQL, robust, secure, and reusable load and transformation modules can be developed. PL/SQL syntax is not very far from the syntax being proposed for SQL3, the next generation of SQL. New enhancements such as the ability to read from and write into an O/S level file simplify the implementation of status reporting, data loading, and unloading modules.

- Stored Triggers: Stored triggers are stored in compiled form which improves their run-time execution. Database-level stored triggers are very important in the implementation of data replication modules.
- Improved Shared Memory Management: Only the parsed format of the PL/SQL and SQL is stored in SGA, SHARED_POOL_AREA. This results in 40 percent less memory usage compared to the previous version of PL/SQL where the text of PL/SQL was also stored.
- Serializable Transactions: SQL92 extends the read consistency model and helps developers reach a high degree of isolation in concurrent environments.
- Improved PL/SQL TABLE Data Types: PL/SQL TABLE data types can contain composite data types. In the past, a PL/SQL TABLE could have been made up of only one data type. As a result, developers had to use multiple tables in parallel and maintain the synchronization among them. Stored procedures can now return result sets that contain more than one set.

8.2.8 OTHER I/O ENHANCEMENTS

The following features have also been added to the Oracle 7.3 feature set and can be indirectly beneficial.

- Fast-Path Direct Export: The Oracle Server data export utility called "exp" is generally used as a logical backup utility. Its function is to extract the definition and data content of objects from Oracle data files and store the result in an ASCII format in an O/S level file. Data is collected using regular SQL queries, like SELECT * FROM table_X; therefore, they have to contend for system resources with other user sessions. This has been enhanced to avoid contention for SQL buffer and SGA mechanisms when reading data from the database. The new option fast-path DIRECT allows "exp", the export utility, to skip Oracle's buffer management and directly read the database files into its own export I/O buffer. The size of this I/O buffer can be specified using the RECORDLENGTH parameter. For example,

```
exp USERID = DW_ADMIN/DW_PASS FULL=Y DIRECT=Y
```

- Direct-Write Sorts: When a large sort operation occurs, it uses the (SORT_AREA_SIZE) memory space in PGA. If it is larger than that memory space, it uses the block buffer areas, DB_BLOCK BUFFER, in (SGA) using temporary segments. If it is still greater they are written to disk. This option helps I/O performance by avoiding the block buffer cache section and going directly to its dedicated sort-write buffers and later to disk. The initialization parameter that activates this feature is DIRECT_SORT_WRITES. It can be set to TRUE, FALSE, and AUTO. If it is set to AUTO, the configuration of the sort-direct-write operation can be done automatically. If it is set to TRUE, the DBA has to configure the number and size of the sort-write buffers.
- Free Space Management: The background process, SMON, performs free space management as needed, in some instances, once every 12 hours. As mentioned in Section 8.2.6, the automatic defragmentation of all contiguous free extents can be done by a database administrator using the initialization parameter: DBA_FREE_SPACE_COALESCED. It De-Allocates unused space in a Table.[3]

8.3 STAR QUERY TIPS

In Chapter 4 we discussed the concept of star schema and star query in detail. In such a model, there is a central table called a fact or star table. This table has to be added to the data model to resolve the many-to-many relationship that exists among the dimensions and actual transactions involved in a particular query. This table has a concatenated index that consists of all the dimensions' primary keys. End users' DSS type queries are often translated into these complex and large intersections of data sets. This type of selection operation that involves the joining of the large fact table with a number of smaller dimension tables is known as a **star query**.

In order to see the implementation of the solution better, let's consider a generic star model example (see Figure 8.1). Dimension tables are REGIONS, PERIODS, CUSTOMERS, SUPPLIERS, STORES. The fact table is SALES_TRX. Dimensions are related to the fact table through their primary keys. The primary key for table_star is a concatenated key composed of the other five primary keys.

[3]Kevin Loney, *Oracle DBA Handbook*, McGraw-Hill, Berkeley, 1994, p. 104.

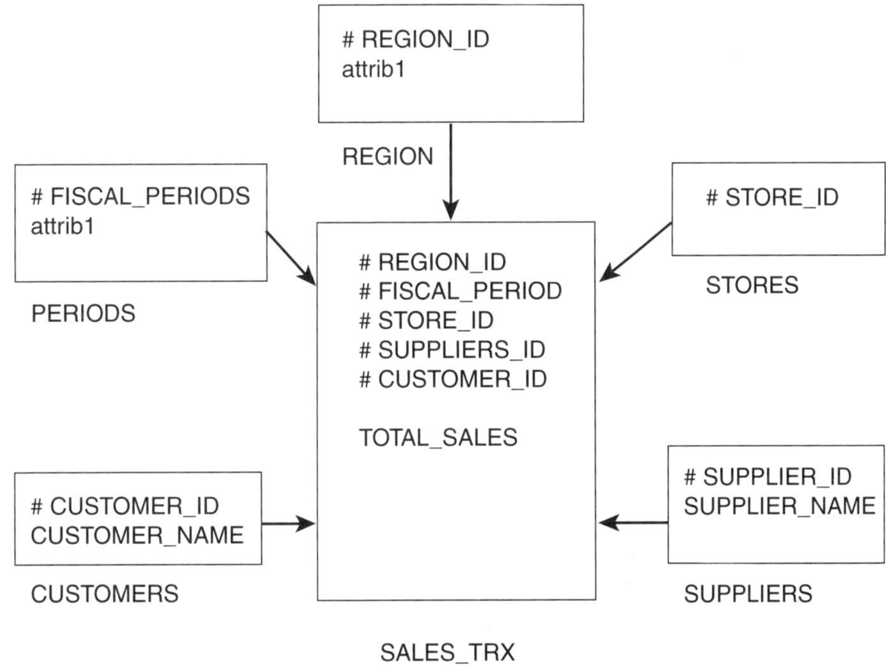

FIGURE 8.1 Star Schema Scenario: One large FACT Table and Multiple Smaller Tables or DIMENSIONS.

In this example, the following notations are used:

- Primary keys are identified using #
- aggregated_value_ stands for the attributes of the transaction table that once aggregated across different categories and dimensions can provide a quantitative measure

Example: Sales Table

```
SELECT      SUPPLIER.NAME ,STORE.NAME, SUM(TOTAL_SALES)
FROM        SALES_TRX S,CUSTOMERS C,SUPPLIERS P ,STORES O,
            REGIONS R, PERIODS F
WHERE       C.CUSTOMER              = S.CUSTOMER
AND         O.STORE                 = S.STORE
AND         P.SUPPLIER              = S.SUPPLIERS
AND         F.FISCAL_PERIOD         = S.FISCAL_PERIOD
AND         R.REGION_ID             = S.REGION_ID
GROUP BY SUPPLIER.NAME ,STORE.NAME;
```

The execution path of a star query can get quite complex and data intensive especially when all the primary keys and foreign keys used in the join are all indexed. By default, without using the star query option, the optimizer first travels through the index structure of a dimension table and identifies all the records as matched records. It then scans the fact table and selects all the rows from the table again. Therefore, the scan of indexes and sort and merge operations do not help performance and they impact it through unnecessary index range operations. As a result of this operation, potentially five full table scans of the large table can occur.

The Oracle 7.3 solution to this challenge is to create the Cartesian product result set of all the dimension tables restricted by the conditions in the WHERE clause. The matching rows are found between the Cartesian product result set that is cached with the fact table in parallel using the concatenated index on the star or fact table. Thus, the joining to the fact table is postponed until the end of the process.

Oracle 7.3 has enhanced the optimizer by recognizing these types of multi-join as a star query and handling it using the star query technique. This enhancement is said to potentially produce ten times better performance.

The star query optimizer hint is a new feature in Oracle 7.3 and must be used with cost-based optimizer mode. It looks and sounds promising. Whenever five or more tables are joined and there is one large central fact table whose key is the concatenation of the other tables' keys, it decides to use the star query technique. One can also enforce the use of the star algorithm using an optimizer hint: /*STAR hint */.

Example: Sales Table

```
SELECT /* star hint*/   SUPPLIER.NAME ,STORE.NAME,
                        sum(TOTAL_SALES)
FROM                    SALES_TRX S,CUSTOMERS C,SUPPLIERS P
                        ,STORES O, REGIONS R, PERIODS F
WHERE                   C.CUSTOMER           = S.CUSTOMER
AND                     O.STORE              = S.STORE
AND                     P.SUPPLIER           = S.SUPPLIERS
AND                     F.FISCAL_PERIOD      = S.FISCAL_PERIOD
AND                     R.REGION_ID          = S.REGION_ID
GROUP BY                SUPPLIER.NAME ,STORE.NAME;
```

The performance benefit is said to be at least ten times better.

8.4 IMPROVED INDEXING SCHEME

The Oracle 7.3 feature set has a number of enhancements in regard to indexing. We are going to briefly look into them and explain the concept used.

8.4.1 FAST INDEX REBUILD

Oracle's primary index structure is based on the B-tree indexes. They are generally good for all data manipulation language (DML), operations, Insert Update, Delete, as well as Select. B-tree indexes are used to support two purposes: as an implementation of UNIQUE and PRIMARY key constraints and as a means to have fast access to select data records. Let's take a quick look at the internal structure of a B-tree index. Suppose the following B-tree represents the index called CUSTOMER_NAME_INDEX on the CUSTOMER_NAME column in the CUSTOMER table.

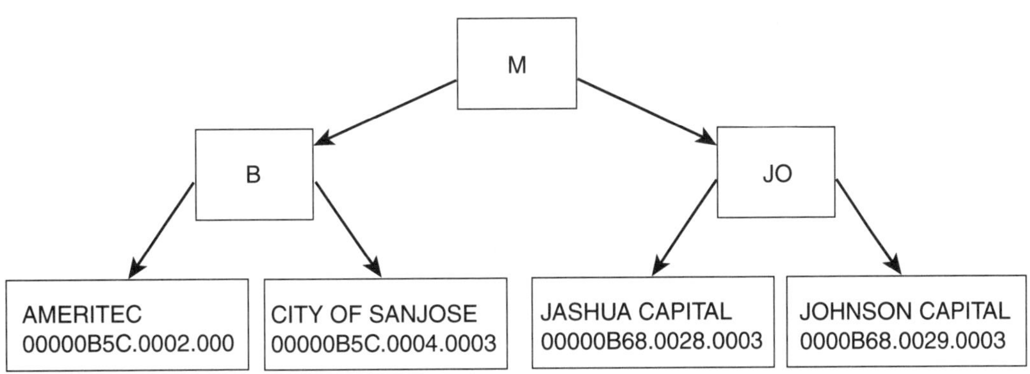

Each box is considered a node. The bottom nodes are called leaf nodes. Consider the following query:

```
SELECT    CORPORATE_ID
FROM      CUSTOMERS
WHERE     CUSTOMER_NAME like 'J%';
```

Records in the CUSTOMERS table:

ROWID	CORPORATE ID	CUSTOMER NAME
00000B5C.0002.0003	AMERITEC	AMERITECH KNOWLEDGE DATA
00000B5C.0004.0003	CITYOFSANCLARA	CITY & COUNTY OF SANTA CLARA
00000B5C.0005.0003	CDATECH	CDA TECHNOLOGIES
00000B5C.0006.0003	CAPITALSOLUTIONS	CAPITAL COMPUTER SOLUTIONS
00000B5C.0007.0003	APPLIEDMASS	APPLIED MASS ELECTRONICS
00000B5C.0008.0003	ARTERS	ARTER & PACKARD
00000B5C.0009.0003	AUSTRALIANPORTER	AUSTRALIAN PORTER
00000B68.0028.0003	JASHUACAPITAL	JASHUA CAPITAL
00000B68.0029.0003	OHNSONCAPITAL	JOHNSON CAPITAL

This query is restricting the result set, the list of corporate customers, to only those customers whose name starts with "J." The data blocks in the CUSTOMERS table will not be searched first since there is an index structure on the CUSTOMER_NAME column. The optimizer plans the retrieval and execution path and includes the following two steps:

- an INDEX RANGE SCAN of CUSTOMER_NAME_INDEX
- followed by a TABLE ACCESS BY ROWID of CUSTOMERS table

The search starts from the top of the index, node "M." It searches the index for rows which satisfy the retrieval condition. It has to traverse down to the right of node "M" to the leaf nodes. Using the index search, first the list of qualified ROWIDs (physical address of data) is retrieved. This list is used to quickly locate the actual records and will be used as a list of pointers to the physical location of customer records.

As new records are added and deleted from the table, the B-tree structure develops intrablock space fragmentation, which is when the leaf nodes (end nodes) are half filled and are not sequentially sorted any more. This index level fragmentation impacts the retrieval process and degrades performance. The traditional solution has been to drop the index and rebuild which can be a time-consuming and resource-intensive task.

Oracle 7.3 has a more practical solution to this problem which is the fast index rebuild functionality. It allows a new optimized index to be built by reading and evaluating the existing index structure. As a result, there is no need to read from the table which means using less I/O and fewer sort operations. Once the rebuild is complete the old structure is dropped. For example,

```
ALTER INDEX  customer_name_index  REBUILD
TABLESPACE  appl_x_idx;
```

This index rebuild can even be faster using the "PARALLEL" and "UNRECOVERABLE" options introduced in the previous versions:

```
ALTER INDEX  customer_name_index  REBUILD
PARALLEL
UNRECOVERABLE
TABLESPACE appl_x_idx;
```

Bitmapped Indexes. Bitmapped indexing is a new feature that is intended to help accessing records that can be selected through low-cardinality attributes. An attribute is said to have low-cardinality when the values are rarely updated and have a small number of distinct values. For instance, columns that indicate some kind of status code or gender or rate are good candidates for bitmapped indexing. For example,

```
Column: Gender
Total number of records: 14
<F:          10001101111001>
<M:          01110010000110>

Column:      Student_category
Total number of records: 26

<FRESHMAN,       10100101010101010010100101>
<SOPHOMORE,      01011000000000001100000000>
<JUNIOR,         00000010100000100000000010>
<SENIOR,         01000000001010000001011000>
```

A table can have both regular and bitmap indexes. Once a bitmap index is created in a column, a bitmap (a collection of bits 0 and 1) is created for every distinct value in the column. A bitmap representation consists of a distinct column value and bit positions for every record in the table. If the column value of a record matches the value for the bitmap table, the bit is set to "1"; otherwise it is "0." Every pair of bitmaps are ordered in turn and linked together using a B-tree index.

Bitmap index implementation in Oracle 7.3 is integrated with the server using an extension to the SQL CREATE INDEX command. Bitmap indexes are especially beneficial as a concatenated index when the combinations of values have a small number of distinct outcomes. The storage requirements are low and it is more appropriate for read-only or rarely updated attributes. Here is an example showing this feature:

```
CREATE BITMAP INDEX student_catg_index ON students
(student_category);
```

Bitmap indexes can also be used as an alternative to those concatenated indexes whose columns, when accessed together, have low cardinality. The important point to note here is to select the appropriate candidate attribute for bitmap indexing. The presence of these bitmaps impacts the performance of INSERT, UPDATE, and DELETE.

8.5 ORACLE SERVER CONFIGURATION

8.5.1 MEASURING QUALITY OF TUNING EFFORTS

Now that we have looked into some of the relevant features of Oracle7 and specifically the Oracle7.3 Enterprise data warehouse option, it may have become clearer that there are quite a number of ways to configure an Oracle Server to meet performance and scalability requirements of a data warehousing application. One may even ask, What is the tangible and measurable objective when it comes to tuning and configuration? What is the easily measurable and visible sign of a well-tuned and configured environment? Of course, the immediate and tactical response would be; Tuning objectives are met when we achieved the processing performance that was required. A more strategic response would be; The system is well tuned and will scale when database transactions (submitted through application code, on-line ad hoc access, and Oracle background processes) have the following criteria:

- I/O efficiency
- near CPU bound
- near memory bound

The reason is clear. I/O inefficiency and bottlenecks are the primary reasons for poor database performance and are much more difficult to correct when a sudden growth occurs in the load. The solution is not always in the hardware; it requires design level decision making and planning. Resolving the database performance issues when faced with a sudden increase in load when the bottleneck is memory or CPU is simpler and predictable. Therefore, this has to be kept in mind during configuration and tuning. Database administrators have to make a lot of trade-offs. Using the above criteria will make configuration decisions become simpler.

8.5.2 INIT.ORA INITIALIZATION PARAMETERS

As will be mentioned in Chapter 14, the activation, synchronization, and configuration of all internal functions of Oracle Server are managed through the database server initialization parameters listed in the INIT.ORA file. Configuring Oracle7.3 features is not an exception and involves a new set of parameters which are briefly stated here.

Configuration Parameter	Value	Usage
COMPATIBLE	7.3	It must be set in order to activate features like UNLIMITED MAXEXTENTS.
OPTIMIZER_MODE	CHOOSE or RULE or COST	If set to CHOOSE, the optimizer is free to use either algorithm, provided tables and indexes are profiled using the ANALYZE command. The cautious approach is to set it to CHOOSE at the system level. On a case-by-case basis, use the ALTER SESSION to enforce the optimizer mode that has been benchmarked and produces better performance. COST and CHOOSE modes require that the tables and indexes involved be explicitly and regularly analyzed.

Configuration Parameter	Value	Usage
HASH_JOINED_ENABLED	TRUE or FALSE	Enables the use of hash join at the system level for all queries. A cautious approach is to leave it at FALSE. Only for those tested cases where it is effective. Turn it on at the session level using ALTER SESSION statement.
HASH_AREA_SIZE	132K	Determines the maximum size (in bytes) of the hash table in memory. It should be at least twice as much as SORT_AREA_SIZE.
HASH_MULTIBLOCK_IO_ COUNT	8	It is defaulted and used like the value for the INIT.ORA parameter DB_FILE_MULTI_BLOCK_READ_COUNT. It determines the number of database blocks the hash join should read and write at a time.
SORT_DIRECT_WRITES	AUTO or TRUE or FALSE	If it is set to AUTO , the configuration of the sort-direct-write operation can be done automatically. If it is set to TRUE, the DBA has to configure the number and size of the sort-write buffers.
ASYNC_READ	TRUE or FALSE	If it is supported by the platform, it pro vides concurrent read from disk while earlier batch is being processed.
ASYNC_WRITE	TRUE or FALSE	If it is supported by the platform, it provides concurrent writes to disk while earlier batch is being processed.

This chapter provided the most interesting features of Oracle 7.3 as it relates to Data Warehousing. Subsequent chapters will present detailed practical considerations and the implementation of optimization techniques.

Chapter 9

PLANNING THE INFRASTRUCTURE

9.1 SCOPE OF THE DATABASE ADMINISTRATOR'S DUTIES

In the previous chapter, the challenges and complexities involved in building and configuring an Oracle Data Warehouse were covered in detail. The materials covered from this chapter onward focus on practical approaches and resolutions that are applicable in most scenarios. Nonetheless, the complexity of managing and administering an Oracle Data Warehouse demands a specific framework for the roles and responsibilities of a data warehouse Database Administrator (DBA).

According to the ANSI database model, the database user community can be divided into three groups:

- End users
- Application developers
- Database administrators

Each group interacts with the database from a different perspective. This interaction is defined and scoped based on their usage and perception of the data and functions captured in the database. Database administrators are primarily responsible for the integrity, health, and operation of the database in the framework of the application requirements. The DBA's responsibilities and services are generally defined in many database textbooks. Nevertheless, as the database technology evolves and the DBMS server gets more complex, the DBA's responsibilities need to be refined and evolve as well. Otherwise, end users and application developers may not benefit from a DBA's optimum skills and services quality of service. As database applications get specialized and rely on specific features of DBMS servers, a DBA has to become more aware of the subtleties and be prepared to meet the unique challenges of that application. It is in this framework that an Oracle-based Data Warehouse should be considered. It requires a DBA's careful administration with an eye on providing the following qualities:

- Scalability
- Performance
- Security
- High availability
- Extensibility

Data warehouses that overlook one or more of the above criteria have had slower success rates. Minimally, these data warehouses suffer from maintenance cost overruns and unhappy end users. First, we are going to review a DBA's general responsibilities and later those aspects of the database administration that are essential for an Oracle data warehouse will be emphasized.

The following is a minimum set of qualifications and responsibilities that a data warehouse DBA should possess and focus on.

Qualifications

- Understand relational and object database concepts
- Understand Oracle Server architecture and technologies
- Practice Oracle's optimal flexible architecture
- Understand computer system architecture and its subsystems
- Expertise in SQL and familiarity with PL/SQL languages
- Understand data warehousing and data mining concepts
- Strong communication, time management, and customer service skills

- Practice quality engineering principles
- Open minded towards the use of automation in system monitoring

Responsibilities

- Keep the Oracle Server up and running
- Identify DBA tasks in the data warehouse project plans
- Install Oracle software and patches
- Investigate Oracle Server issues
- Define platform requirements suitable for data warehousing
- Plan the physical and logical layout of the database
- Create and modify database structures
- Implement the database design
- Back up the database
- Recover the database
- Configure the database optimally
- Prepare capacity plan based on peak requirements
- Establish security policies
- Tune database performance
- Collect metrics on load, usage, growth, throughput, and availability
- Provide technical support to other Oracle users and developers
- Prepare scripts and documents in support of DBA procedures

9.2 PROCESS MANAGEMENT

According to the Software Engineering Institute,[1] the majority of information systems organizations, nearly 76 percent, suffer from a so-called software engineering immaturity. The symptoms of such immaturity are:

- Poor quality
- Cost overruns

[1]Kevin Loney, *Oracle DBA Handbook*, McGraw-Hill, Berkeley, 1994. p.123.

- ❑ Late delivery
- ❑ Project cancellation
- ❑ Huge backlog of enhancements
- ❑ Outdated technology
- ❑ Employee turnover

Data warehouse projects are no exception. In fact, the business impact of any of the above incapabilities is greater for a data warehouse project. After all, it is intended to bring together the most optimal hardware, software, business, technical, and management talents to contribute directly to the enterprise's mission statement. The question is: How can one plan to avoid this "IS application dilemma?" In this section we present our subjective perspective and opinions that have emerged from years of direct experience in this industry and academia.

Software development, like other engineering disciplines, needs strong project management. An effective data warehouse project plan has a threefold objective: methodology management, project management, and process resource management. A data warehouse application starts as a new project once and is expected to go through enhancements continuously to directly support the enterprise's mission-critical goals. The heart of process management is regular and adequate communication. It is vital for the project manager to customize the standards and methodologies, establish a practical and effective process, and deliver a successful project. There are a number of tools that can help facilitate this process that have been found to be effective. Regardless of the tools being used, the following factors should always be included in a data warehouse project plan:

- ❑ Estimating cost and resource
- ❑ Planning
- ❑ Tracking
- ❑ Quality control

We have found that once we separate the technical leadership role of the project from the pure project management role, the ability to focus on all of the above areas increases dramatically. The technical leader identifies the architecture, components, tasks, risks, and success factors using an accepted methodology involved in the technical implementation of the data warehouse. The project manager, on the other hand, receives these inputs coupling them with strong project management skills delivers a plan that supports the project strategy, resources, and delivery requirements.

One effective methodology is Oracle's application development methodology called the CASE*Method. This methodology consists of a complete set of templates, guidelines, models, maps, techniques, and tools. The life cycle of a project in the CASE*Method consists of the following phases:

- Strategy
- Analysis
- Design
- Build and Documentation
- Testing (systems and user acceptance)
- Training
- Production release
- Enhancement (Start over from the top but focus on a specific subsection of a subject area.)

Due to the nature of a data warehouse application and the fact that it is expected to go through regular enhancements, a rigid version of the methodology can be unproductive and impractical. An adaptation of Rapid Application Development (RAD), and Joint Application Development (JAD), which are based on the best practices in the industry, has been shown to be very effective. It is not uncommon to see developers, managers, and DBAs resistance to the use of any methodology. This is probably due to past experiences with endless and exhaustive bureaucratic processes that cause bottlenecks rather than facilitate. We have found the RAD approach quite efficient in the development of a data warehouse application.

As described in detail in Part I, one of the primary application developments of a data warehouse consists of the following three layers of the architecture:

- INTERIM
- ATOMIC
- COLLECTION (summarization)

Data and process modeling efforts should cover all three areas of the architecture. Depending on the delivery requirements and the infrastructure, each of these layers can be simple (thin) or extensive (thick). The following checklist represents our adaptation of the Oracle CASE*Method RAD approach, called FASTPATH for a data warehouse application's development requirements.[2]

- ❑ Time is of the essence
- ❑ Strong partnership and respect between business and IS teams
- ❑ Business goals and process awareness
- ❑ System development skills
- ❑ Communication/team management skills

Here is a list of best practices and checklists we have found to be very helpful:

- ❑ Become very familiar with the business processes and the users who will be the beneficiaries of this application
- ❑ Make an educated guess of what is required based on existing knowledge, then check to make sure the guess is reasonable
- ❑ Define the application architecture, partitions, layers, and components
- ❑ Identify high-level tasks and the resources required for each
- ❑ Focus rapidly on key aspects of a system that can be achieved without much exposure
- ❑ Establish the business model via interviews and meetings
- ❑ Aggressively decide what to implement, leave room in the design for future maneuvers, and deliver a prototype of the data warehouse project very quickly
- ❑ Eventually replace initial development by planning a replacement system
- ❑ Prepare the end user's data dictionary (metadata) and submit for approval. Preferably, link this layer with the developer's view in CASE or a modeling tool

[2]Richard Barker, *CASE*Method Function and Process Modeling*, Addison Wesley, Oracle Corporation 1992.

Best Practice Techniques

- ❑ Define business subject areas of the ATOMIC layer
- ❑ Use entity relationship and hierarchy modeling of data sets to set the scope of the ATOMIC layer very quickly
- ❑ Use dimensional modeling of COLLECTION and SUMMARIZATION layers
- ❑ Model critical core processing components using dependency diagrams
- ❑ Define join, aggregation, and time series in the data
- ❑ Use good CASE, database query, and OLAP tools to prototype
- ❑ Enhance requirements and business data definitions using prototype and user acceptance testing
- ❑ Adopt standards to cut down disagreements on esoteric styles
- ❑ Use diagrams to illustrate data warehouse concepts and front-end tool navigation

Reverse Engineering

- ❑ Prepare data flow charts of what is already in existence.
- ❑ Use data flow charts to communicate and share ideas. Modify them to be the basis of the development of the new/replacement system.

Quality and completeness check

- ❑ Test the model and present ideas to the users for feedback
- ❑ Check to see if the model is complete and accurate
- ❑ Ask the **what if** and **does it** questions
- ❑ Consider flexibility, reusability, robustness, ease of use, performance, and high availability
- ❑ Are the business reasons for developing the system clear?
- ❑ How can we measure whether the system helps the relevant business objectives?
- ❑ Is the purpose clearly described?
- ❑ Are the system's objectives and critical success factors clear?
- ❑ Is the boundary clearly defined? Which delivery is "meeting expectations,"? Which one is "exceeding expectation"?
- ❑ Are the interfaces to other systems clearly and minimally defined?

- ❑ Are the different user groups clearly defined?
- ❑ Have you provided a complete list of functions to be implemented?
- ❑ Is there a description of the system architecture?
- ❑ Are the client's acceptance criteria for the system defined and documented?
- ❑ What are the cost/benefit/time scale/scope?
- ❑ Have the executive users and systems people bought into the concept?
- ❑ Is the user's data dictionary or metadata documented and on-line?
- ❑ Are the infrastructure and operation ready to support the new code/system?
- ❑ Are there resources to support rollout and general demands (training, installation, security)?

DBA's additional focus: Performance Management

- ❑ audit the usage
- ❑ identify bottlenecks
- ❑ tune the bottlenecks
- ❑ use the above to develop proactive maintenance strategy

9.3 INFRASTRUCTURE SUITABLE FOR THE DATA WAREHOUSE USING ORACLE OPTIMAL FLEXIBLE ARCHITECTURE (OFA)[3] GUIDELINES

9.3.1 IDENTIFYING INFRASTRUCTURE REQUIREMENTS

The data warehouse infrastructure plan should be based on its critical success and failure factors. At a minimum, an infrastructure plan should be used to observe the following:

[3] Chidori Boeheim, Tony Duarte, Mark Johnson, *Oracle for UNIX Performance Tuning Tips*, Oracle Corporation, 1993.

Critical Success Factors

- ❑ End users' needs
- ❑ Project must be within the time frame and budget
- ❑ Cost of maintenance and support
- ❑ Infrastructure readiness
- ❑ Source data volume and growth rate
- ❑ Collaborative decision making
- ❑ Operational aspect of the production environment
- ❑ Availability within the production time frame

Critical Failure Factors

- ❑ Poor quality data delivered to end users, that is, decision makers.
- ❑ Inaccurate forecast and plans.
- ❑ Loss of profit and productivity due to inaccurate analytical data as a result of using the data warehouse

The infrastructure requirements can be divided into two distinct categories: quantifiable and nonquantifiable. In this age of performance-based management, even the infrastructure performance should be measured. Change in any of these measures can impact the performance of the infrastructure.

Directly Quantifiable Measures: It is generally easier to identify the quantifiable measures. Here is a list of suggested measures:

- ❑ resource capacity
- ❑ batch job elapsed time
- ❑ concurrent number of users
- ❑ maximum number of users
- ❑ transaction response time
- ❑ number of times service level agreement requirements are met
- ❑ number of applications/system/user/network/HW/database server failures
- ❑ backup schedule

- ❏ number of requests and paging or contacting on-call personnel
- ❏ number of escalation of issues to management

Nonquantifiable Measures: On the other hand, nonquantifiable measures are more abstract and do not have definitions that are formally polished. They are more of a perception that is a uniquely identifiable condition. They should generally be associated with a tangible and quantifiable measure. For instance, the system is reliable when it meets the service level agreement delivery time window 90 percent of the time. The important point is that they should be considered and defined within the boundaries of the enterprise and data warehouse deliverables, such as:

- ❏ reliability
- ❏ scalability
- ❏ extensibility
- ❏ flexibility
- ❏ maintainability
- ❏ ease of use
- ❏ security
- ❏ recoverability
- ❏ optimized
- ❏ tuned
- ❏ dependable
- ❏ supportable
- ❏ usable
- ❏ available

9.3.2 IMPLEMENT INFRASTRUCTURE REQUIREMENTS

Once the requirements are defined, they need to be turned into **flexible** and **practical procedures** that can be adopted and enforced easily. Of course, they cannot all happen overnight, especially in an environment that is more in a reactive mode than a proactive mode. The point here is that a data warehouse cannot afford **not** to have a planned infrastructure. We have seen that it is possible to establish and implement these procedures for just the data warehouse application. Due to its special and actually quite expensive resource needs, the data warehouse team is encouraged to be a pioneer in the infrastructure arena. Eventually, the benefits and the return on investment will not go unnoticed by management and the developers. It then becomes more of a norm rather than an exception. Once again, it is the role of the data warehouse technical lead and database administrator to jointly drive the following procedures:

- ❑ Review existing standards and procedures
- ❑ Prepare/identify problem/bug/issue management procedures
- ❑ Prepare/identify source code management procedures
- ❑ Prepare/identify change control procedures
- ❑ Prepare/identify software distribution and migration procedures
- ❑ Prepare/identify database object migration procedures
- ❑ Prepare/identify database/file patch installation procedures
- ❑ Prepare/identify providing secure access procedures

9.3.3 ORACLE'S OPTIMAL FLEXIBLE ARCHITECTURE (OFA) GUIDELINES

The optimal flexible architecture guidelines[4] is a set of comprehensive recommendations that Oracle has been publishing since Version 6 of Oracle Server. It is meant to provide a road map of the best practices when it comes to configuration of a medium to large Oracle Server. The information presented here has been gathered from a number of Oracle Server documents.

At a high level, OFA is based on a set of directory structures and Oracle physical layout and configuration parameters that facilitate the management and administration of the Oracle database. The following summarized set of practical guidelines is partly based on OFA and partly based on actual data warehouse experience. The guidelines can increase permanent and general performance gain and facilitate database maintenance.

[4]*GRACIE for UNIX Performance Tuning Tips*, Oracle Corporation, 1993. p. 47.

- ❑ Organize directories and subdirectories in a hierarchical fashion
- ❑ Keep ORACLE_HOME clean from non-Oracle scripts and files
- ❑ Name disk drives storing Oracle data such that a wild card can be used when referring to all of them
- ❑ Keep directories storing database data files at the same level as file system hierarchies
- ❑ In a multidatabase environment, organize data files in directories named after database names
- ❑ Store control file, redo file, and data files in separate directories
- ❑ Minimize disk fragmentation:
  - Use striping, detect datase "bubbles" and "honeycombs"
  - Separate application objects into business subject areas. Use subject-area-specifc table spaces to store the database objects. This can be beneficial during data access, ease of backup/recovery, and storage configuration optimization
  - Keep temporary, rollback, and nonsystem data segments out of the SYSTEM table space and subject-area-specific table-spaces
  - Separate rollback segment from temporary, data, and index segments by storing them in separate table spaces
  - Separate data segments that have high volatility or different purge/backup/recovery needs from other data segments in separate table spaces
  - Keep at least three copies of control files in three different locations (preferably, different disks and different controllers)
  - Have at least three redo log files and isolate them by placing them on low-activity disks
  - Use software-level mirroring of redo logs instead of hardware level
  - Avoid the I/O performance hit of RAID disks on redo log groups by storing Oracle level mirroring and placing them on non-RAID disks
  - Use operating system-level disk striping as much as possible. If that is not available, use Oracle table-/table-space-level striping

9.3.4 DETAILED DATABASE ADMINISTRATION CHECKLIST

Use the following checklist to evaluate your Oracle Data Warehouse configuration to check its conformity with OFA and other best practice guidelines.

1. DBA Performance Analysis Checklist

1.1 Optimum flexible architecture rules

1. Operating system administration standards
   a. volume naming standards and consistency
   b. separate user home directory from Oracle 7 files
   c. Oracle O/S account as owner of files
   d. separate individual DBA account with DBA group privileges
   e. separate O/S owner for database application files
   f. individualized O/S account for each application user
   g. Oracle owns oraenv, coraenv, dbhome, dbaenv, cdbaenv, oratab
2. Oracle software installation standards
   a. use Oracle login only for upgrade and installation
   b. keep Oracle login home directory clean
   c. separate Oracle data files into version-named directories
   d. version-based $ORACLE_HOME directory
   e. create and use an on-line Oracle/TAR directory for future reference
   f. maintain oraenv, coraenv, dbhome,dbaenv, cdbaenv, oratab, sqlnet
3. Oracle database creation standards
   a. Oracle database name
   b. Oracle instance name
   c. value of environment variable: $DBA
   d. administrative directory for each database
   e. structure of administrative directory
   f. configuration file config.ora

g. content of config.ora
control_files,init_sql_files,db_block_size,db_name ... dump destinations

h. instance parameter files: initX.ora, initX_0.ora , initX_1.ora

i. Oracle directory on each disk

j. restriction on content of Oracle directory: control file, redo log file, database file

k. table spaces: SYSTEM, RBSnn, TEMPnn, TOOLS, USERS

l. database segment separation based on fragmentation,I/O contention, project focus

m. number, name, and location of control files

n. number, size, location, and name of redo log files

o. data files' name and location

p. segments in SYSTEM

q. table space resource privilege setup and administration

r. using SYSTEM as default table space

s. TEMP table space initialization (ks+b)

t. rollback segment R0

u. other rollback segments' name and location

1.2 Distribution of data segments across different table spaces

1.3 Data and index Segments' Initialization

1.4 Temporary and rollback initialization based on active transactions

Application Design

1.5 Use of CHAR and VARCHAR2

1.6 Location of LONG columns

1.7 SQL statements reuse

Data Access Analysis

1.8 1. SQL statement tkprof

2. Analyze concurrent read/ rows returned

3. Run bstat/estat report

1.9 Oracle parallel query option analysis

Memory Management Analysis

1.10 Oracle block size should be multiple of O/S block size
1.11 Number of database block buffers with respect to hit ratio
1.12 Number of redo log buffers
1.13 Data dictionary cache based on object get/object miss ratio
1.14 O/S swap-out activities
1.15 O/S page-out activities
1.16 O/S swap-space allocation
1.17 O/S ability to allow more control of SGA swapping
1.18 SGA fragmentation
1.19 O/S ability to lock SGA in physical memory
1.20 Library cache misses analysis

Disk I/O Analysis

1.21 Redo log's disk location
1.22 Striping disks at O/S level
1.23 Striping at the database level
1.24 RAID disks' analysis for WRITE activities (Rollback +, Redo logs -)
1.25 Database writers based on number of disks
1.26 O/S support for "list I/O"
1.27 O/S support for "asynchronous I/O"
1.28 Large disk request queue
1.29 Hot files analysis
1.30 Location of hot files
1.31 Hot segment analysis
1.32 Disk fragmentation analysis
1.33 Other applications on the server
1.34 Table space fragmentation analysis
1.35 Capacity for more database block buffers
1.36 File system type and performance rating
1.37 O/S support for "raw disks"
1.38 Capacity for additional disks

CPU Usage Analysis

1.39 CPU load balance analysis
1.40 Oracle user/processes priority
1.41 Query server analysis
1.42 Batch scheduling control and capability analysis
1.43 Usage patterns analysis
1.44 O/S support for processor affinity/binding on SMP
1.45 Degree of client/server process distribution
1.46 O/S support of "post-wait driver"
1.47 O/S and Oracle support for Single_task
1.48 Overall current and future expansion plans of system (CPU, CACHE, faster CPU)

Tuning Resource Contention

1.49 Rollback segment contention hit rate analysis
1.50 Redo log buffer latch contention analysis
1.51 Parallel query contention analysis
1.52 Analysis of "spin-count" on SMP
1.53 Analysis of O/S system parameters

2. Documentation

2.1 Record the result of all the analysis and the findings

3. Overall Oracle 7 Database Administration Plan

3.1 OFA-based configuration plan
3.2 Backup and recovery plan
3.3 Database expansion plan
3.4 Fragmentation monitoring
3.5 Performance monitoring

4. Results and Adjusting the Scope Going Forward

9.4 DATA WAREHOUSE CAPACITY PLANNING

9.4.1 CAPACITY PLANNING CONCEPTS

The ultimate goal of capacity planning is to design the system so that under peak CPU and disk utilization the ideal response times can still be met. The method we are proposing here is capacity planning by studying and taking into account the following criteria:

- IS organization platform, tools, standards, and limitations
- Data warehouse application's current requirements and future plans
- User acceptance testing
- General ad hoc and batch usage
- Company's growth and its impact on data warehouse subject area and usage

Often, capacity planning in an IS environment is done based on the first criteria. This approach will not result in adequate infrastructure when it comes to a resource-intensive application like a data warehouse. We have found that the data warehouse technical leaders and database administrators can cooperate and proactively take into account the other criteria. Generally, data warehouse project managers can also provide information on future needs of the project and the impact of the company's growth on the application in terms of number of users, and the end users' perceptions and expectations.

9.4.2 THE RIGHT APPROACH: GATHER DATA PRIOR TO ANALYZING

- Define the functions performed by end users
- Determine how often such functions will be performed
- Define end-users' performance expectations (response time)
- Measure or estimate the resource requirements

The tangible delivery of capacity planning is a platform and database configuration that can meet the future peak conditions. As a result of the study of the above criteria, the present peak conditions at every server level (O/S, Oracle Server, OLAP server) are quantitatively described in the following resources:

- ❑ Workload
- ❑ Logical I/O
- ❑ Physical I/O
- ❑ Response time
- ❑ CPU usage
- ❑ Memory usage
- ❑ Disk usage

The basic system monitoring tools are generally adequate to collect the above statistics. Of course, this step of the process can be tedious and time consuming. Effort has to be spent to prepare customized DBA scripts that collect statistics on the platform. A more efficient way of accomplishing this step is to take advantage of advances in automated system monitoring and use an off-the-shelf tool rather than preparing customized scripts and tons of log files.

The above data values can then be analyzed using the following formulas:

- ❑ Sum up the total resource requirements (all users and frequencies)
- ❑ Decompose response time into CPU and disk
- ❑ Study the effects of CPU and disk utilization on overall response time (What portion is spent in internal queues?)

Response Time = Service Time/(1% utilization of the resource)

- ❑ Choose the type and number of disks
- ❑ Choose the power and the number of CPUs (SMP)
- ❑ Choose the overall size and segmentation configuration of main memory

The above information can be tracked, trended, and summarized in spreadsheets. Using basic probability and statistics techniques, it will be possible to produce a more practical capacity plan for your data warehouse.

9.4.3 GROWTH FORECAST AND MONITORING

A server's capacity forecast cannot be independent of the entire organization's growth forecast. At the time of capacity planning we should ask such a question: Is this a very successful and fast-growing organization whose overall company goal is to grow at a minimum rate of 50 percent? If not properly planned, this can be a problem for the data warehouse application with inadequate data transportation **channels** and infrastructure. From a higher perspective it may be a "good" position to be in. It is wise to plan as aggressively as the operational arm of the organization is generating data.

The server administrator of the data warehouse is generally responsible for the hardware configuration and capacity. The data warehouse team can provide valuable input to this process. As new projects are planned for data warehouse customers, the impact of these projects at a high level should be made known to the data warehouse server administrators as early in the process as possible. It should generally include elements that can impact the growth, such as:

- ❑ Anticipated data volume
- ❑ Data subject area variety
- ❑ Anticipated users
- ❑ An estimate of data growth by month

We have found the estimated data growth to be the most challenging. One method to estimate is to find a dependable correlation between the growth at the database table level and the corresponding business process. For instance, if a total of 10K can be stored in various tables for every new sales order (and let's assume that the business strategist estimates a rate of 3000 orders per day), that will correlate to about a 30 megabyte per day increase in the database volume.

This correlation can always be checked with business contacts and can be updated as new projects are added to the data warehouse. Surely there are other big-picture strategic factors that can impact the data growth from the high-level goals of an organization. For instance, the growth of the enterprise from the following perspectives can provide a quantitative means to measure the growth impact of the infrastructure:

- orders booked
- products shipped
- head counts
- impact of acquisitions and mergers
- distributed multisite source systems

One of the effective and easy methods of monitoring the growth impact is to proactively, on an ongoing basis, monitor the data volume of end user access and the variety of subject areas that are regularly loaded into the data warehouse. By trending these numbers over time we can scientifically be prepared for sudden changes in the data volume.

9.4.4 DEVELOPMENT AND TEST ENVIRONMENT

In addition to capacity planning, the data warehouse infrastructure needs to cover a few other issues. The productivity of the development and test environment is one of those issues. The data warehouse development team needs to count on the availability of the development and test environments that support their RAD approach in the project life cycle. For the RAD approach, time is of the essence and any delay due to the unavailability or limitation of the concurrent development and test environments can have a negative impact. This issue can be addressed by using a scaled-down version of the production environment with adequate system and database administration support.

9.4.5 DEVELOPMENT ENVIRONMENT, TOOLS, FACILITIES, AND PROCEDURES

The following is a list of some of the fundamental elements of the infrastructure that need to be planned for:

- Define release procedure and source code control
- Implement batch scheduler capable of parallel processing and job monitoring
- Define directory structures for the application and users on the server and client

- ❑ Define environment variables and paths
- ❑ Define database resource quotas
- ❑ Prepare development environment for functional and standard testing
- ❑ Prepare/install tools:
  - Set up CASE repository server
  - Configure SQL*NET
  - Create data dictionary objects for EXPort and IMPort utilities
  - Configure SQL TRACE, SVRMGR, TKPROF, EXPLAIN plan
  - Provide read access to dynamic performance V$ tables to all
- ❑ Prepare test environment for load and integrity testing
- ❑ Plan resources for operational support:
  - Produce an SLA with each cross-functional group that requires or provides services with respect to the data warehouse on a regular basis
  - Establish off-hour monitoring of jobs and escalation of infrastructure issues
  - Monitor and document issues through metadata modules
- ❑ Standardize archival strategy
  - How long should the backups be kept?
  - How often is the backup done?
  - Back up downtime, if possible, use third mirrored disk for cold backups
  - Schedule a regular logical backup
  - Schedule a regular cold backup
  - Back up audit process
  - Regular test of backup copies
  - Back up the development and test environmentsregularly
  - Regular testing of backup power supply

The next chapter illustrates the implementation of the concepts presented in this chapter.

Chapter 10

IMPLEMENTATION OF THE APPLICATION DESIGN

10.1 DESIGN FOR SCALABILITY, PERFORMANCE, SECURITY, AND HIGH AVAILABILITY

10.1.1 OPERATIONAL QUALITY CRITERIA

As mentioned earlier, to achieve a high quality data warehouse application, upfront planning and design are key. If one is not familiar with the technical challenges of data warehouses, consider topics such as scalability, performance, security, and high availablility as typical DBA topics that can be addressed whenever there are problems, most often after an application rollout. It is common to see a data warehouse application designed, built, and rolled out with high expectations and visibility show the first signs of scalability and performance issues six months later. End users become disappointed with the performance and a crisis is at hand! A special task force is called to **tune** and **scale** the application. Some level of performance tuning is applied, but usually those fixes are temporary and the next wave of increased volume can create another crisis all over again.

Therfore, in case of a data warehouse, the application design should formally address the typical operational quality issues. This provision makes the architicture less vulnerable to volume and query increases. The following set of sample criteria illustrates the type of changes that can occur after the data warehouse is rolled out.

Operational Quality Requirements	Current state	In 6 months	In 12 months
Availability	12 hours/day	12 hours/day	18 hours/day
Refresh rate	500 Mb/day	800 Mb/day	1600 Mb/day
Transformation batch function	20 jobs/day	30 jobs/day	60 jobs/day
Optimal refresh elapsed time	11 hrs	11 hrs	6 hrs
Data volume	30 gigabytes	40 gigabytes	80 gigabytes
User access rate	50 users/day	70 users/day	140 users/day
Concurrent user access rate	20 users	40 users	100 users
SGA size	0.5 gigabytes	1.0 gigabytes	3 gigabytes
Throughput(Mbytes/hr) (refresh rate/elapsed time)	500 Mb/11 hrs = 45	800 Mb/11 hrs = 73	1600 Mb/6 hrs. = 266

The above table represents some of the operation criteria of a real-life data warehouse application. As you can see, the rate of growth is such that unless the platform and the Oracle Server configuration continue to scale and reach higher limits, the operation quality will start to decline. These criteria can be analyzed in two disctinct data access scenarios:

- data load and transformation—refresh batch processing
- data access—end user querying

10.1.2 DATA LOAD AND TRANSFORMATION BATCH PROCESSING

As described in Chapter 7, data in the data warehouse gets refreshed periodically. This refresh is done through the data load and transformation modules. The time it takes to process these batch jobs is often one of the major quality issues. Suppose the batch processing of data warehouse X consists of loading and processing six subject areas on a daily basis. Figure 10.1 shows how one approach will look.

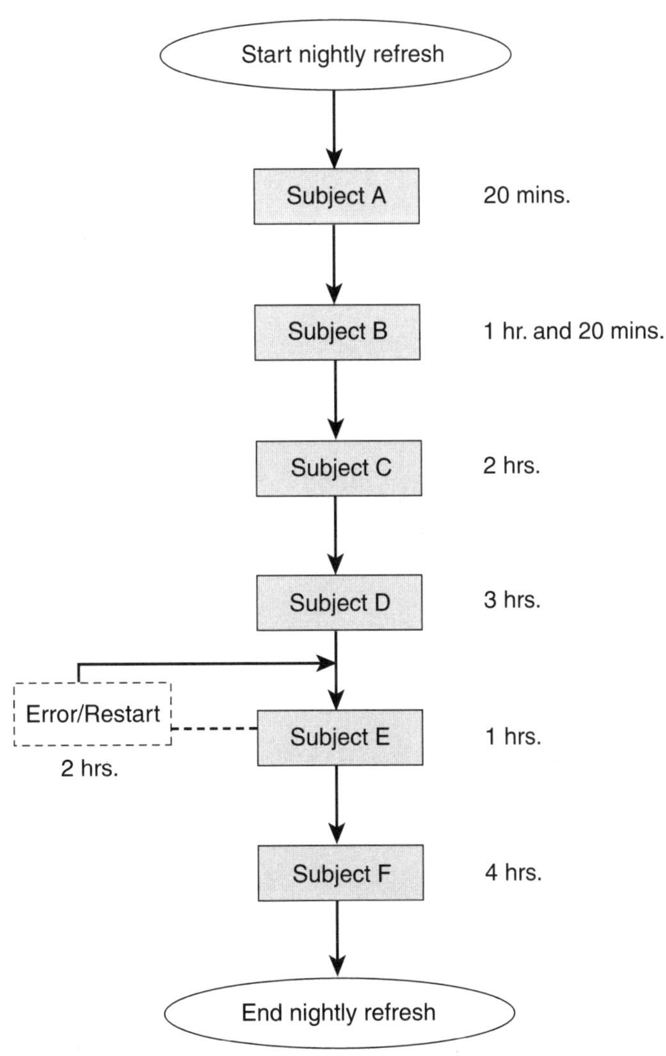

FIGURE 10.1 Sequential Batch Processing of Refresh Modules.

The above batch processing will take about 11 hours and 40 minutes and another hour for a backup job, thus leaving only 11 hours of data warehouse availability to end users. As long as (1) the volume of data, (2) the load on the data warehouse host server, and (3) Oracle continues to be the same, one can probably expect throughput to remain unchanged. Consider the case where a data/system/database/operator error has occurred along the critical path and the module responsible for subject area E is impacted. Supposing it takes 2 hours to correct the problem and the refresh job needs to be restarted. Hopefully with the way the batch job is set up the restart run will start only from subject area E. Assuming the rest of the processing goes well, data availability in the data warehouse will be about 1 hour late. As you can see, it takes only a very small glitch in this type of batch processing to miss the service level agreement which consequently impacts the overall data warehouse quality.

One effective approach in dealing with this common issue of scalability and performance problems in a data warehouse is using the following proven design considerations and techniques.

Design Techniques	Description	Benefit
Fine-grain functional modularity **Method:** Use PL/SQL stored procedure and packages along with strong exception handling standards to handle the refresh of one data set at a time.	Load and transformation modules are broken down into smaller and independent modules which can be grouped together. Each module is responsible for its own job run status logging and exception handling.	**Restorability:** Efficient batch job recovery is made possible when job rerun becomes necessary. Instead of restarting from an earlier stage in the process, only the impacted data sets are reprocessed.
Minimum functional dependency among the batch jobs and modules **Method:** Keep the PL/SQL stored procedures independent unless there is a semantic dependency.	Independent small component-based approach that allows a high degree of independent and parallel runs of each functional module.	**Performance and Scalability:** System throughput is greatly increased as more system resources are used for user processes and less system idle time is reported. This technique demands an SMP or MPP platform.

Design Techniques	Description	Benefit
Avoid writing into ROLL-BACK segments and redo logs, if possible **Method:** In cases where an empty table is populated or an index is rebuilt, use the UNRECOVERABLE option of CREATE TABLE or CRE-ATE INDEX.	By default Oracle uses the ROLLBACK segments and redo logs when populating an empty table or creating an index. This overhead that includes disk I/O can be avoided when transac-tion-level recovery is not needed.	**Peformance** It improves INSERT, UPDATE, and DELETE operations performance.
Isolating *published* data from *being processed* data **Method:** Suppose table X has the published result. RENAME TABLE x_work to x_temp; RENAME TABLE x to x_work; RENAME TABLE x_temp to x;	As data sets are processed, a set of work tables are used. Once the refresh is completed, the data are published through the renaming of database objects which occurs at the memory level and not at the disk I/O level. Therefore, it is not dependent on the vol-ume of data being pub-lished to end users.	**High-availability** End users and OLAP tools can continue to access the previously refreshed data from the data warehouse until the new data are com-pletely refreshed and made available to them.
Intermediate work tables **Method:** When preparing a many-to-many table join, aggrega-tion, and summarization, use intermediate work tables. Reset them first using TRUNCATE TABLE x STORAGE REUSE.	Often using work tables is much easier than sorting and resorting the same set of large amounts of data.	**Performance** It improves join opeations performance.

Design Techniques	Description	Benefit
Store aggregated STAR query results **Method:** Create fact tables using STAR query. Hint at different aggregated and trended levels.	Precalculate the heavy aggregations and publish the end result for other data warehouse tools.	**Scalability** Improves the information querying operations regardless of the number of dimensions involved.
Release resources as soon as the work is done **Method:** When updating, inserting, and deleting from very isolated work tables, use cursors to commit records in batches. Also use UNRECOVERABLE option when creating /populating work tables	Granted the content of these tables is not going to be referenced by another concurrent transaction, there is no reason to use ROLLBACK segments and other system resources.	**Improve Peformance**

Now let's consider the long-running data warehouse batch jobs. The objective is to apply a technique that can shorten the batch jobs' elapsed time and improve performance. The following two techniques can save a few hours and provide enough recovery time in case of an error in the refresh process.

1. Fine-grain functional modularity.
2. Minimum functional dependency among the batch jobs and modules can be used to parallelize processing.

As shown in Figure 10.2, load modules of subject areas B and C are running in parallel.

10.1.3 DATA ACCESS—END-USER AD HOC QUERY

This area of the architecture can be designed for high performance using a number of tested and proven techniques. The list below presents some of the readily available and useful techniques in the Oracle environment.

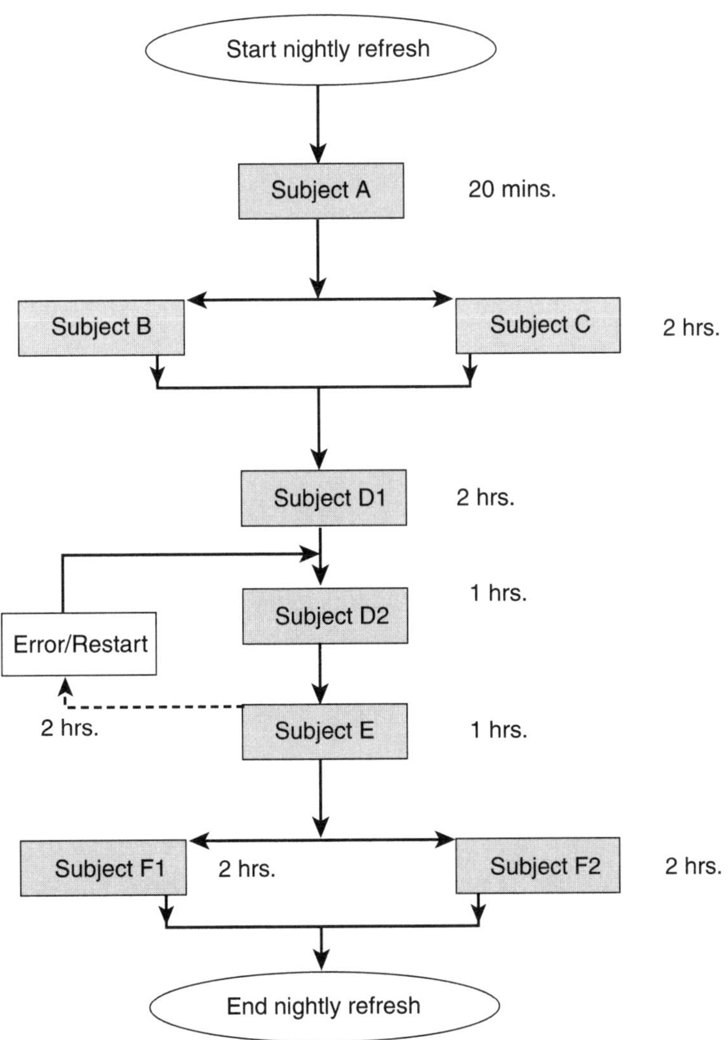

FIGURE 10.2 Parallel Processing of Fine-Grained Batch Jobs.

Design Techniques	Description	Benefit
Partitioning large tables **Method:** Create a table that stores all records belonging to a particular fiscal period. Build views to encompass tables two at a time using UNION ALL operation. This method can be further enhanced by placing tables in separate TABLESPACES and disk drives to further distribute I/O.	To avoid scanning vast amount of records all stored in one physical table, split them into mutually exclusive physical tables. The split criteria can be based on an attribute that is very commonly used and has low cardinality like fiscal year.	**Improves Performance** Queries will not necessarily pay the price for a large consolidated table.
Cache small and medium tables **Method:** Depending on the SGA and database block buffer size, use the CACHE option of the CREATE TABLE or ALTER TABLE commands. Use the init.ora parameter SMALL_TABLE_THRESHOLD to automatically keep the small table in cache.	Keeping the content of a table in SGA improves query performance. The server process responsible for that transaction does not have to go to disk to try to read the content of that table. This avoids unnecessary I/O.	**Improves Peformance**
Avoid scanning long data types **Method:** During the implementation of physical model, arrange columns by placing LONG column as the last column of a table. Preferably normalize the table with a LONG column per tables.	Every time there is a table scan, all rows of a table are scanned. In cases where the SELECT clause does not include any long data type, the unnecessary I/O can be avoided by isolating long data type attributes.	**Improves Peformance**

Design Techniques	Description	Benefit
Avoid row chaining **Method:** During the implementation of a physical model, arrange columns of a table by placing the NULL columns after all the NOT NULL columns. Use the ANALYZE TABLE command to identify the chained rows. They can be corrected by deleting and reinserting them into the same table.	Row chaining can seriously impair time spent executing a table scan. A row is chained when it does not fit entirely in a database block. DBWR has to perform a recursive function call to find the rest of a row.	**Improves Peformance**
Avoid fragmentation, honeycomb **Method:** Size the storage parameters of tables, indexes, and snapshots by setting optimal values for INITIAL EXTENT, NEXT EXTENT, PCTFREE, PCTUSED, and PCTINCREASE	Oracle dynamically allocates space whenever it needs to fit more rows that it can fit. If the initial estimates of the storage clause are not set to a large enough value, new records are fit into newly created extents. Both the dynamic creation of next extents and locating them can be an I/O overhead.	**Improves Performance**
Optimizer options and views **Method:** Views are stored at the database level and they can include Oracle optimizer hints. Turn common queries into tuned views to be used	Not all database ad hoc query tools use Oracle Optimizer. Using Views we can hide the optimizer hints at the database level.	**Enhances Scalability**

Design Techniques	Description	Benefit
Creative indexing **Method:** Using bit maps, hash indexing, clusters, and histograms in addition to B-tree to provide fast access.	Low cardinality and rarely changed attributes can benefit from bitmap indexing, clustering, and hash indexes.	**Improves Performance**
Mutlilevel security **Method:** Use Oracle database ROLES, GRANTs, ADMIN OPTION, and AUDIT facility to manage the security. Use Stored PL/SQL functions to provide data-slice-level security based on lookup values.	Provide access to only what is intended to be published and not all the other database objects. Using the Oracle database ROLES object, system privileges can be comprehensively managed.	**Enhances Security Management**
Aggregate aware access **Method:** Use metadata tools like Discover 2000 to define relationships, join conditions, and aggregate hierarchies.	End users do not need to know about the details of the data warehouse logical model in order to submit a sound and meaningful query. Using a metadata layer, they can leave that job to the database. This can avoid possible Cartesian products, unnecessary queries that can impact everyone on the system.	**Enhances Scalability**

10.2 PHYSICAL DATABASE SCHEMA MODEL

As shown in Figure 10.3, the concept of following the blueprint during a construction project is the only accepted and standard practiced technique among construction engineers. Using this analogy in the context

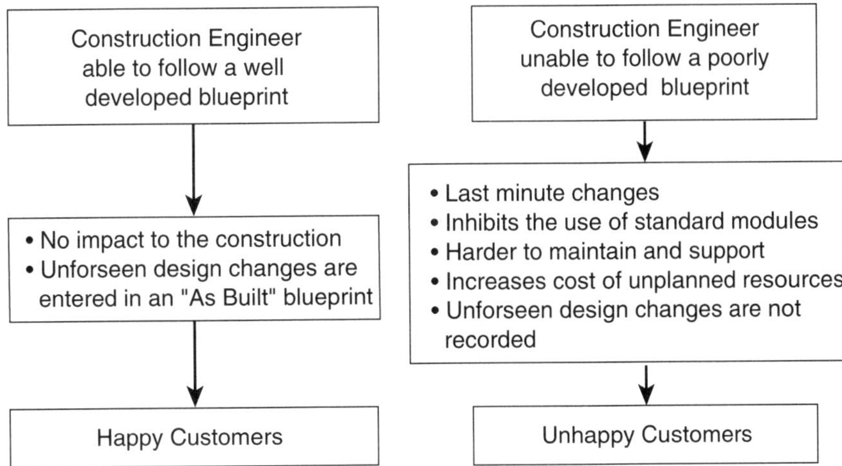

FIGURE 10.3 Outcomes of a Clear versus Poor Building Blueprint.

of software engineering, one of the basic blueprints or mapping techniques is the proper planning, allocation, and distribution of database objects in the database. What follows are two such mapping tables, namely:

- Table space and table mappings
- Table space and disk mappings

10.2.1 TABLE SPACE AND TABLE MAPPINGS

The table below illustrates the physical layout of database tables with respect to table spaces. The purpose of this planning and mapping is to achieve the following:

- Separate summarized data from detail data [summarized (SUMTAB) vs. atomic (ATMTAB)]
- Separate interim work data from atomic or summarized data [work data (INTMTAB)]
- Separate highly updated data (sales order data) from those that are not changed as often (dimensions)
- Minimize the impact of a media hit and increase the ease of recovery; do not let table space sizes get too large

- ❑ Plan the storage clause of every table space by allocating homogeneous data in a table space

The following table illustrates simple table to table-space-level mappings:

	ATMTAB	INTMTAB	DIMTAB	SUMTAB
SO_HEADERS	1000 Mb			
SO_LINES	5000 Mb			
THEATERS			100 Mb	
CHANNELS			10 Mb	
CALENDAR			1 Mb	
PRODUCTS			200 Mb	
CUSTOMERS			500 Mb	
STAR_PRODUCT				200 Mb
STAR_WORK		800 Mb		

10.2.2 TABLE SPACE AND DISK MAPPINGS

The following table illustrates the layout plan of table spaces with respect to physical disks and controllers (e.g., /c1/d1 can be read as disk 1 on controller 1). The purpose of this planning and mapping is to allocate so that hot (heavy I/O) files are kept away from each other. Increase parallel I/O by distributing a table space over a number of disks and controllers. This can be done at both the operating system level (disk striping) and at the table space level (table space soft striping or table partitioning).

	SYSTEM	ROLLBACK	TEMP	ATMTAB	INTMTAB	SUMTAB	SUMNDX
/c1/d1	100 Mb						
/c1/d2		1500 Mb					
/c1/d3							
/c1/d4							
/c2/d1			2000 Mb				

	SYSTEM	ROLLBACK	TEMP	ATMTAB	INTMTAB	SUMTAB	SUMNDX
/c2/d2				2600 Mb			
/c2/d3							
/c2/d4		1500 Mb					
/c1/d5						500 Mb	
/c1/d6							
/c1/d7					1000 Mb		
/c1/d8			2000 Mb				
/c2/d5							
/c2/d6						500 Mb	
/c2/d7							500 Mb
/c2/d8							

10.3 DATABASE CREATION SCRIPTS

Oracle software installation and configuration have certain standard phases that are described here. In general, the details of Oracle software installation are a function of the platform the software is going to be running on. The *Oracle 7 Installation and Configuration Guide*[1] for every supported operating system is the best up-to-date reference. It is essential to perform your installation using the procedures described in *The Guide* and the following on-line documents in $ORACLE_HOME /rdbms/doc directory:

- readmeunix.doc
- README.doc
- readmedlm.doc

For clarification and an introduction to the subtleties involved in installation, we describe installing Oracle on a UNIX environment. For instance, $ORACLE_HOME is an environment variable that is pointing to the location of Oracle software on disk.

[1]*Oracle 7 Installation and Configuration Guide*, Oracle Corporation, 1992.

10.3.1 ORACLE'S ENVIRONMENT VARIABLE

The following environment variables are used by Oracle executables to identify certain specifics about the targeted database. They must be set to valid values before a connection to the database is attempted.

Variable Names	Purpose
ORACLE_SID	Oracle instance name
ORACLE_HOME	Oracle software directories
DBA	DBA work directories
ORACLE_BASE	Oracle account home
ORACLE_TERM	Terminal emulation
ORACLE_DOC	Oracle documentation on line
ORACLE_PATH	Oracle executables
TWO_TASK	Client/server protocol
ORACLE_LINK	Points to CD-ROM drive

10.3.2 PREPARATION AND CONFIGURATION

Start the installation of the Oracle software by setting up the following configuration steps as adapted to a UNIX environment:

1. Create one UNIX GROUP ID, for example, dba::103.
2. Create one UNIX USER ID like the following:
   Oracle:x:119:103:ORACLE user id:/usr/opt/oracle:/usr/bin/ksh
3. If you are installing from a CD-ROM, the CD-ROM can serve as your permanent staging area and you can get the installer started. Otherwise, if you are installing from tape, you need a temporary staging area. Prepare a staging area on disk and transfer the installer bootstrap from tape to the staging area. Run the installer program and install the appropriate modules in Oracle's software directory. It consists of the following basic milestones:
   - Start the installer
   - Load Oracle software from tape or CD-ROM
   - Install Oracle

4. SQL*Plus uses "@" to execute or "start" a SQL script. In some UNIX systems, the character @, is the default command to do "line kill." This must be changed before moving forward. Use the UNIX shell "stty" command to redefine it. It is best to remove any special definition that is assigned to "@" and let it be used by Oracle in SQL*Plus to "start" a SQL script.
5. Copy the following files from $ORACLE_HOME/bin to /usr/local/bin:

   ```
   oraenv,coraenv,dbhome,dbaenv,cdbaenv
   ```
6. Copy the file "oratab" from $ORACLE_HOME/bin to directories:

   /etc and /var/opt/oracle:
7. The following steps show how you can create your X instance of Oracle. In the following instructions, X represents the 6 char or less Oracle SID of your system. You need to replace that with your choice of instance name. The necessary UNIX environment level setups are first mentioned. They must be in place before starting the database creation procedure.
8. Set the environment variables TERM, ORACLE_TERM, ORACLE_SID,ORACLE_HOME, and DBA, ORACLE_BASE in ".profile" so that it uniquely and properly defines your X system. Here is an example:

   ```
   TERM=vt100;export TERM
   ORACLE_TERM=vt100;export ORACLE_TERM
   ORACLE_SID=X;export ORACLE_SID
   ORACLE_HOME=/usr/opt/oracle/product/7.1.4;export
   ORACLE_HOME
   PATH=$ORACLE_HOME/bin:$PATH ; export PATH
   ORACLE_BASE=/usr/opt/oracle;export ORACLE_BASE
   DBA=/usr/opt/oracle/admin/X
   ```
9. Create the following directories for database X specific dump/script files:

   ```
   $ORACLE_BASE/admin/X/bdump
   $ORACLE_BASE/admin/X/cdump
   $ORACLE_BASE/admin/X/udump
   $ORACLE_BASE/admin/X/create
   $ORACLE_BASE/admin/X/arch
   $ORACLE_BASE/admin/X/pfile
   $ORACLE_BASE/admin/X/perf
   ```
10. Create a directory /var/opt/oracle and move "oratab" there. This file should contain the name of the valid Oracle SIDs on your system.

11. Check the PATH in the "profile" file of "oracle." Make sure the following precedence order exists. The lack of this order may cause Oracle or some of its tools to call improper binaries.

    /usr/bin:/usr/ccs/bin:/usr/ucb:/usr/opt/oracle/bin/usr/sbin:/opt/bin:

12. Database files should have: owner "oracle," group "dba," and mode 660.

10.3.3 DATABASE CREATION PROCEDURE

1. Decide on the location and size of each of your database files on the file system and make sure there is disk space available for them (set aside appropriate swap space on disks). The goal in database file layout is to minimize the contention and isolate the risk of media failure. Therefore, database files should be carefully sized and laid out. It is important for the DBA to be aware of the physical disks/logical volumes/controller maps. As much as possible, redo log files, DATA, INDEX, ROLLBACK, or TEMPORARY segments should be separated. Decide on the destination of archived redo log files, Oracle log, and alert files. Prepare a file called "create_ts.sql" that has all the CREATE TABLESPACE statements.
2. Log in as "oracle," and change directory to $DBA/pfile. Set up parameter files, "initX.ora," "initX_0.ora," "initX_1.ora," with database name, archive file's destination, Oracle's log files, multiple copies of control files, and appropriate rollback segments.

   All three parameter files should contain the following parameters:

   ```
   DB_NAME=X
   CONTROL_FILE=(/ora01/X/cntrlX.dbf,/.....)
   DB_BLOCK_SIZE= 8192
   BACKGROUND_DUMP_DEST=$DBA/bdump
   CORE_DUMP_DEST=$DBA/cdump
   LOG_ARCHIVE_DEST=$DBA/arch/arch
   USER_DUMP_DEST=$DBA/udump
   ```

   These three init.ora files will differ on the values assigned to the ROLLBACK_SEGMENT parameter, as explained here.

   file name: initX_0.ora

   Has no ROLLBACK_SEGMENTS entry. It is the default parameter file.

file name: initX.ora

ROLLBACK_SEGMENTS=(RB1,RB2,RB3,RB4,RB5,RB6,RB7, RB8,RB9,RB10)

file name: initX_1.ora

ROLLBACK_SEGMENTS=RB0 # Temporary rollback segment

3. At the UNIX shell prompt, set ORACLE_SID to X and prepare the script "create_X.sql," which includes the proper "CREATE DATABASE" command.
4. Invoke server manager line mode (svrmgrl) from the shell and issue:

   CONNECT INTERNAL.

   Full screen user interface with menu on top of the screen:

   % sqldba

   Line mode user interface:

   %sqldba lmode=y
5. From the top menu, select INSTANCE and then "Start Instance Only." Enter the name of the parameter file, "initX_0.ora."
6. Upon successful "Startup Nomount" in step 5, select "File" from the menu and open a spool file.
7. Run the script that creates the "X" database, "create_X.sql." This step may take about 5 to 10 minutes.

```
DATABASE Schema creation
REM: filename : CRE_DB.SQL
REM:CREATING A DATABASE- DB_NAME= UCSC
REM:login to SQLDBA or Server manager, and startup the
database "nomount".
spool creat_db.lis
CREATE DATABASE X
CONTROLFILE REUSE
DATAFILE "/oradata/data/7.2/X/SYSTEM01_X.dbf" SIZE 40M
REUSE,
LOGFILE "/oradata/log/7.2/X/LOG1_X" SIZE 2M REUSE,
    "/oradata/log/7.2/x/LOG2_x" SIZE 2M REUSE;
?/rdbms/admin/expvew.sql
?/rdbms/admin/xplainpl.sql
?/rdbms/admin/bstat.sql
?/rdbms/admin/helpgrnt.sql
spool off
```

8. The response "Statement Processed" announces the successful creation of the initial phase of the database.
9. Next, the following scripts in "/usr/opt/oracle/rdbms/admin" need to be run while still logged in SQLDBA as SYS. From directory:

   /usr/opt/oracle/rdbms/admin
   catalog.sql,catproc.sql,standard.sql,catblock.sql
   Note: Ignore "not exists" errors such as
   ora-2289,4043,1919,942,1434,1432.
10. It may be easier to log in in "sqldba lmode=y," rather than the full-screen mode.
11. From the shell prompt, check the new database background processes using

   %ps -ef I grep ora
12. Create the "RB0" temporary rollback segment and restart the database using "initX_1.ora" parameters. RB0 must have already been added to the parameter file "initX_1.ora."
    a. Run the following while logged in as SYSTEM/MANAGER:

       create public rollback segment rb0
    b. From directory;

       /usr/opt/oracle/rdbms/admin catdbsyn.sql
    c. Create an RBS table space for rollback segments to reside in.
    d. Restart the database using initX_1.ora.
    e. Create rollback segments in RBS.
13. Verify the file name, sizes, and paths in the DDL scripts in your "create_ts.sql."
14. Create all the other table spaces by calling the scripts from a "sqlplus system/manager" session using your "create_ts.sql" script.
15. Restart the database using "initX.ora." New rollback segments, RB1,...,RB10, must have already been added to this parameter file.
16. Modify the default table space of SYSTEM to be TOOLS.
17. Create application server's SCHEMA by running all the corresponding scripts as the owner of the application. Use the following order:

   create_table
   create_index

create_view
create_trigger
create_database_links
compile_SQL_package_procedures
create_inititial_data

18. The initial data (a.k.a. day 0) can be entered using a set of pre-written INSERT statement scripts. If the data already exists in a test system, an export file can be generated from the test system. Import it in X_PROD.
19. Next, you need to create database objects for each of the Oracle tools and Oracle Server. Invoke "orainst" from /usr/opt/oracle/install and select the option "Upgrade database objects." It prompts for the tool name and the system ID.
20. Shut down and start up the database.
21. Look for all the log files in $DBA/bdump, cdump, udump users.
22. Review the "cold" or "full" backup strategies. You need to update them so they can find all your database files.
23. Make a complete cold backup and full export dump file of the database while it is in its initial stage before it is changed through general use.

10.4 LOGICAL MAPPING

10.4.1 DATA INTEGRITY SUPPORT

Oracle's primary data types are as follows:

Data Type	Description
CHAR(n)	Fixed-length character data of length n. Default size is 1, maximum is 255 bytes.
VARCHAR2(n)	Variable-length character data. Default size is 1 and maximum size is 2000 bytes.
NUMBER(P,S)	Variable-length numeric data. P, precision or the total number of digits, can range from 1 to 38. S, sacle or the number of decimal places, can range from -84 to +127.

Data Type	Description
FLOAT(P)	A floating point number with binary precision P. FLOAT with no precison is the same as FLOAT(126).
DATE	Fixed-length date and time, from January 1, 4712 B.C. to December 31, 4712 A.D. NLS_DATE_FORMAT init.ora parameter or ALTER SESSION command can change the default date format.
LONG	Variable-length character data up to 2 gigabytes to 1 byte, limited by program memory. Can not be used in subqueries. It is stored on disk in row pieces. An entire LONG field is INSERTed or UPDATEd with one "bind" variable.
RAW(n)	Variable-length raw binary data. A maximum size n up to 255 must be set.
LONG RAW(n)	Variable-length raw binary data up to 2 gigabytes to 1 byte limited by program memory. Does not use character set translation (ASCII/EBCDIC). It is not suitable for character data. It is automatically converted to raw types, if entered as bytes or hexadecimal character strings. It is used for storing images and sound. They are also called Binary Large Objects (BLOBs).
ROWID	Binary data representing row addresses.

To improve data type consistency, adopt a set of standard data types with appropriate sizes that can be used throughout the data warehouse. For instance, define $ values as data type number (20,2) or define flag values as CHAR(1).

10.4.2 ENTITY INTEGRITY MAPPING

The Oracle data dictionary controls the data content of every record through the basic integrity constraints.

- ❑ PRIMARY KEY
- ❑ NOT NULL
- ❑ DEFAULT
- ❑ UNIQUE
- ❑ CHECK

Identify the attributes that are part of the primary and unique key at the database level. The activation will guard the data integrity of the database engine. They automatically provide data cleansing at the sever data load level and not at the interface level. It is important to mention here that in cases of massive data load, the presence of indexes can impact performance. In that scenario, it is best to drop the indexes before the load job and re-create them after the load job using the PARALLEL and UNRECOVERABLE options.

10.4.3 REFERENTIAL INTEGRITY

Referential integrity constraints enforce master/detail relationship between tables based on primary keys and foreign keys. It prevents invalid INSERTs, UPDATEs, and DELETEs by requiring that the detail record always have a corresponding master. It also propagates valid changes and restricts invalid changes by taking one of the following actions in case of DELETE or UPDATE:

- ❑ CASCADE
- ❑ SET NULL (must be implemented using triggers)
- ❑ SET DEFAULT (must be implemented using triggers)

10.5 MODULE AND DATABASE OBJECT MAPPINGS

The following mapping table illustrates the association between database objects and data warehouse batch modules.

Module	Object1	Object2	Object3	Object4
Load subject area A	Yes	No	Yes	No
Transform/integrate data set A	Yes	No	Yes	Yes
Load subject area C	Yes	Yes		
Transform C data		Yes		
Load subject area E		No		

The following mapping illustrates the referernce between data warehouse tables and source data sets.

Data Warehouse Entities	Source Entity
Sales_order_lines	so_lines
Sales_order headers	so_headers
Products	mtl_system_items
Customers	RA_CUSTOMERS
And so on	

Depending upon the data modeling or metadata tool used, the above mappings can be addressed effortlessly as part of the design process. Maintaining such mappings will be very useful during impact analysis.

10.5.1 END USERS' SECURITY GROUPINGS

The implementation of data security in the data warehouse has two aspects:

- ❑ Database-level security using ROLE and GRANT statements
- ❑ Data-slice-level security that can be implemented using custom security groupings

Nevertheless, the association of every user with the security groups must be defined and enforced as an ongoing administration function. The following table provides an example of user security group mapping.

End users	Security Group 1	Security Group 2	Security Group 3	Security Group 4
Scott	Yes	No	Yes	No
Tim	No	No	Yes	Yes
Mary	Yes	Yes		
Karen		Yes		
Tim		No		

10.6 THE NECESSITY OF DATA WAREHOUSE METADATA

The purpose of metadata is to provide an easy to use communication vehicle and information repository that links the developer's data dictionary to the end user's world. Regardless of the tools used to build the metadata, the data warehouse team needs to define the scope, depth, and breadth of the information that is going to be recorded in the metadata repository. The key is to phase the implementation of the data warehouse with short-term deliverables that have tangible results. The success of each phase will facilitate the progress of the subsequent phase.

10.6.1 KEY ROLE OF METADATA

As mentioned earlier metadata if scoped effectively, plays a key role in the success of the data warehouse. The most simple metadata implementation should provide the following:

- ❑ application of hidden knowledge/assumptions/calculations
- ❑ definitions that help IT understand the business or end-user domain
- ❑ business user's dictionary of systems, modules, data sets, and elements
- ❑ a hierarchical related set of business concepts that is somehow being represented or inferred to from data in the data warehouse
- ❑ Example:
    - Orders from a source system perspective (SO_LINES and SO_HEADERS)
    - Orders from an application perspective (order entry module of the source operational system)
    - Orders from regional sales managers' perspective: Orders of U.S. vs. orders of subsidiaries
    - Orders from business units and executives' perspective: Orders of their flagship product family
    - Orders from the corporate executives' perspective: company's first quarter orders

10.6.2 CHALLENGES OF METADATA ACCURACY

Keeping metadata content up to date requires planning and standard procedures. These procedures should address the following challenges:

- Must be current and up to date
- Use of consistent naming conventions and definitions across the tools and metadata
- Versioning and documenting changes to the metadata
- Intuitive structure, categorization, and navigational paths
- Information to help end users estimate how large or small the result or processing time of a query or report can be
- Reports on volume, ratio, and sparsity of data as a continuous capacity matrix and auditing process
- Role and content of the source system of record as they evolve and expand their functionalities
- Synchronization between data definition, integration, assumptions and implemented logic and code
- History of data warehouse refreshes and level of changes in data volume
- Location and description of data warehouse servers, databases, tables, and summarized structures
- Rules of automatic **drill-up** and **drill-down** in the OLAP tools; for example, how to traverse the sales hierarchy tree going from sales agent ID to sales theater
- Rules and guidelines for end users' defined custom calculations and models

There are currently a variety of tools in the market that address the above needs. At a minimum, an intuitive spreadsheet can play the key role of the data warehouse's metadata. The final solution may very well be the integration of a number of tools and technologies. In our opinion, the combination of Oracle Designer 2000, Discover 3.0, and Web front-end pages can provide an adequate, affordable and effective metadata tool in an Oracle data warehouse environment.

10.6.3 DATA WAREHOUSE ADMINISTRATION OF THE METADATA DATABASE MODEL

Consider the magnitude of the data's movement, processing, querying, and access that takes place. It is feasible to think of the following ongoing administration-related items:

- ❑ Capture statistics about how the job segment runs
- ❑ Start and stop time
- ❑ Number of records processed in each segment
- ❑ Success or failure status
- ❑ Error message encountered
- ❑ Capture statistics about the database system performance statistics
- ❑ Capture statistics about the database usage level
- ❑ Capture statistics about data distribution
- ❑ Capture statistics about system performance

In this chapter we provided practical considerations, techniques, and solutions that can make the administration of a data warehouse easier and more manageable. The next chapter dicusses how to optimize the performance of the data warehouse back-end Oracle server.

Chapter 11

Performance Optimization

11.1 CONTROL-SYSTEM-BASED OPTIMIZATION

11.1.1 PRIORITY BASED APPROACH

Performance optimization of a database is both challenging and rewarding. Optimization efforts are generally triggered by some unsatisfied performance expectations. Once the optimization efforts are applied and the outcome is relatively closer to the expectation, it is a gratifying experience to see how happy customers can now stop worrying about the system performance and can focus on their main job functions. Database performance tuning generally follows a set of principles that can be used as the framework for the procedures. The challenge is, given a specific tuning issue in a specific environment, how one should distribute the available technical resources, that is, time and effort, to obtain more optimized performance.

The information offered in this chapter is based on recommendations in Oracle's product documentation, technical books, articles, and our own personal experiences. It emphasizes the proven techniques gathered through research and actual data warehousing efforts. Therefore, rather than providing exact ready-to-run scripts that can become obsolete as Oracle Server goes through enhancements, we have chosen to provide a practical framework that is applicable to most platforms and situations. We decided to take advantage of the published features and did not include any so-called "undocumented" features.

At a high level, we all know that computer systems—hardware or software—follow the laws of physics and mathematics. In that context we can think of an Oracle server as an engine that behaves more like a "fluid control system." Transactions and the resources required to process those transactions run through the system via specially designed pipes, valves, and paths. The speed with which this engine processes these transactions has a lot to do with the size of those pipes, valves, additional resources, and volume of transactions. Once we start imagining Oracle Server as a big pipe structure and start identifying which "valve" controls which "flow," we are on our way to do effective and objective database tuning.

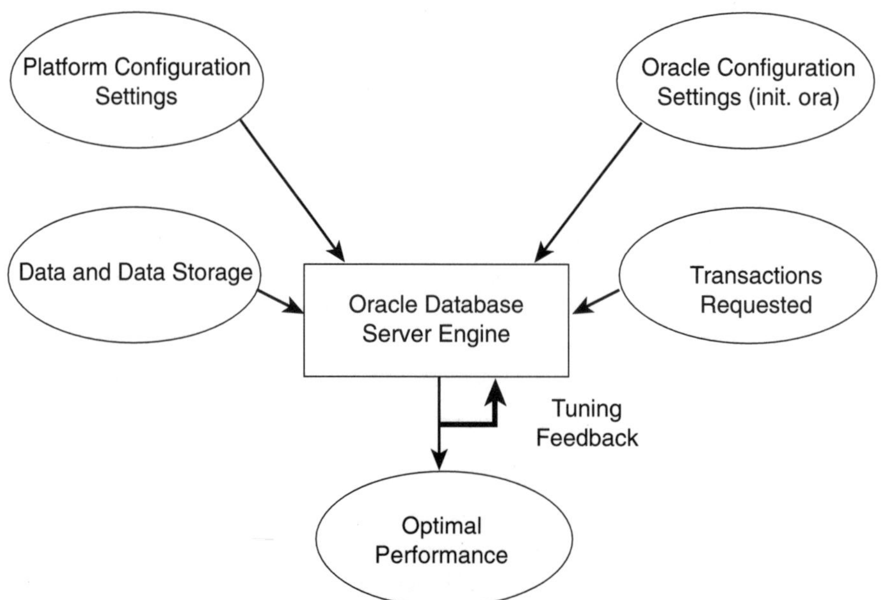

FIGURE 11.1 Tuning Oracle Using Control System Model.

This conceptual model emphasizes the fact that the performance of the Oracle database server is a function of the input feeds:

- Platform configuration (O/S system parameters, system, resources, etc.)
- Oracle configuration (Init.ora parameters, etc.) physical layout
- Data (volume, distribution, layout, etc.) and data storage
- Transactions (application code, volume, size , etc.) requested

The model also emphasizes that to reach optimum performance results, the outputs of the system should be monitored and analyzed. This analysis can identify the deficiencies, bottlenecks, contentions and inefficient use of resources within the Oracle database server. This information and **feedback** will help determine the kinds of changes that need to take place and identify the contention or bottleneck that needs to be removed. As one can see from Figure 11.1, optimization can very well be an iterative process. We cannot change the way the engine routes the transaction through the system; that is done by Oracle Corporation's product engineering divisions. As database administrators we will treat Oracle Server as a closed box and change the throughput by providing the appropriate feedbacks to the system.

This iterative process of applying the change and checking the results for further configuration is the framework of Oracle tuning. Compared to many other general DBMS servers, Oracle Server has probably the highest number of tunable and configurable factors. As such, it is much more effective in defining the framework and the structured approach that can be applied at any level, namely, application, database logical and physical models, and instance.

Due to the complexity involved in the Oracle Server engine, inappropriate modification of any tuning factor can have a noticeable negative impact. Oracle tuning almost always involves some sort of compromise and trade-off. The requirements of the application can help us make trade-off decisions. All the major differences of an OLTP application that were mentioned in Part I can now become useful. For instance, one of the major requirements of a data warehouse is the access performance. Ad hoc or batch access performance is much more important than the ease and speed of database recovery. The reason is that the database is not used for running the enterprise's daily operation but for long term decision support and to help focus on the enterprise's direction. So, a basic, solid and dependable recovery plan may be good enough for an Oracle data warehouse database. It is not necessary to have a sophisticated **point-in-time** recovery plan which involves resource-intensive operations such as, frequent transaction logging and archiving. This requirement alone opens many tuning doors for a data warehouse database administrator. The objective is to perform **targeted tuning** and avoid **blind** tuning.

The initial system installation and configuration based on data warehouse application requirements establish the baseline and the starting point. At this initial stage, a DBA has to ensure that the configuration is appropriate for the data warehouse application and not necessarily one that is used for an OLTP system. Applying OFA architectural rules has major significance at this stage. Configuring the server based on OFA rules is one of the most important optimization steps a data warehouse DBA can take to reach optimum performance.

11.1.2 OPTIMIZATION AT THE APPLICATION CODE LEVEL

The next step in the process is the application code that submits transactions to the database server. As illustrated in Figure 11.1, database transactions are one of the input feeds of the system. We should always attempt to start with an optimum design based on the type of data and volume of transactions involved. Some strategic techniques applicable at this level are:

- ❑ Compose the application code using modules that are self-sufficient and restartable
- ❑ Process large numbers of records by dividing them into multiple partitions that are processed in parallel and merged later
- ❑ Preprocess the static data sets and use the end result repeatedly
- ❑ Design modules so that while manipulating the data they do not hold on to database resources longer than necessary. COMMIT or ROLLBACK as soon as it is safe
- ❑ Plan the process hierarchy and network dependency
- ❑ Identify processes that can be parallelized early in the design cycle. Data warehouse load and transformation jobs are the best candidates to run in parallel
- ❑ Avoid unnecessary specialization in the application interfaces. Use stored procedures for common functions as much as possible; for example, **instead of**

```
INSERT INTO EMP (employee_no , employee_name , mgr, job)
VALUES (:V_employee_no , :V_name, :V_manager, :V_job);
```

Use

```
EMPLOYEE.NEW_EMPLOYEE(:V_employee_no, :V_name, :V_
manager, :V_job);
```

Where EMPLOYEE is a PL/SQL package containing a number of PL/SQL procedures. NEW_EMPLOYEE is one of the procedures in that package that handles the job of entering new employee information into the database.

This technique uses the object-orientation technique of defining classes (stored packages) and objects. Objects, for example, EMP, can be accessed only through the object methods, for example, NEW_EMPLOYEE( ).

11.1.3 OPTIMIZATION AT THE LOGICAL MODEL LEVEL

As seen in Part II, the logical model of the data warehouse can consist of two types of models:

- ❑ Entity Relationship (ER) model of the atomic layer
- ❑ Dimensional model of the aggregated and summary layer

The ER model of the atomic layer can be optimized to include a moderate level of denormalized tables. This denormalization can help avoid too many table joins. As we will see in Chapter 12, one of the challenging areas of SQL tuning is optimizing the multitable joins. Intermediate work tables that hold the result of mutlitable joins can help create an optimized and scalable application code.

The dimensional model can be optimized and enhanced over time to include the basis for a number of popular aggregated and summarized queries. This can help avoid the on-line and resource-intensive processing of multiple table joins and sorts. By nature, once the data in a data warehouse are refreshed they will stay static until the next refresh cycle. Therefore, there is no need to have end users issue the same query using their ad hoc query tool over and over again. These resource-intensive operations will return the same results anyway.

By monitoring the SQL statement in the shared SQL area over time, a data warehouse administrator can identify the popular aggregates and propose enhancements to the dimensional model. SQL statements including UNION and GROUP BY are very good candidates for using parallel queries.

```
REM
REM name:          collect_queries.sql
REM Purpose:       capture the ad-hoc queries.
REM Table:         USER_QUERIES
REM                       (STATUS,USERNAME,OSUSER,
REM                       PROGRAM,SQL_TEXT, TIMESTAMP)
REM
insert into user_queries
select sess.status
       ,sess.username
       ,decode(osuser,'daemon',machine,osuser) osuser
       ,sess.program
       ,text.sql_text /* active processes have text */
       ,a.timestamp
from v$session sess ,v$sqltext text , sys.aud$ a
where sess.sql_address = text.address
and sess.type = 'USER'
and text.piece = 0
and sess.audsid = a.sessionid
/
commit;
```

11.1.4 OPTIMIZATION AT THE PHYSICAL I/O LEVEL

The most expensive activity on the critical path of a transaction is the time needed to perform a physical I/O operation. I/O activities are specially singled out because of the lower rate of read/write compared to the memory rate of read/write (see Figure 11.2). Some effective strategies are:

1. Reduce the percent of the total time spent in performing a physical I/O operation.

2. Use buffer cache as much as possible.
3. Distribute I/O. Let I/O tasks be performed in parallel by many disks heads.
4. Don't let the CPU wait for I/O completion; process data as they are read into memory.
5. Avoid I/O operations over noncontiguous database blocks.
6. Let Oracle blocks be a multiple of operating system-level blocks.
7. Reuse the work and temporary structures; avoid frequent dynamic allocation of disks.
8. Configure queues (CPU, disk, controller, memory) to lower average waiting.
9. Have many large redo logs and place them on very fast disks.
10. Be aware of the I/O performance overhead of the RAID disks. It may be more optimal to place redo logs on regular mirrored disks than placing them on RAID along with other database files.

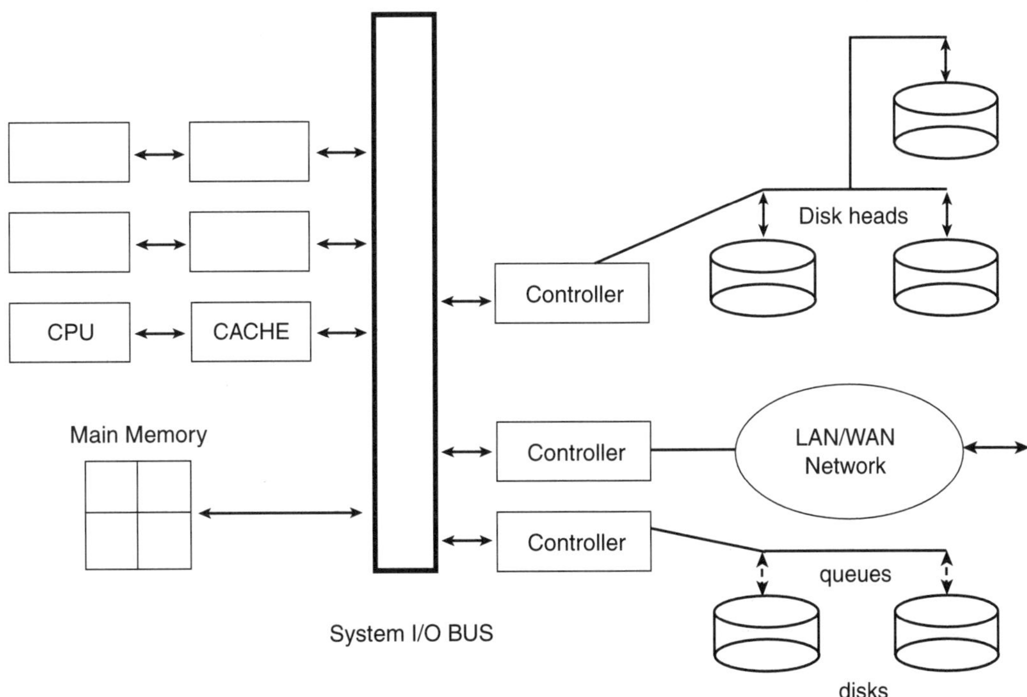

FIGURE 11.2 Conceptual Model of Main Components of a Computer System.

11.2 OPTIMIZATION TOOLS AND TECHNIQUES

In order to identify bottlenecks, we can turn to Oracle Server and take advantage of the massive amounts of system data collected in the Oracle system data dictionary.

11.2.1 DATA DICTIONARY OBJECTS

Almost any Oracle optimization effort involves the use of data dictionary objects. The reliance on a data dictionary will continue to grow as more object-oriented features are added to Oracle Server. Data dictionary serves as a registry of all the system activities and services.[1] Basically, a user program **requests database services** and Oracle Server **provides** those **database services**.

Figure 11.3 illustrates the main subsystems of the Oracle architecture that are on the critical path of a database transaction. The goal of any level of Oracle optimization is to reduce the overhead of one or more of each of these subsystems. As a quick reference, Chapter 14 provides more in-depth discussion on Oracle Server architecture. The approach proposed here is to become familiar with the role of each of these components so we can start asking ourselves analytical questions about the performance of the system. Often, starting with the right question is already half of the solution. Here are some examples.

- How fast is a particular service being performed on average or during a time window?
- How long does a particular service request have to wait in the queue before it is processed?
- How effective is a specific cache pool?
- What is the chance of finding a class of objects in cache?
- How can logical I/O be increased and physical I/O reduced?
- How optimized is the log writer process?
- How optimized is the database writer?
- Does the database configuration fit with the O/S configuration?

[1]For further detailed discussion, please refer to Chapter 15.

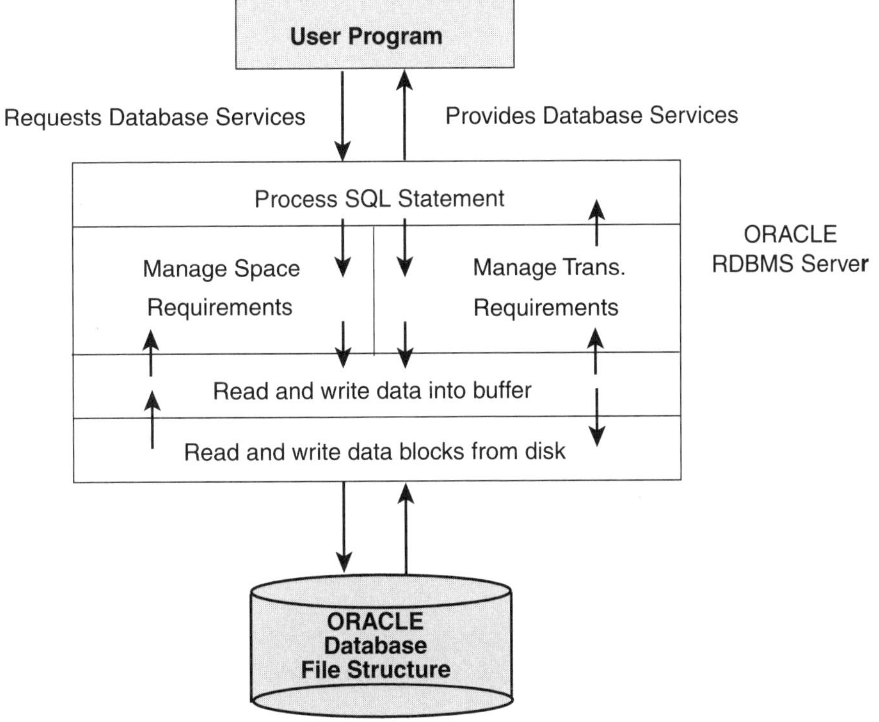

FIGURE 11.3 Subsystems of Oracle RDBMS Server Architecture.

- Does the data dictionary have enough information to intelligently find the best path to data?
- What is the throughput of the system per a particular set of SQL code and data sets?
- What percentage of the elapsed time of a SQL code is spent for CPU, FETCH, EXECUTE, and PARSE work?
- How effective are the indexes?
- What percent of total transactions involves full table scan of large tables?

The ability to identify and prioritize the tuning questions is definitely an art and an essential phase of Oracle database tuning.[2] Once that is done, using tuning tools and scripts, information in the data

[2]*Oracle for UNIX Performance Training Tips Manual*, Oracle Corporation.

dictionary, and the basic statistical methods, we can scientifically quantify the performance gain of a tuning enhancement. This is an iterative process until the optimum result is obtained. The good news is DBAs can use basic SQL queries to reach this objective. The down side is this search and analysis can be time consuming and cumbersome.

Oracle's default DBA utilities, SQL*DBA or Server Manager, come with all Oracle software and can serve as good starting points. They provide tabular information about the state of the Oracle Server from different perspectives and can aid in the monitoring of an active Oracle database. In recent years, the market of database administration tools has been growing rapidly. There are many third-party tools that can be used to assist in this analysis and monitoring. Very few of these products provide tuning suggestions. We do anticipate this area will continue to grow into a specialized DBA decision support system that treats the Oracle Server data dictionary as the source of its operational data. There are a number of promising tools in the market that collect, store, trend, alarm, and proactively suggest corrective action for the problem areas. They definitely deserve a fair evaluation and selection, but they are outside of the scope of this book.

Additionally, Oracle 7.3 provides a comprehensive system management tool called Oracle Enterprise Manager that can simplify the database administration and management of an Oracle-based Data Warehouse. It is an optional Graphical User Interface (GUI) client/server management system that has its own database to serve as the main repository of system information. The advantage of this tool is that it is native to Oracle technology and it can be used to manage more than one Oracle database at a time. It collects the system statistics, traces transactions, schedules jobs, monitors the data dictionary, and provides heuristic tuning recommendations. This tool can perform standard DBA tasks such as backup, recovery, export, import, database alteration, security management, and data replication. It is an administration tool that all Oracle-based Data Warehouses should use.

Much of the information displayed and analyzed by the DBA tools is obtained from the Oracle data dictionary. The status of each request is represented by information stored in the dynamic data dictionary objects. These objects are named with a prefix of V$ or X$ and since our focus is on the art of tuning we will focus on how to use them. In Chapter 15 we will cover some of the important data dictionary objects that are used to assess the state of the objects in the database. Based on that coverage and the architecture of Oracle Server, we are going to present the correlation between the top tuning issues and the data dictionary.

Source of Information	Analysis	Tuning Technique	Tuning Question
V$SQLAREA	Views the recent SQL entries and sees the amount of work that has been done by the server to service those requests.	• Provides **logical reads**, **disk gets**, **buffer gets**, **disk reads** • **Identifies** the statements that have a high number of **buffer gets** and **disk reads**	• What are the specific long-running SQL codes? • What are the most "offensive" SQL codes?
V$SQLTEXT	The full text of the SQL statements.	• Joins V$SQLAREA, V$SESSION, and V$OPEN_CURSORS to retrieve the most active SQL codes	• How is the SQL statement worded?
V$SESSION	The session information of the current SQL statements.		
V$OPEN_ CURSORS	The data activity of a session.		
V$FILESTAT		• Provides "**Buffer busy**" rates	• What is the disk I/O rate? Has it reached saturation?
SQLDBA utility	Uses file I/O monitor screen.	• Locates table spaces and data files that have an I/O Ratio of 0.90 or less	• How is the I/O rate? Is there an I/O bottleneck?

Source of Information	Analysis	Tuning Technique	Tuning Question
		• I/O distribution: Identifies if the heavily used table space spread is across physically separate disks or not	• Are the heavily used tables cached with CACHE option?
V$SYSSTAT SQLDBA or SERVER MANAGER system statistics screen	Provides information about Oracle's SGA ability in caching data blocks by storing information about Oracle's buffer cache activities.	• **Buffer cache hit ratio:** Selects name, value from V$SYSSTAT where name in [db block gets, consistent gets, physical reads (PR)]: Logical Reads(LR)= db block gets+ consistent gets Hit ratio=(LR-PR)*100 / PR	• How effective is Oracle's data cache (DB_BLOCK_BUFFER cache pool)? • Is the buffer cache hit ratio less than 70%? • What is the "buffer gets" rate? Are there any chained rows?
V$ROWCACHE SQLDBA or SERVER MANAGER system statistics screen V$SGASTAT	Provides information on cached database objects.	• Excessive **recursive calls** indicates insufficient cached dictionary data • If the number of recursive calls grows rapidly during ad hoc access it is an indication that SHARED_POOL_SIZE is low.	• How effective is the data dictionary cache?

Source of Information	Analysis	Tuning Technique	Tuning Question
V$SYSTEM_EVENT V$SESSION_WAIT	Indicates if DBWR has been a bottleneck.	• Checks the value of **free buffer waits**. If this value is significantly higher than normal, indicates there is a DBWR bottleneck. • Depending on the platform, DBWR bandwidth can be increased through one of the following: 1. In a multidisk configuration, start more than one database writer using **DB_WRITERS** parameter. 2. Use O/S **list I/O** feature (execute and write in parallel). 3. Enable Asynchronous I/O Do not wait for write acknowledgement to do CPU work by using	• Is the DBWR optimized? • Does the DBWR have enough bandwidth to handle the flow of requests?

11.2.2 INSTANCE STATISTICS REPORTS

Every Oracle installation includes a set of SQL administration scripts that are located in the Oracle software administration directory, $ORACLE_HOME/rdbms/admin subdirectory (in UNIX environment, $ORACLE_HOME is the O/S level environment variable that refers to the Oracle software top home directory). The scripts in this directory are generally run by SYS, SYSTEM, or a DBA privileged account. They include all the prepackaged SQL scripts that are used to create data dictionary objects, any additional options, patches, or upgrades. Examples of these scripts are:

- ❑ catalog.sql
- ❑ catproc.sql

The Oracle software administration directory also includes another set of scripts that is intended to aid the DBA in extracting some of the most useful system diagnostic statistics. These scripts relevant to tuning topics are listed below.

Administration script	Benefit/Usage
utlmontr.sql	This script provides read access to dynamic views V$ to all users
utllockt.sql	Who is waiting for which lock
utldidxs.sql	How effective are the indexes
utlxplan.sql	Create base table for EXPLAIN plan tool
utltkprf.sql	Create base table for tkprof trace logs
utlexp6.sql	Create base export/import views
dbmspool.sql prvtpool.sql	Lock a PL/SQL code in cache area of SGA
utlbstat.sql, utlestat.sql	bstat/estat diagnostic reporting

Using bstat/estat Report. A report known as the **bstat/estat** report (in UNIX utlbstat.sql and utlestat.sql) is the best place to start. The name of the report may vary slightly from platform to platform even though the functionality is the same across all platforms. These reports are always used together. The bstat report marks the beginning of a monitoring session. The other, estat report, ends the statistics collection session and produces a concluding report called "report.txt." The time period selected for bstat/estat monitoring should be long enough to include a good representation of transaction volume.

It is possible to use the SQL statements in bstat/estat reports and build a simple database that can collect this information as **operational data** over time. This effort can enhance the ability of the DBA to form a performance baseline. This baseline can help quantify the unquantifiable requirement of **database performance**. Once an adequate set of statistics is collected, the data warehouse DBA can quantify what is the **normal** and what is **poor** performance using automatic and batch scripts that can proactively alert if the performance in certain areas start falling below the **normal line.**

The following are sample SQL queries used in the bstat/estat report.

1. Begin taking statistics:
   SQLDBA>@$ORACLE_HOME/rdbms/admin/utlbstat
2. End taking statistics and prepare performance analysis report called "report.txt":
   SQLDBA>@$ORACLE_HOME/rdbms/admin/utlestat

Interpretation of bstat/estat Report. One of the primary uses of the bstat report is to form a general picture of the Database Writer's (DBWR) performance. If DBWR does not clean out the buffer cache fast enough, other user foreground processes will wait for DBWR. This always impacts the performance.

Bstat/Estat Performance Indicators	Interpretation
Inspect dirty buffers	This value should be low and near 0. The time spent in scanning the buffer is an overhead. It should be kept to a minimum.
Summed dirty queue length	The total length of the dirty queue after writer requests have completed.
DBWR summed scan depth	It should be close to the DBWR buffers scanned which show DBWR is keeping up with the rate at which DBWR buffers are filling up.

Bstat/Estat Performance Indicators	Interpretation
Summed dirty queue length/write requests	Average number of buffers in the dirty list after writing completes. It needs to be lower than _DB_BLOCK_WRITE_BATCH (X$KSPPI). If it is not lower, try to increase DB_BLOCK_WRITE_BATCH.
DBWR timeouts	Increments as there is no DBWR activity since the last timeout.
DBWR makes free segments	The number of messages received requesting DBWR to make some more free buffers for the LRU selection process: average number of reusable buffers = DBWR free buffers/DBWR make free segments
DBWR LRU scans	The number of times DBWR scans db buffer and looks for LRU queue, looking for more buffers to write.
Dirty buffers inspected	The number of times a process is looking for a buffer to reuse and encounters a dirty buffer that had aged out through the LRU algorithm.

Note: LRU stands for Least Recently Used and it is an algorithm used often in Oracle for implementing process scheduling and resource allocation.

11.3 OPTIMIZE SQL CODE

In the last section we stressed the concept of Oracle database tuning and pointed out some of the most common areas that can be the focus of Oracle performance tuning. We directed your attention to a number of data dictionary sources of information that can identify the bottlenecks, and contention or constraint of system resources. We also looked into how to resolve them once the tuning problem is actually diagnosed. Now that the framework of performance tuning is defined we need to look into the efficiency of the application code. We need to ask ourselves if it is necessary to use so much I/O or CPU to reach this end result.

11.3.1 EXPLAIN PLAN COMMAND AND SQL TRACE FACILITY

SQL Optimizer, the query processing subsystem in the Oracle engine, is responsible for identifying the best path to the desired data. Using EXPLAIN PLAN and the SQL TRACE tkprof facility, we can observe the major milestones that Optimizer goes through when processing a SQL. They both generate information that makes it easier to identify the unnecessary resource-intensive SQL codes. For instance, we can see if the intended performance index is actually being used or not. Therefore, it is essential to include the use of the EXPLAIN PLAN SQL command and SQL TRACE facility part of code review and the SQL optimization process.[3]

Using EXPLAIN PLAN. The script $ORACLE_HOME/rdbms /admin/utlxpln.sql (note, the script name may be different on different platforms) creates the base table PLAN_TABLE. This table will store the results of the analysis that the EXPLAIN STATEMENT (SQL extension) command performs on a specific SQL statement. The SQL statement provided to the EXPLAIN command is not executed. Instead, it is analyzed using the optimizer and its query plan is described through a series of records in the PLAN_TABLE.

Create the PLAN_TABLE table using the following Oracle supplied administration script.

```
SQL>@$ORACLE_HOME/rdbms/admin/utlxplan.sql
```

The structure of the PLAN_TABLE is shown here:

```
SQL>DESC PLAN_TABLE

Name                                 Null?    Type
------------------------------------ -------- ----
STATEMENT_ID                                  VARCHAR2(30)
TIMESTAMP                                     DATE
REMARKS                                       VARCHAR2(80)
OPERATION                                     VARCHAR2(30)
OPTIONS                                       VARCHAR2(30)
```

[3] *Oracle Server Application Developer's Guide*, Oracle Corporation, Appendix B, "Performance Diagnostic Tools," page B-10, 1992.

```
OBJECT_NODE           VARCHAR2(128)
OBJECT_OWNER          VARCHAR2(30)
OBJECT_NAME           VARCHAR2(30)
OBJECT_INSTANCE       NUMBER(38)
OBJECT_TYPE           VARCHAR2(30)
OPTIMIZER             VARCHAR2(255)
SEARCH_COLUMNS        NUMBER(38)
ID                    NUMBER(38)
PARENT_ID             NUMBER(38)
POSITION              NUMBER(38)
OTHER                 LONG
```

For example:
SQL>EXPLAIN PLAN SET STATEMENT ID = 'stmts' FOR
SELECT———-

In this example, EXPLAIN PLAN facility analyzes the targeted SELECT statement. The outcome of this analysis which is the optimizer path, sometimes refered to as query plan, is recorded in the PLAN_TABLE. Notice that the query is only parsed and analyzed by the optimizer and is not actually executed.

The information stored in the plan table tells us about the order in which the referenced data sets are searched, merged, and sorted before the results are achieved. This information identifies the methods used to access data. Further analysis of this information can point out opportunities for performance improvement. As mentioned earlier, the objective is to reduce unnecessary I/O, sorting, and full scans. The following example illustrates the use of EXPLAIN PLAN with a relatively long and complex query.

```
SQL> ALTER SESSION SET OPTIMIZER_GOAL=RULE;

SQL> EXPLAIN PLAN SET statement_id = 'MERGE1' for
SELECT
 P.BUSN_SECTOR_ID,P.PROD_TYPE_ID,P.PROD_FMLY_ID,P.PROD_SUB_GROUP_ID,
 P.PRODUCT_ID,P.DESCN,C.CORP_ID,C.CHANNEL_CD,C.CUST_UID,C.CUST_NAME,
 CST.THEATER,BCT.TERRITORY_ID,BCT.SO_LINE_UID,
 SUM(NVL(BCT.EXTNDD_QTY,0)) ORDERED,0.00 SHIPPED,
```

```
SUM(NVL(BCT.EXTNDD_NET_PRICE,0)) EXTNDD_NET_PRICE,
SUM(NVL(BCT.ROLLED_UP_NET_PRICE,0)) ROLLED_UP_NET_PRICE,0.00
ORIG_BKG,0.00
ORIG_EXTNDD_NET_PRICE,0.00 ORIG_ROLLED_UP_NET_PRICE,
DECODE
(SOT.SALES_ORDER_TYPE_UID,1004,0,1034,0,SUM(NVL(BCT.EXTNDD_QTY,0)) -
SUM(0.00) ) BACKLOG
FROM
MTD_TRX_W BCT, MTD_SHIP_W SH, PRODUCTS P, CUSTOMERS C,
CRNT_SALES_HIERARCHY CST, SALES_CREDIT_TYPES SCT, SALES_ORDER_TYPES
SOT
WHERE
BCT.TRANS_DT >= :b1 AND BCT.TRANS_DT <= :b2 AND
BCT.SO_LINE_UID = SH.SO_LINE_UID (+) AND
BCT.TERRITORY_ID = SH.TERRITORY_ID (+) AND BCT.PRODUCT_ID = P.PRODUCT_ID
AND
BCT.PO_CUST_UID = C.CUST_UID AND
BCT.SALES_CREDIT_TYPE_UID = SCT.SALES_CREDIT_TYPE_UID AND
BCT.SALES_ORDER_TYPE_UID = SOT.SALES_ORDER_TYPE_UID AND
BCT.TRANSFER_PRICE_IND != 'Y' AND
SOT.INCL_BKG_IND = 'Y' AND
SOT.SALES_ORDER_TYPE_UID NOT IN ( 1008,1010,1001,1006,1011,1014 ) AND
SCT.REVENUE_IND = 'Y' AND BCT.TERRITORY_ID = CST.REGION (+) AND
P.PROD_FMLY_ID != 'SERVICE' AND BCT.SALES_AGT_ID != 1000
GROUP BY
P.BUSN_SECTOR_ID,P.PROD_TYPE_ID,P.PROD_FMLY_ID,
P.PROD_SUB_GROUP_ID,P.PRODUCT_ID,P.DESCN,C.CORP_ID,C.CHANNEL_CD,C.CUST_UID,
C.CUST_NAME,CST.THEATER,BCT.SO_LINE_UID,BCT.TERRITORY_ID,
SOT.SALES_ORDER_TYPE_UID
UNION
SELECT
P.BUSN_SECTOR_ID,P.PROD_TYPE_ID, P.PROD_FMLY_ID, P.PROD_SUB_GROUP_ID,
P.PRODUCT_ID,P.DESCN,C.CORP_ID, C.CHANNEL_CD, C.CUST_UID,
C.CUST_NAME,CST.THEATER,BCT.TERRITORY_ID,
BCT.SO_LINE_UID,0.00 ORDERED,MAX(NVL(SH.SHIPPED_QTY,0)) SHIPPED,
0.00 EXTNDD_NET_PRICE,0.00 ROLLED_UP_NET_PRICE,
MAX(NVL(SH.ORIG_BKG,0)) ORIG_BKG,
MAX(SH.EXTNDD_NET_PRICE) ORIG_EXTNDD_NET_PRICE,
MAX(SH.ROLLED_UP_NET_PRICE)
ORIG_ROLLED_UP_NET_PRICE,
DECODE
(SOT.SALES_ORDER_TYPE_UID,1004,0,1034,0,SUM(0.00)-
MAX(NVL(SH.SHIPPED_QTY,0))) BACKLOG
```

```
FROM MTD_TRX_W BCT, MTD_SHIP_W SH, PRODUCTS P, CUSTOMERS C,
 CRNT_SALES_HIERARCHY CST, SALES_CREDIT_TYPES SCT,
 SALES_ORDER_TYPES SOT
WHERE SH.SO_LINE_UID = BCT.SO_LINE_UID AND
 SH.TERRITORY_ID = BCT.TERRITORY_ID AND
 BCT.PRODUCT_ID = P.PRODUCT_ID AND
 BCT.PO_CUST_UID = C.CUST_UID AND
 BCT.SALES_CREDIT_TYPE_UID =SCT.SALES_CREDIT_TYPE_UID AND
 BCT.SALES_ORDER_TYPE_UID = SOT.SALES_ORDER_TYPE_UID AND
 BCT.TRANSFER_PRICE_IND != 'Y' AND SOT.INCL_BKG_IND = 'Y' AND
 SOT.SALES_ORDER_TYPE_UID NOT IN ( 1008,1010,1001,1006,1011,1014 ) AND
 SCT.REVENUE_IND = 'Y' AND BCT.TERRITORY_ID = CST.REGION (+) AND
 P.PROD_FMLY_ID != 'SERVICE' AND BCT.SALES_AGT_ID != 1000
GROUP BY
 P.BUSN_SECTOR_ID,P.PROD_TYPE_ID,P.PROD_FMLY_ID,P.PROD_SUB_GROUP_ID,
 P.PRODUCT_ID,P.DESCN,C.CORP_ID,C.CHANNEL_CD,C.CUST_UID,C.CUST_NAME,
 CST.THEATER,BCT.SO_LINE_UID,BCT.TERRITORY_ID,SOT.SALES_ORDER_TYPE_UID
```

Once the EXPLAIN plan is generated, we can view the result in the PLAN_TABLE using a query similar to the following:

```
set term off ver off
spool xpl
select decode(id,0,'',
lpad(' ', 2*(level-1))||level||'.'||(position)||' '||
operation||' '||options||' '||object_name||' '||
object_type||' '||
decode(id,0,'Cost = '||position) Query_plan
from plan_table
connect by prior id = parent_id
and statement_id = upper('&statement_id')
start with id = 0 and statement_id = upper('&statement_id');
spool off
set term on
/
```

The formatted query plan of the above SQL statement with OPTIMIZER_GOAL=RULE is as follows:

```
QUERY_PLAN 1
--------------------------------------------------------------------------------
SELECT STATEMENT Cost =
  2.1 PROJECTION
   3.1 SORT UNIQUE
    4.1 UNION-ALL
     5.1 SORT GROUP BY
      6.1 MERGE JOIN OUTER
       7.1 SORT JOIN
        8.1 NESTED LOOPS OUTER
         9.1 NESTED LOOPS
          10.1 NESTED LOOPS
           11.1 NESTED LOOPS
            12.1 NESTED LOOPS
             13.1 TABLE ACCESS FULL MTD_TRX_W
             13.2 TABLE ACCESS BY ROWID SALES_ORDER_TYPES
              14.1 INDEX UNIQUE SCAN SOTP_PK UNIQUE
            12.2 TABLE ACCESS BY ROWID SALES_CREDIT_TYPES
             13.1 INDEX UNIQUE SCAN SCT_PK UNIQUE
           11.2 TABLE ACCESS BY ROWID CUSTOMERS
            12.1 INDEX UNIQUE SCAN C_UK UNIQUE
          10.2 TABLE ACCESS BY ROWID PRODUCTS
           11.1 INDEX UNIQUE SCAN PROD_PK UNIQUE
         9.2 INDEX RANGE SCAN MTD_SHIP_W_N1 NON-UNIQUE
       7.2 SORT JOIN
        8.1 TABLE ACCESS FULL CRNT_SALES_HIERARCHY
     5.2 SORT GROUP BY
      6.1 MERGE JOIN OUTER
       7.1 SORT JOIN
        8.1 NESTED LOOPS
         9.1 NESTED LOOPS
          10.1 NESTED LOOPS
           11.1 NESTED LOOPS
            12.1 NESTED LOOPS
             13.1 TABLE ACCESS FULL MTD_SHIPTHEATER_W
             13.2 TABLE ACCESS BY ROWID MTD_BKG_TRX_W
              14.1 INDEX RANGE SCAN MTD_BKG_TRX_W_N1 NON-UNIQUE
            12.2 TABLE ACCESS BY ROWID SALES_ORDER_TYPES
             13.1 INDEX UNIQUE SCAN SOTP_PK UNIQUE
           11.2 TABLE ACCESS BY ROWID SALES_CREDIT_TYPES
            12.1 INDEX UNIQUE SCAN SCT_PK UNIQUE
          10.2 TABLE ACCESS BY ROWID CUSTOMERS
           11.1 INDEX UNIQUE SCAN C_UK UNIQUE
```

```
        9.2 TABLE ACCESS BY ROWID PRODUCTS
          10.1 INDEX UNIQUE SCAN PROD_PK UNIQUE
      7.2 SORT JOIN
        8.1 TABLE ACCESS FULL CRNT_SALES_HIERARCHY
```

Notice that if the above query was really being executed, the same statement can be analyzed with the Cost-base optimizer (CBO):

```
QUERY_PLAN2
--------------------------------------------------------------------------------
SELECT STATEMENT Cost = 1395   <------
  2.1 PROJECTION
   3.1 SORT UNIQUE
    4.1 UNION-ALL
     5.1 SORT GROUP BY
      6.1 NESTED LOOPS
       7.1 NESTED LOOPS
        8.1 NESTED LOOPS OUTER
         9.1 NESTED LOOPS
          10.1 NESTED LOOPS
           11.1 NESTED LOOPS OUTER
            12.1 TABLE ACCESS FULL MTD_BKG_TRX_W
            12.2 INDEX RANGE SCAN MTD_SHIPTHEATER_W_N1 NON-UNIQUE
           11.2 TABLE ACCESS BY ROWID DW_PRODUCTS
            12.1 INDEX UNIQUE SCAN PROD_PK UNIQUE
          10.2 TABLE ACCESS BY ROWID DW_CUSTOMERS
           11.1 INDEX UNIQUE SCAN C_UK UNIQUE
         9.2 TABLE ACCESS FULL CRNT_SALES_HIERARCHY
        8.2 TABLE ACCESS BY ROWID SALES_CREDIT_TYPES
         9.1 INDEX UNIQUE SCAN SCT_PK UNIQUE
       7.2 TABLE ACCESS BY ROWID SALES_ORDER_TYPES
        8.1 INDEX UNIQUE SCAN SOTP_PK UNIQUE
     5.2 SORT GROUP BY
      6.1 NESTED LOOPS
       7.1 NESTED LOOPS
        8.1 NESTED LOOPS OUTER
         9.1 NESTED LOOPS
          10.1 NESTED LOOPS
           11.1 NESTED LOOPS
            12.1 TABLE ACCESS FULL MTD_BKG_TRX_W
```

```
          12.2 TABLE ACCESS BY ROWID MTD_SHIPTHEATER_W
            13.1 INDEX RANGE SCAN MTD_SHIPTHEATER_W_N1 NON-UNIQUE
        11.2 TABLE ACCESS BY ROWID PRODUCTS
          12.1 INDEX UNIQUE SCAN PROD_PK UNIQUE
      10.2 TABLE ACCESS BY ROWID CUSTOMERS
        11.1 INDEX UNIQUE SCAN C_UK UNIQUE
    9.2 TABLE ACCESS FULL CRNT_SALES_HIERARCHY
  8.2 TABLE ACCESS BY ROWID SALES_CREDIT_TYPES
    9.1 INDEX UNIQUE SCAN SCT_PK UNIQUE
7.2 TABLE ACCESS BY ROWID SALES_ORDER_TYPES
  8.1 INDEX UNIQUE SCAN SOTP_PK UNIQUE
```

Notice QUERY_PLAN2 using the Cost-base optimizer has a numerical value representing the **cost** of this query plan unlike QUERY_PLAN1 with no cost value. As tuning enhancements are applied, this value can increase or decrease which helps quantify the improvement.

Using SQL Trace TKPROF facility. On all platforms the following on-line usage definition can be obtained by entering **tkprof** at the command:

```
$tkprof
Usage: tkprof tracefile outputfile [explain= ] [table= ]
   [print= ] [insert= ] [sys= ] [sort= ]
table=schema.tablename Use 'schema.tablename' with 'explain=' option.
explain=user/password Connect to ORACLE and issue EXPLAIN PLAN.
print=integer List only the first 'integer' SQL statements.
aggregate=yeslno insert=filename List SQL statements and data inside INSERT state-
ments.
sys=no TKPROF does not list SQL statements run as user SYS.
record=filename Record non-recursive statements found in the trace file.
sort=option Set of zero or more of the following sort options:
 prscnt number of times parse was called
 prscpu cpu time parsing
 prsela elapsed time parsing
 prsdsk number of disk reads during parse
 prsqry number of buffers for consistent read during parse
```

```
prscu number of buffers for current read during parse
prsmis number of misses in library cache during parse
execnt number of execute was called
execpu cpu time spent executing
exeela elapsed time executing
exedsk number of disk reads during execute
exeqry number of buffers for consistent read during execute
execu number of buffers for current read during execute
exerow number of rows processed during execute
exemis number of library cache misses during execute
fchcnt number of times fetch was called
fchcpu cpu time spent fetching
fchela elapsed time fetching
fchdsk number of disk reads during fetch
fchqry number of buffers for consistent read during fetch
fchcu number of buffers for current read during fetch
fchrow number of rows fetched
userid userid of user that parsed the cursor
```

The TKPROF facility is a diagnostic tool that can be used during the execution of one or more SQL or PL/SQL statements. This facility can be used at the session level and it produces a report that provides run-time information about the resources involved. It can be used to measure the performance of one or more SQL codes. Use the following procedures to run this facility.

1. Enable the system level diagnostic by including the following parameter in the init.ora file prior to the database startup:
   TIMED_STATISTICS = TRUE
2. At the session level (foreground program, SQL*PLUS, etc.), mark the beginning of the diagnostic session:
   SQL> ALTER SESSION SET SQL_TRACE = TRUE;
   This particular session is now being monitored by the SQL trace facility in the Oracle engine. At this point, the particular SQL application code can be executed (any SQL or PL/SQL code,etc.) in the same session.
3. Once the application code is processed, the end of the diagnostic session is announced:
   SQL> ALTER SESSION SET SQL_TRACE=FALSE;

4. At this point, a trace report is generated in the user process trace dump destination known as the "udump" area (identified by USER_DUMP_DEST in init.ora file).
5. This file has the raw information about the activities in the monitored session. It needs to be put in a format that can be read using the tkprof utility:

   ```
   $tkprof <tracefile> <formatted file> EXPLAIN=username/password
   ```

   For example:

```
% tkprof dwprod_ora_10934.trc /tmp/trace_10934.tkp
EXPLAIN=dw/dwpass
TKPROF: Release 7.2.3.0.0 - Production on Sun Dec 15 12:26:58 1996
Copyright (c) Oracle Corporation 1979, 1994. All rights reserved.
%
```

The tkprof report generated in the above example is called "/tmp/trace_10934_tkp" which records the diagnostic run-time information of the traced session.

Interpreting SQL Trace Utility. Though this report is not very easy to read, it can point out some important facts about the efficiency of the application code. Every SQL code issued in the traced session will be reported along with its EXPLAIN PLAN and run-time statistics. This information is reported at each of the milestones of SQL processing:

- ❑ Parsing
- ❑ Executing
- ❑ Fetching

The following statistics are important to track and analyze:

tkprof Indicator	Interpretation
CPU	number of 100th of seconds spent in CPU
elap	number of 100th of seconds elapsed time
phys	number of disk reads (physical I/O)

tkprof Indicator	Interpretation
cr (in some platform query)	Number of consistent reads from SGA (logical I/O)
cur	Number of records reserved for update
rows	Number of rows processed

The goal in tuning should be to lower the "phys," cr/rows ratio, and CPU. Often as tuning steps are applied, indexes are used, caching is increased, I/O is distributed, or a parallel query is used, we can see how the cr/rows ratio gets dropped. Through an iterative process, quantify the impact of the tuning step applied in order to reach an optimum performance tuning scenario.

Statement ID	CR/ROWS	PHYS	CPU	Tuning applied
Merge 1	2265555/94446	5940	208.55	RULE based at session level
Merge 1	2265555/12134343	232131	98834	CHOOSE at system level

Example: The portion of the tkprof report that analyzes the Statement ID = Merge 1.

```
call       count    cpu      elapsed   disk    query     current  rows
-------    -----    -----    -------   -----   -------   -------  -----
Parse      1        0.04     0.04      0       0         0        0
Execute    2        0.03     0.03      0       0         0        0
Fetch      94447    208.48   250.05    5940    2265555   12442    94446
-------- -------- -------- --------- -------- -------- -------- --------
total      94450    208.55   250.12    5940    2265555   12442    94446
Misses in library cache during parse: 1
Optimizer goal: RULE
Parsing user id: 9 (CDWADM) (recursive depth: 1)
***********************************************************************************
```

One effective method to reduce the parsing time of the SQL statement is to increase the possibility of finding previously parsed version of that SQL statement in SGA. This is done by expanding the caching ability of the data dictionary (row cache) and the shared SQL and PL/SQL (library cache) in the shared pool area. This can be done in a number of different ways:

- ❑ Use PL/SQL stored procedures
- ❑ Increase the size of SHARED_POOL_SIZE
- ❑ Lock the frequently used PL/SQL code in SGA using the DBMS_SHARED_POOL procedure

The last method provides a mechanism to instruct the Oracle engine not to remove the parsed format of a specific PL/SQL code and continue to keep it in cache:

```
SQL>$ORACLE_HOME/rdbms/admin/dbmspool.sql
SQL>$ORACLE_HOME/rdbms/admin/prvtpool.sql
```

Chapter 12

Database Administration Techniques

12.1 HOW TO MANAGE DATABASE SYSTEM RESOURCES EFFICIENTLY

In the previous chapters we have analyzed many technical aspects of a data warehouse application using an Oracle server as its repository. Due to the resource-intensive nature of a data warehouse application, the emphasis has been on planning for scalability, performance, and extensibility. Generally, these can be considered as the toughest technical challenges of a data warehouse. In this chapter we are going to look at the other aspects of database administration, namely, resource management, backup recovery, and security. System resources can be seen as reusable fuels of an Oracle server. It is every DBA's goal to always have enough resources available to be able to support the needs of a demanding application. As we noticed in the previous chapter, when it comes to optimization we should always make sure that the application code is as efficient as it can be.

Start with the following basic queries to identify the data files, logs, and tablespaces.

```
COLUMN NAME FORMAT A50 TRUNC;
COLUMN FILE_NAME FORMAT A30 TRUNC;
SET PAGES 60;
spool check_db_files.log;

TTITLE 'LIST OF ALL THE DATABASE FILES';
SELECT name
FROM V$DBFILE;
TTITLE 'LIST OF ALL THE REDO LOG FILES';

SELECT name
FROM V$LOGFILE;

SET PAGES 60;
CLEAR COLUMN;
COLUMN FILE_NAME FORMAT A35 TRUNC;
column file_id format 99 trunc;
COLUMN TABLESPACE_NAME FORMAT A15 TRUNC;
TTITLE 'DATABASE FILES STATUS';

SELECT *
FROM DBA_DATA_FILES;

SET PAGES 60;
CLEAR COLUMN;
COLUMN FILE_NAME FORMAT A35 TRUNC;
COLUMN TABLESPACE_NAME FORMAT A15 TRUNC;

TTITLE 'TABLESPACE STATUS';
SELECT *
FROM DBA_TABLESPACES;
SET PAGES 60;
CLEAR COLUMN;
COLUMN FILE_NAME FORMAT A35 TRUNC;
COLUMN TABLESPACE_NAME FORMAT A15 TRUNC;
BREAK ON TABLESPACE_NAME skip 1 on report skip 1;
COMPUTE SUM AVG of blocks on tablespace_name report;
COMPUTE SUM AVG of bytes on tablespace_name report;

TTITLE 'TABLESPACE FRAGMENTATION OF FREE SPACES';
SELECT *
FROM DBA_FREE_SPACE
ORDER BY TABLESPACE_NAME,BYTES;
spool off
```

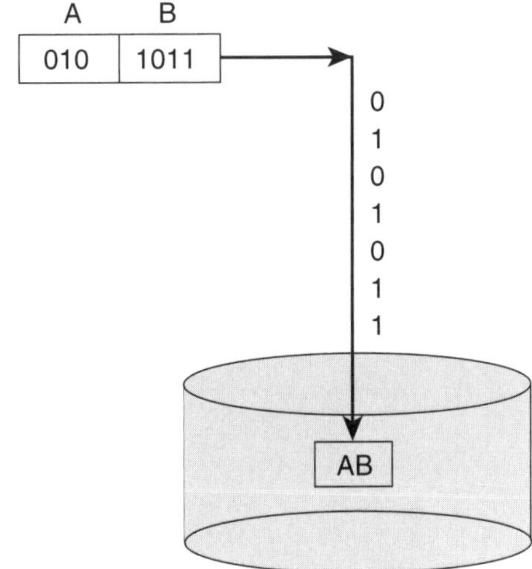

FIGURE 12.1 Single I/O Stream to a Single File on one Physical Disk.

12.1.1 I/O DISTRIBUTION

One of the costliest resources in terms of time spent, is the I/O subsystem. Regardless of what type of permanent storage system and technology is used, the reduction of I/O bottlenecks and distribution of the load have always been cornerstones of database administration and configuration. I/O distribution can be done in a number of different ways. Figure 12.1 and Figure 12.2 illustrate the use of multiple disks to parallelize the I/O stream.

12.1.2 I/O DISTRIBUTION TECHNIQUES[1]

Depending on the severity of the I/O bottleneck and the availability of resource one of the following options can be used:

[1]*Oracle 7 Server Administrator's Guide*, Appendix A. Oracle Corporation, 1992, p. 22-1.

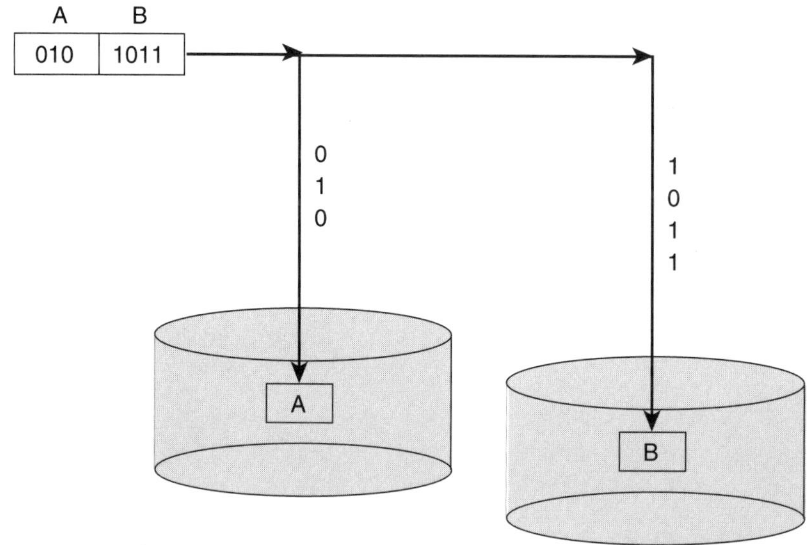

FIGURE 12.2 Parallel I/O Stream to a Single File on Two Physical Disks.

I/O Distribution Option	Description
Table and index isolation	Tables and their associated indexes should be placed (1) on separate table spaces, and (2) table spaces should be placed on separate physical disks.
Tablespace striping	An entire table space is created across a number of physical disks. By default, all objects stored on that table space have a chance to be split across more than one physical disk.
Table striping	A specific table that is heavily used and has been identified as a data access bottleneck is created in its dedicated table space. The table space is based on at least two equal-sized data files. Each of those data files are placed on a separate disk. Size the initial extent and next extent of the table so that each file contains only one table extent. As the table grows, add additional data files and place them on alternate disks.

I/O Distribution Option	Description
O/S striping	At the operating system, create logical disks that actually span across at least two disks. By default, any file including the database data files have a chance to be split across at least two physical disks.
Use more controllers	Disk controllers like disks also have a queuing mechanism. Place hot files on separate disks and if possible, separate controllers. Do not attach the maximum number of disks per controller.
Increase Init.ora parameter DB_FILE_MULTIBLOCK_READ_COUNT	Increase the related init.ora parameters to increase the maximum number of blocks in one I/O operation as Oracle goes to disk and reads data.
Isolate checkpoint background process from database writer background process	Monitor checkpoint activities: When **checkpoint, CKPT**, occurs, database writer, **DBWR**, stops reading new blocks and writes all the dirty blocks in SGA to the data files. This guarantees that the information recorded in the redo log up until this point is not needed for instance recovery. The init.ora parameter CHECKPOINT_PROCESS= TRUE before start-up ensures that checkpoint activity is performed independent of the database writer.

12.1.3 FILE I/O STATISTICS FROM DATA DICTIONARY

Use the following views and queries to measure the physical reads/writes. Use the following information to balance the load evenly across all your disks and disk controllers.

```
CREATE VIEW stats$file_view
AS SELECT
   ts.name table_space , i.name file_name , x.phyrds phys_reads,
   x.phywrts phys_writes, x.readtim phys_rd_time, x.writetim phys_wrt_tim,
   x.phyblkrd phys_blks_rd,
   x.phyblkwrt phys_blks_wr from v$filestat x, ts$ ts, v$datafile I, file$ f
WHERE
   i.file#= f.file# AND ts.ts# = f.ts# AND x.file#=f.file#;
```

```
SELECT
   table_space, sum(phys_reads) phys_reads, sum(phys_blks_rd)
phys_blks_rd,
   sum(phys_rd_time) phys_rd_time, sum(phys_writes) phys_writes,
   sum(phys_blks_wr) phys_blks_wr,
   sum(phys_wrt_tim) phys_wrt_tim
FROM stats$file_view
GROUP BY table_space order by table_space;
```

```
SELECT name filename, phyrds phys_reads, phywrts phys_writes
FROM v$datafile df , v$filestat fs
WHERE df.file# =fs.file#;
```

12.1.4 CHECKPOINT EFFICIENCY

The checkpoint process is a CPU- and I/O-intensive activity. The more frequent the checkpoint activity occurs, the less time required to perform an instance recovery in case of a system crash. The frequency of this activity is configurable. We can increase or decrease its occurence by modifying two init.ora parameters, LOG_CHECKPOINT_TIMOUT and DB_BLOCK_CHECKPOINT_BATCH.

The checkpoint throughput can be measured by comparing the value for the init.ora parameter DB_BLOCK_WRITE_BATCH and the "Average Write Queue Length." DB_BLOCK_WRITE_BATCH should be larger than the average waiting period; otherwise there is a CHECKPOINT bottleneck.

```
DB_BLOCK_WRITE_BATCH = DB_BLOCK_CHECKPOINT_BATCH X
DB_BLOCK_SIZE
```

```
SELECT      queue.change/writes.change
            "Average Write Queue Length"
FROM        stats$stats queue, stats$stats writes
WHERE       queue.name = 'summed dirty queue length'
AND         writes.name = 'write requests';
```

In the case of a data warehouse application, as opposed to an OLTP application, we can compromise ease of recovery in favor of performance. Therefore, it is desirable to have a checkpoint process as minimal as possible. DBAs can reduce checkpoint activity occurrence by setting the two init.ora parameters. For instance, LOG_CHECK-POINT_TIMOUT =600 causes a checkpoint to take place after every 600 seconds or 10 minutes. DB_BLOCK_CHECKPOINT_BATCH is derived from DB_BLOCK_WRITE_BATCH divided by 4 and causes a checkpoint to take place after so many database blocks are ready to be written as a batch.[2]

12.2 HOW TO MANAGE SGA RESOURCES

When it comes to Oracle Server optimization, the most important structures in SGA, like buffer cache, the redo log buffer and shared pool area need the most attention. When managing memory resources, DBAs have to identify the optimization strategy. Is it increasing successful **hits** or saving memory? The following queries will help identify the memory bottlenecks or usage inefficiencies. They are based on the dynamic data dictionary objects.

Source of status	SGA structure	Analysis and monitoring

V$SGASTAT	• All structures in SGA.
	• The size of a number of init.ora parameters can be directly linked to SGA structure.
		Monitor wasted/unused areas in SGA known as **free memory**
		`SELECT * FROM V$SGASTAT WHERE name = 'free memory';`
		`SELECT name, byte FROM V$SGASTAT WHERE name IN ('db_block_buffers','log_buffer', 'dictionary cache','sql area','library cache');`

[2]Ibid, page 13.

Source of status	SGA structure	Analysis and monitoring
V$LIBRARYCACHE	• Shared SQL, PL/SQL area • Controlled by init.ora parameter: SHARED_POOL_SIZE	*Monitor:* **Library cache PIN HIT ratio** SELECT (SUM(reloads)/SUM(pins)) * 100 'Number of library cache miss %' FROM V$LIBRARYCACHE; SELECT sum(pins) "executions", sum (reloads) "cache misses during execu-tions", FROM V$LIBRARYCACHE; SELECT namespace, gets round(decode(gethits,0,1,gethits)/ decode(gets,0,1,gets),3) "GET HIT RATIO" , pins, round(decode(pinhits,0,1,pinhits)/ decode(pins,0,1,pins),3) "PIN HIT RATIO" , reloads , invalidations FROM V$LIBRARYCACHE;
V$ROWCACHE	• Dictionary cache • Controlled by init.ora parameter: SHARED_POOL_SIZE	SELECT SUM(gets) "Data Dictionary Gets" , Sum(getmisses) " Data Dictionary Cache get misses" FROM V$ROWCACHE;

Source of status	SGA structure	Analysis and monitoring
V$SYSSTAT		SELECT ((SUM(gets)- SUM(getmisses))/SUM(gets))* 100 FROM V$ROWCACHE; SELECT parameter "name", gets "get requests", getmisses, scans "scan requests" , scanmisses, modifications, count, usage "Current Usage" FROM V$ROWCACHE WHERE gets != 0 OR scans !=0 OR modifications != 0 ORDER BY GETMISSES DESC , SCANMISSES DESC;
	• Database block Buffer Cache • It is controlled by init.ora parameter DB_BLOCK_BUFFER	Monitor effectiveness of Buffer cache : **DB Buffer Cache hit ratio** = 1- (physical reads / (db block gets + consistent gets)) SELECT name, value FROM V$SYSSTAT WHERE name IN 'dbblock gets', 'consistent gets', 'physical reads');

SGA

Shared SQL Area / Data dictionary buffer cache	Shared database buffer cache	Redo log block buffer

PGA

Stack space	Cursor stat	User session data sorting area

12.2.1 LIBRARY CACHE AREA[3]

Consider the following criteria when managing shared pool area SGA resources.

- The frequency of parse calls should be kept to a minimum. It is usually controlled at the user tools and interface levels, for example, precompilers, Oracle Call Interface, SQL*Forms. The size of init.ora parameter OPEN_CURSOR determines how many cursors (execution information) should be kept allocated in user session memory area. Increasing the value of OPEN_CURSER reduces frequency of parsing and improves the performance
- At times, keeping SQL information in Shared SQL area is not beneficial and it should be cleaned up soon after. The overhead associated with searching and scanning the Shared SQL area and looking for an already parsed statement can be more cost-effective than skipping the parsing of that statement. By enabling an init.ora parameter, the CURSOR_SPACE_FOR_TIME = TRUE Oracle kernel de-allocates the Shared SQL area after the application cursors are all closed
- The V$LIBRARYCACHE table records statistics about SQL executions. **Pin hit ratio** is the number of times the parsed representation of a SQL statement was found. This ratio should be near 1.0 and the number of "misses" should be very low. If the hit ratio is small, increase the SHARED_POOL_SIZE. If the pin hit ratio is always 1.0

[3]*Oracle 7 Server Administrator's Guide*, Oracle Corporation, 1992, page 21-9.

and there are no misses, then set timeout criteria as CURSOR_SPACE_FOR_TIME = TRUE

- Encourage the reuse of code through standardization, naming conventions, and style. Use bind variables rather than explicit use of constants. Also use stored procedures where possible
- The Least Recently Used (LRU) algorithm is used to age out the entities in the shared pool even when the parsed representation still exists in library cache
- One of the tuning goals is to avoid misses in the library cache. It is optimal to keep the ratio of reloads to pins < 10%

12.2.2 DICTIONARY CACHE

Consider the following criteria when managing dictionary cache SGA resources.

- The V$ROWCACHE table records statistics for data dictionary activities.[4] The goal is to keep the ratio of total get misses to total gets below 10%
- Unlike the operating system, it is important to have **low free memory**. **Large free memory** is an indication of a fragmented shared pool due to the age-out SQL statements
- The ratio of get misses/gets indicates the percentage of requests that resulted in cache misses. It should be under 0.15
- Increase SHARED_POOLSIZE if there are misses only after you have determined there is no **free memory** in Shared SQL area
- Use the view and X$KSMSP. The V$DB_OBJECT_CACHE view shows library cache objects and their usage. The X$KSMSP table is used to construct the map of the shared pool. Using these two we can determine which objects are taking relatively large chunks of memory. These objects can be "kept" in the shared pool using the procedure **dbms-shared_pool.keep**( ), and they can get "pinned" to library cache. This way the object is not going to age-out or be "flushed out" of cache area

[4] *Application Developer's Guide*, Oracle Corporation, page D-62.

```
SELECT *
FROM       V$DB_OBJECT_CACHE
WHERE      sharable_mem > <threshold>;

Create a map:

SELECT     ksmchcom "Entity", ksmchsiz "shared memory",
           ksmchcls "freeable/pinned/recreatable"

FROM       X$KSMSP
ORDER BY   ksmchptr;

SELECT     namespace,name "object", owner, sharable_mem "Memory
           used"
FROM       V$DB_OBJECT_CACHE
ORDER BY   sharable_mem;
```

12.2.3 BUFFER CACHE

Consider the following criteria when managing database block buffer cache resources in SGA.

- ❑ Upon receipt of every request for a database block, Oracle kernel first searches (scans) the database buffer cache. If it finds the block in memory, it is counted as Logical Read. If it is not found, it will access data in the data file and it counts as a **physical read**. It will read the block from disk to cache. This physical read activity can impact performance. In order to measure the number of reads from disk we can analyze the information in V$SYSSTAT
- ❑ The hit ratio should be closed to 1.0 as much as possible. Increase init.ora parameter DB_BLOCK_BUFFERS to improve the hit ratio. Increasing the database buffer can reach a diminishing return point.
- ❑ Perform a what-if analysis before expanding the buffer cache to make sure the expansion of buffer cache will actually help the current level of I/O activity. For diagnostic purposes, set init.ora parameter: DB_BLOCK_LRU_EXTENDED_STATISTICS = n, a nonzero value, in which case **n** is an integer indicating extra database buffers. Measure the "cache_hits" factor which indicates how many additional cache hits (performance improvement) can be achieved

if more database block buffers are used. Query from X$KCBRBH to measure the additional misses if the database block buffers are reduced by **n**.

- Use the following query to measure the improvements that can be achieved by adding 250 block buffers at a time

```
SELECT        250 *trunc(indx /250) + 1 || ' to' ||
              250 * (trunc(indx/250)+1) 'interval ',
        sum(count) 'cache-hits'
 FROM sys.x$kcbrbh group by trunc (indx/250);
```

12.2.4 FRAGMENTATION OF SGA IN O/S SHARED MEMORY SEGMENT

The Oracle Server's SGA is generally the largest shared memory segment running on a server. The default values for maximum and minimum limits of shared memory segments set at the operating system level are usually not enough and must be expanded before any Oracle installation and subsequent database creation.

The SGA of an Oracle database is preallocated at startup time from the pool of available O/S shared memory segments. It is desirable to have a single shared memory segment to hold the entire SGA. This can be overlooked as ongoing tuning enhancements call for more pool and buffer area in SGA. Every time the size of SGA grows, DBAs have to make sure it will continue to stay in one single shared memory segment. The O/S shared memory segments are sized as part of O/S configuration. The platform-specific Oracle installation guide identifies which O/S configuration parameter should be used to size the shared memory segment. In the UNIX environment SHMMAX, SHMMIN, SHMMNI, and SHMSEG kernel parameters are used for this purpose. The size of the major components of SGA can be retrieved with the following command using SQLDBA or SERVER MANAGER utilities:

```
> SHOW SGA
Total System   Global Area          4408616 bytes
               Fixed Size           52120 bytes
               Variable Size        3938704 bytes
               Database Buffers     409600 bytes
               Redo Buffers         892 bytes
```

The SGA and configuration information of the data warehouse instance can be made available to application developers using the following commands executed by a DBA privileged account:

```
Rem Enables SHOW SGA command
GRANT SELECT on V$SGA to public;
Rem Enables 'SHOW PARAMETER'
GRANT SELECT on V$PARAMETER to public;
set echo off;
```

12.2.5 AVOID SGA SWAPPING AND PAGING

The SGA should be monitored at the O/S level for possible "swap" or "paging" activities. Swapping and paging are done by the O/S as part of its CPU scheduling algorithm.

Paging and Swaping: In UNIX, whenever physical memory is not enough for all processes, it moves pages of memory to a disk called **swap space**. In the event that the SGA of an Oracle instance is swapped or paged, a temporary total freeze is seen across the database. The performance will drop to its lowest possible point. Therefore, ensure that the SGA and O/S shared memory segments are sized such that swapping and paging of SGA almost never happens. Also, hanging is most detrimental and should be completely avoided. In case of sudden poor performance after a recent SGA tuning, DBAs can use the O/S monitoring tool to see if any swapping or paging is taking place. If that is the case, SGA size should be reduced to avoid paging and swapping in worst conditions.

- Monitoring swapping in UNIX:
  `vmstat -S 5 5`
- Monitoring paging in UNIX:
  `sar -p 5`
- Monitoring swap space in use:
  `swap -l or pstat -s`

System swap space = 4 times the system's physical memory

Recently, some platforms (AT&T, Data General, Sequent,etc.) have provided a mechanism to guarantee the allocation of a specific portion of physical memory to SGA, referred to as "locking" the SGA. This can be an effective measure for an Oracle data warehouse that has a large active database portion and therefore needs a large cache. It is preferable to have the platform configured specifically toward the requirements of the data warehouse.

12.3 HOW TO MANAGE REDO LOGS, TEMPORARY SEGMENTS, AND ROLLBACK SEGMENTS

12.3.1 REDO LOGS

Redo logs, by design, are very frequent, short lived, and sequential write activities. Any bottleneck on redo log activity can impact all active users of the Oracle instance at the time and not just one transaction. Therefore, one of the primary configuration steps is to place them on disk with minimum activities. This can decrease the mechanical movement of the disk head which translates to fast redo log writes.

In case of a data warehouse application which is primarily used for decision support, the redo log transactions are small during end-user ad hoc access. On the other hand, during the refresh cycle where massive amounts of data are being refreshed, the redo log transactions will be large. Depending on the prioritization of performance issues:

1. Optimize it for optimal batch jobs
2. Optimize on-line decision support system (DSS) users

In cases where the checkpoint activity does not complete fast enough for the Redo Log Writer (LGWR) which is ready to reuse and switch into the redo log file, the following message appears in the system alert file in the "bdump" directory:

```
Thread 1 cannot allocate new log, sequence 160
Checkpoint not complete
 Current log# 4 seq# 159 mem# 0:
/db318/CDW2PROD_db/log4_CDW2PROD.dbf
  Mon Mar 6 13:03:06 1995
```

There could be a number of causes and solutions to this problem. In any case, the alert message indicates that the database writer or checkpoint background processor is not fast enough for the redo log writer. If this message continues to be generated, then one of the following can take place to remedy the problem:

- ❑ Increase the number of redo log files
- ❑ Extend the size of the redo log files
- ❑ Isolate checkpoint from database writer
- ❑ Have more than one database writer
- ❑ Increase the frequency of checkpoint activity

As we saw in the structure of the SGA, redo log transactions are first collected in the redo log buffer structure. The init.ora parameter LOG_BUFFER controls the size of this structure in bytes. Its size is platform dependent, although the larger it is, the lower redo log disk activities will be. In case of a data warehousing application, we recommend a high value like 100 * database block size.

One of the configurable redo log parameters is the redo log buffer latch. Any contention at this level indicates slower redo log transactions. We can identify the contention using the following query from bstat/estat. The value of redo log space requests should be near 0. If it is not near zero, increase the size of the redo log buffer (LOG_BUFFER). The units are in bytes and the recommendation is to have them increased 5% at a time.

```
REM: Redo log buffer latch contention

SELECT       name,value
FROM         v$SYSSTAT
WHERE        name='redo log space requests';
```

To reduce redo log allocation latch contention, reduce the value set for LOG_SMALL_ENTRY_MAX_SIZE.

By checking the value set in init.ora or in V$PARAMETER DBAs can dynamically obtain the value. When the redo log entry is too large, the user process can't get the redo allocation latch; instead it gets the redo copy latch. There can be multiple processes writing entries into the redo log buffer. It is determined by LOG_SIMULTANEOUS_COPIES. For good performance, we recommend that it be configured to about twice as much as the CPU counts on the server. If the server has 10 CPU then, LOG_SIMULTANEOUS_COPIES = 10 * 2 = 20.

```
LOG_SMALL_ENTRY_MAX_SIZE = 800 — bytes
LOG_SIMULTANEOUS_COPIES = 10 — default= CPU_COUNT, which is
set by RDBMS autom
......
```

To ensure good throughput through the redo log buffer, monitor the ratio of misses/gets. It is desirable to keep it below 1%.

```
SELECT      ln.name,gets,misses,immediate_gets, immediate_misses
FROM         v$latch l, v$latchname ln
WHERE       ln.name IN ('redo allocation','redo copy')
AND         ln.latch# =l.latch#;
```

12.3.2 TEMPORARY SEGMENTS

The temporary sort activities take place in a number of data manipulation languages (DML) and data definition languages (DDL) statements.

- Sometimes when there is a large SORT operation, Oracle performs the sorting in the **temporary tablespace**.

```
SELECT      name , value
FROM        v$sysstat
WHERE       name in ('sorts(memory)' , sorts(disk));
```

- The init.ora parameter SORT_AREA_SIZE can be used to increase the sort area size in memory. This will take place at the **per process** level. So, the increase in SORT_AREA_SIZE can have a major impact on the available system memory.

- The init.ora parameter SORT_READ_FAC = DB_FILE_MULTI-BLOCK_READ_COUNT facilitates bigger merges during the cost-based optimizer sort merge joins.
- Since the ORACLE 7.2.2 sorting operation has been improved, SORT_DIRECT_WRITE=TRUE reduces the load on DBWR caused by sort processes. This is done by writing sort runs directly to disk and bypassing the database block buffer cache.
- Configure SORT_AREA_SIZE and the storage definition of the table space assigned for temporary and sort activities. The goal is to minimize dynamic allocation of extents of TEMP segments once the sort activity is too large to fit in the memory, in which case, the temporary segments are formed and expanded to fit the data sets involved in sorting.

```
SELECT      INITIAL_EXTENT NEXT_EXTENT
FROM        dba_tablespaces
WHERE       tablespace_name='TEMP';
```

Optimize TEMP tablespace using the following extent size consideration:

INITIAL= ks+b , NEXT = ks

Where **k** can be from 1 . . . 20, **s** is the SORT_AREA in blocks, and b is one data block.

12.3.3 ROLLBACK SEGMENTS

Identify the storage definition of the existing rollback segments:

```
SELECT      segment_name, status, initial_extent, next_extent
FROM        sys.dba_rollback_segs;
```

In a data warehouse application the transactions that are very rollback intensive are included in the data warehouse refresh batch jobs. During the massive data load, rollback segments are used heavily. Once rollback segments are created they can be reused by other transactions. If a transaction size is larger than the size of the rollback segment, the rollback segment will expand dynamically. This dynamic expansion can have an impact on the performance and it should be kept to a minimum. In case of a data warehouse application where one wants to avoid dynamic expansion of rollback segments, we recommend that one large rollback segment be created to hold at least half of the largest table in the database. This large rollback segment can be explicitly assigned to a user session like the following:

```
ALTER SESSION USE ROLLBACK SEGMENT= 'MERGEI';
```

Monitor rollback (undo) block contention activities. V$WAITSTAT is populated only when the TIMED_STATISTICS is enabled in init.ora file.

```
SELECT      class, count
FROM        v$waitstat
WHERE       class IN
('system undo header','system undo block', 'undo header','undo block')/
```

12.4 DATA SECURITY CONCEPTS

12.4.1 SECURITY CONSCIOUS DATA WAREHOUSE TEAM

Data Warehouse security requirements are usually more complex than merely requiring a password at login to limit the data warehouse user to a set of operations that can be done over certain database objects. In reality, it often involves limited viewing access to certain subsets of the published data of the warehouse. Data warehouses, if built right, are supposed to make it easier to access the critical data which sometimes include performance indicators. Actually, one of the success factors of a data warehouse implementation is to make it very easy for the analyst to access its business data. The challenge is how to continue to provide this service without jeopardizing the ownership and data access entitlement that existed prior to the data warehouse.

Often, even data warehouse developers lose sight of this subtle complexity of the data-slice/user-function-based security requirement and say that the data they are providing to users are **theirs** and that they are not going to **destroy** their own data. As a result of this inaccurate perception, the implementation of the security requirements gets lower priority and is left to be handled by the end-user tool or at some later stage of the life cycle. Using this approach, "later" is often too late to implement the granular level of security. We have seen how applications are designed, developed, ready to be tested by the end users when someone, possibly the corporate controller, brings up the topic of **data security**, at which point the delivery of the project is impacted until this security issue is resolved.

In most data warehouses, security and integrity of the data goes beyond the restriction of certain operations on database objects or their attribute values. The following table illustrates three different aspects of data warehouse security.

Scope of Security	Description
Object- or attribute-value-based restriction	User *X* has a SELECT or UPDATE access to nonfinancial attributes of table A.
Data-slice/user-function-based restriction	User *X* from department Y has access to only data belonging to department Y in table A.
System-resource-limit-based restriction	User *X* is allowed to use X CPU cycle, Y open sessions, and query Z megabytes of data.

We recommend that DBAs drive the documentation of the detailed definition of the security requirement and plan to implement it using a combination of Oracle features and application logic. Only then can security be administered and monitored on a regular and effective basis. In this section we are going to introduce Oracle's security facilities along with a simple application-level data slice security design.

12.4.2 ORACLE SECURITY FACILITY

The security features can be divided into five security privilege categories:

- Manage object access privilege on object types: table, view, column, database link, sequence, package
- Provide database ROLEs to group of USERs
- Provide system privilege granted to USERs and ROLEs
- Control usage through configuring user PROFILEs
- Take advantage of Oracle tool/SQL operation-based security using Product User Profile database level audit facility

It is quite common to receive user requirements that call for both basic and granular-level data security especially with financial or Web-based data warehouses. In this section we are going to cover Oracle's security features which are at the object and operation levels.

12.4.3 GROUPING USERS INTO DATABASE ROLES

A properly privileged account can create a database object called a ROLE. This object can be the recipient of a number of objects and operation-based access rights.

```
SQL> REM DBA creates the application ROLE "uc_student"
SQL> CREATE ROLE uc_student NOT IDENTIFIED;
SQL> REM add user "tjohnson" to group known as "uc_student"
SQL> GRANT uc_student TO tjohnson;
.................
SQL> REM Provide access right as the owner of the object UC_CLASSES
SQL>GRANT SELECT,INSERT ON uc_classes to uc_student;
```

Database ROLES of an application can be based on the functional hierarchy of the application and the types of end-user tools used. They can represent the conceptual security and access level of the end-user community. Assign object access to end users by assigning the appropriate grants to the database roles. The maintenance and expansion of this new scheme are much easier than on a user-by-user basis. Using database ROLE, DBAs can centrally administer or delegate the administration of data security. Using the database ROLE concept, the database object owner needs only to be concerned about assigning or revoking access rights to/from a group. This is regardless of how many end users are associated with the database ROLE. A user can belong to more than one database ROLE.

All Oracle installations come with a set of precreated database roles. A set of database administrative system and object privileges are grouped together into a database ROLE called "DBA." A DBA privilege account can assign this role to another Oracle user. Therefore, it is not necessary to perform most of DBA activity as SYSTEM or SYS. It is generally because of traceability and accountability that it is recommended that individualized accounts equipped with proper privileges be used rather than a group and generic account. This can be especially true for application schema owner accounts. An application schema owner account is the one that owns all the application objects.

It is best to create at least two database roles for a Data Warehouse:

- DW_ANALYST
- DW_ADMINISTRATOR

DW_ANALYST role can have CONNECT system privileges and SELECT object privileges on the published data in the data warehouse. Whereas DW_ADMININSTRATOR role can have CONNECT system privileges and UPDATE, INSERT, and SELECT object privileges on all tables owned by the data warehouse application owner. Using this configuration every time a new data warehouse user is created, the DW_ANALYST role is assigned. Also, the individual members of the data warehouse team responsible for the data warehouse operation will need only DW_ADMINISTRATOR role.

12.4.4 MANAGE RESOURCES USAGE USING DATABASE PROFILE

Oracle provides a database object called PROFILE that allows DBAs to identify different types of users and group them according to their system resource needs. This powerful and often unnoticed facility places some control over "killer," "harmful," and "wasteful" ad hoc database requests submitted to a data warehouse. A dimensional data warehouse can very well have large transactional tables. In theory, it is possible to intentionally or unintentionally submit a number of concurrent queries that perform FULL TABLE SCAN (all physical I/O) over these large tables. How can a DBA who is responsible for the performance and availability of the data warehouse control these requests?

Database PROFILE provides DBAs with a mechanism to limit the resources used by a database user at the database level, regardless of the front-end tools used. A database PROFILE can be as simple as limiting the number of open sessions per user and as sophisticated as limiting the logical and physical I/O.

```
ALTER SYSTEM SET RESOURCE_LIMIT TRUE;
CREATE PROFILE STUDENT_PROFILE
        SESSION_PER_USER                    10
        CPU_PER_SESSION                     100
        CPU_PER_CALL                        DEFAULT
        LOGICAL_READS_PER_SESSION           UNLIMITED
        LOGICAL_READS_PER_CALL              100000;
```

12.4.5 CREATING DATABASE USER ACCOUNTS

The SQL command CREATE USER allows DBAs to register authorized users of the database. The SQL syntax calls for two minimum attributes of user name and password. User name/password is the minimum and default security mechanism. The CREATE USER syntax also provides the following options to be specified:

- Assign a default table space
- Assign temporary sort table space
- The space quota on individual table spaces
- Default database ROLES and PROFILE

```
CREATE USER               tjohnson
IDENTIFIED BY             change_your_password
DEFAULT TABLESPACE        users
TEMPORARY TABLESPACE      temp
QUOTA 10M ON              users
PROFILE                   student_profile;
```

Oracle also provides a mechanism that doesn't require passwords to be entered. This feature is called O/S authentication. It relies on the O/S to allow authorized users to log in. This mechanism bypasses Oracle's security at login as long as the user is defined to be authenticated through the operating system. These types of Oracle user names are known as OPS$ accounts. This is because such Oracle accounts are usually prefixed with "OPS$" for easier identification. The benefit of this approach is it eliminates the need to remember too many passwords. Here is how it is done:

1. Enable init.ora parameter OS_AUTHENT_PREFIX="OPS$"
2. Obtain the name used to define the user at the O/S level
3. Create an O/S authenticated account by concatenating OPS$ to the O/S user name

```
CREATE USER OPS$TJOHNSON IDENTIFIED EXTERNALLY;
```

Data access privilege and system privilege can be managed using the following two SQL commands:

- GRANT
- REVOKE

```
GRANT           REFERENCES (deptno),
                SELECT,
                UPDATE(ENAME) ON EMP
      TO        tjohnson ;
```

```
REVOKE          SELECT (SALARY) ON EMP FROM tjohnson;
```

In the event that a user is to be completely purged a powerful DDL command, DROP USER, can be used. A user can be dropped along with all its objects as long as there are no connected sessions at that moment.

```
DROP USER scott CASCADE;
```

It is highly recommended that no ORACLE user account except SYS and SYSTEM have the capability to write into SYSTEM, rollback and temporary table space. This can be performed categorically by including the following option in the default CREATE USER command.

```
CREATE USER scott identified by change_your_password
DEFAULT TABLESPACE                        users
TEMPRARY TABLESPACE                       sort
QUOTAS          0 on     system
QUOTAS          0 on     rollback
QUOTAS          0 on     sort
QUOTAS          10M      ON users ;
```

```
ALTER USER tjohnson
QUOTA           0        ON system
QUOTA           0        ON rollback
QUOTA           0        ON sort;
```

12.4.6 COMMON-SENSE SECURITY MEASURES

The following recommendations are intended to enhance the security aspect of an Oracle database, especially a data warehouse application:

- Unless it is necessary, do not make the database links publicly accessible
- Use the UNIX Oracle account only for shutdown/backup, installation, and upgrades
- Avoid "GRANT RESOURCE " which can provide unlimited access to all table spaces
- Change the initial passwords of SYS and SYSTEM every time the database is created

```
ALTER USER system IDENTIFIED BY new_pwd;
```

12.4.7 DATABASE AUDIT FACILITY

One of the quantifiable benefits of a data warehouse is the end-user access and usage metrics. Oracle's audit facility provides a mechanism to track something as simple as login and logoff attempts and as detailed as actual SQL operation usage. Of course, the audit facility can add to the overhead if too much detailed information is tracked. At a minimum we recommend the monitoring the number of login and logoff attempts. Enable the audit facility by performing the following steps:

Enable Auditing

- Enable the init.ora parameter
- Select the destination for AUDIT reports: database or O/S level
- Define the criteria and the scope for the audit
- Unload the audit table owned by SYS regularly

12.5 DATABASE BACKUP CONCEPTS

12.5.1 DATA WAREHOUSE BACKUP REQUIREMENTS

Oracle has an extensive backup and recovery architecture. Selecting the appropriate backup strategy depends on a number of criteria and available resources on an ongoing basis. Answering the following questions can help one prepare the scope of the data warehouse backup strategy:

- How large is the database?
- How often and for how long can a maintenance downtime be scheduled—once a day, once a week?
- How critical is the data in the database? Is the data for development, test, production, archive, and mission critical?
- How long can we afford to have the database down while it is being recovered; for a day, an hour?

- How many tape drives are available on the system?
- What is the tape drive capacity/performance?
- How resource intensive are the disk-to-disk and disk-to-tape backups?
- How reliable are the backup jobs? Do they need to be audited periodically?
- In case of a crash, how long would it take to completely build the data warehouse using application code and not database recovery?

12.5.2 DATABASE STARTUP AND SHUTDOWN

An Oracle database goes through three different stages every time it starts or shuts down. These stages each have important significance, especially in the context of backup and recovery.

Database Startup

1. When the database instance is started and the database enters a NOMOUNT stage, the specified init.ora file is read. ORACLE_SID and ORACLE_HOME environment variable should have already been defined at the O/S session level. All the background processes get started and SGA is allocated.

   ```
   SQLDBA> STARTUP NOMOUNT
   ```

2. When the database enters a MOUNT stage, the control file is located based on the information in the init.ora file. The content of the control file must be readable. The list of rollback segments, database file names, table spaces, and database characteristics are all read.

   ```
   SQLDBA> ALTER DATABASE MOUNT
   ```

3. When the database enters an open stage, the integrity of the database files are checked. The last log sequence number in the control file is also checked against the content of first block of every data file. If it matches, this means the data file is good; otherwise it flags the file as needing RECOVERY. In case a table space is designated to be a READ ONLY table space, then its first block sequence number does not have to match the control file.

   ```
   SQLDBA> ALTER DATABASE OPEN
   ```

Once all these steps are performed successfully and SMON acknowledges that the database does not need any recovery, the database is officially available for end users to use.

Database shutdown. The database shutdown process involves a number of cleanup steps. It basically takes the database from OPEN stage to CLOSED stage while ensuring no live transaction is lost. Shutdown can be requested in three different modes also.

Modes of SHUTDOWN	Description
SHUTDOWN NORMAL	Once issued, the Oracle kernel does not allow any more login. It will wait until all connected sessions exit voluntarily
SHUTDOWN IMMEDIATE	Once issued, the Oracle kernel does not allow any more logins and rolls back the uncommitted transactions. If a session is executing, it waits until it finishes. Once the last transaction is completed, it will go down. It does not wait for users to exit voluntarily.
SHUTDOWN ABORT	Once issued, all background processes are killed. An image dump of the SGA is created to aid the next instance recovery.

Generally, the SHUTDOWN IMMEDIATE is the most efficient and safe method to bring down an Oracle database.

12.5.3 LOGICAL BACKUP

The content of the database records stored in the database tables are read and stored into an operating system file. This file is generally known as an export dump file and can be stored on disk or transferred to tape. The more data read, the larger the export file will get. This method does not record the physical location of the data and the database files, rather, only the actual data and their logical groupings into extents, segments, and table spaces are captured. This export file is transportable to different hosts and can be used to transfer data from one database to another database.

```
Using "exp" and "imp" Oracle utilities :
exp system/manager file=expdata.dmp compress=y
exp system/manager file=appl_data.dmp owner=appl
exp parfile=exp.par
imp system/manager file=expdata.dmp full=y buffer=64000 commit=y
imp system/manager file=expdat.dmp fromuser=appl_dev
touser=appl_prod
```

Oracle export utility can be used in three different modes: complete, incremental, or cumulative.

Export of the Database

Modes of Export	Description
Compete	It is the default behavior that all tables specified will be exported.
Incremental	Only those tables that have modified since the last full export of any type will be exported.
Cumulative	This option exports all tables whose rows have changed since the last cumulative or complete exports.

12.5.4 PHYSICAL BACKUP

Cold Backup. Once the database is completely shut down and none of the database files are being accessed, we can make a complete set of database file backup copies known as **cold backup**. A physical copy of the following database files are generally all that is required: data files, control files, redo logs, init.ora, and config.ora.

Implementation.

```
e.g., create a new save set
tar -cvf /dev/rmt/0hc /usr[1-4]/oracle/data/DBA0
append the following:
tar -rvf /dev/rmt/0hc $ORACLE_HOME/dbs/initDBA01.ora
```

Hot Backup. While the database is open a system backup takes place. The files that must be backed up are data files, archived redo logs, control files, init.ora, and config.ora.

The database must be running in ARCHIVELOG mode. From SQLDBA issue the following:

```
startup mount
alter database archivelog;
archive log start;
alter database open;
```

The location of archived redo log files are specified in init.ora or config.ora file.

```
log_archive_dest=/usr1/oracle/arch/DBA01/arch
log_archive_start=true
```

The background process Archiver (ARCH) uses this configuration information to archive off the redo logs and name them according to the masking and redo log file sequence number information.

```
arch_100.dbf
arch_101.dbf
```

Implementation. Oracle backup scripts are very platform specific. To demonstrate the steps in the process we are illustrating a simple backup script in the UNIX environment.

```
alter tablespace USER begin backup
!tar -rvf /dev/rmt/0hc /usr1/oracle/data/DBA01/user*_DBA01.dbf
alter tablespace USER end backup
.........
alter database backup controlfile to
'/usr1/oracle/data/DBA01/backup_controlfile_DBA01.dbf';
!tar -rvf /usr1/oracle/data/DBA01/backup_controlfile_DBA01.dbf
.....
```

It is important to become familiar with the basics of all three types of Oracle database backups. Familiarity with the resource requirements and ramifications of HOT/COLD export backup and the recovery time of each method is essential in deriving the backup schedule and policy of your data warehouse repository.

In general, a data warehouse Oracle database does not need to have a HOT backup. HOT backups are more suited for an OLTP environment. The overhead involved in hot backups will impact the performance of both batch jobs and ad hoc query data access. The important thing is to have management involved and get their support. Also, test each method and practice using the recovery methods and the recovery scripts.

Every time a rollback segment or a datafile is added to the database, shut down the database and make a good cold backup of the entire database. Before every shutdown, get a listing of all table spaces, data files, and database links. Every time an export/import takes place, the database links are defined in the target database only after all the other objects are created. Objects like views and stored packages can't be compiled during the import. The workaround is once the import is finished try to define and compile those objects again.

Oracle 7 allows re-creation of control files. Checkpoints can be reduced using the following INIT.ORA parameter which improves the performance but in case of a failure and automatic recovery, it will take SMON longer time to complete the recovery. For example:

```
LOG_CHECKPOINT_TIMEOUT= 300 # timeout every 5 minutes
                      = 0 # timeout disabled.
```

To ensure database synchronization, a user can force one or all instances accessing a database to perform a checkpoint. As a result, DBWR stops all other actions and writes dirty blocks in the SGA to the data files. For example:

```
Write buffers for all instances of the same databases:
          ALTER SYSTEM CHECKPOINT GLOBAL;
Write buffers for the current instance:
          ALTER SYSTEM CHECKPOINT LOCAL;
```

12.5.5 RECOVERY METHODS

Instance Failure. It happens when the host machine has crashed or for some reason the background processes are killed due to an external reason. The recovery is automatic. When the database gets restarted, the aborted transactions can be identified by SMON during the startup process and they will be rolled back, for example; perform complete or incomplete recovery with the command. It applies the redo log files until the user specifies CANCEL to the RECOVER command prompt:

```
RECOVER DATABASE UNTIL CANCEL;
```

Disk Failure. It is also called media failure. The first thing to do is to identify the database files that are affected. The recovery methods differ depending on what database file is lost. If the database files are on shadow disks and one of the shadow disks fails, the RDBMS will continue to operate. Though it is best to shut down the database and perform a cold backup. Once the disk problem is fixed at the O/S level, start the database up again.

In case the disks are not shadowed, and when the disk problem is resolved, the backup copy of the database files that are affected must be recovered from backup disk or tape to put in the proper location. At this point, issue the RECOVER command.

```
From O/S:

cp /backup/oracle/DBA01/user_DBA01.dbf
/usr1/oracle/data/DBA01/user_DBA01.dbf

From SQLDBA:

SQLDBA> startup mount
SQLDBA>recover database;
SQLDBA>alter database open;
```

Object Loss. This happens when an object (table) is accidentally altered or dropped. In order to recover that particular object, depending on how old the data and the object structure are, one can either use the recent export dump file or perform a point-in-time recovery.

1. Back up the current database (cold).
2. Replace it with a prior backup copy of this database.
3. Apply the archived logs to it up to the point of loss.
4. Export the object(s).
5. Restore the database back. Use the backup copies of step 1.
6. Replace the loss objects using the export file.

```
SQLDBA> startup mount
SQLDBA> recover database until '1994-12-1:10:10:00';
SQLDBA >alter database open reset logs;
```

12.6 ADMINISTRATION SCRIPTS

Script 1

```
SQL> COLUMN TABLESPACE_NAME FORMAT A15 TRUNC;
SQL>
SQL> TTITLE 'TABLESPACE STATUS';
SQL> SELECT *
2 FROM DBA_TABLESPACES;
Mon Sep 1 page 1
TABLESPACE STATUS
TABLESPACE_NAME INITIAL_EXTENT NEXT_EXTENT MIN_EXTENTS
MAX_EXTENTS PCT_INCREASE STATUS
--------------- -------------- ----------- ----------- ---------- -----------
SYSTEM      16384       16384       1    505   50   ONLINE
INTMTAB     516096      516096      1    505   1    ONLINE <--
INTMNDX     516096      516096      1    505   1    ONLINE
TOOLS       106496      106496      1    505   1    ONLINE
TEMP        104857600   104857600   1    505   1    ONLINE <--
ROLLBACK    1048576     1048576     2    505   1    ONLINE
HISTTAB     516096      516096      1    505   1    READ ONLY <--
HISTNDX     516096      516096      1    505   1    READ ONLY
SUMNDX      516096      516096      1    505   1    ONLINE
SUMTAB      516096      516096      1    505   1    ONLINE
ATMTAB      516096      516096      1    505   1    ONLINE
ATMNDX      516096      516096      1    505   1    ONLINE
```

```
USERS        516096    516096    1    505    1    ONLINE
13 rows selected.
```

Notes:

- Use simple naming conventions when naming table space and file names.
- Separate tables, indexes, temporary and rollback segments into their dedicated table spaces.
- Set the "INITIAL EXTENT" and "NEXT EXTENT" of temporary table spaces to be a multiple of SORT_AREA_SIZE in SGA.
- Separate those table and index segments that get re-created and repopulated very often into their dedicated tablespaces (INTMTAB and INTMNDX).
- Place static data into a dedicated table space and set them to be "READ ONLY," which demands less integrity checking from Oracle kernel.

Script 2

```
COLUMN TABLESPACE_NAME FORMAT A15 TRUNC;

TTITLE 'TABLESPACE STATUS';
SELECT *
FROM DBA_TABLESPACES;

SET PAGES 60;
CLEAR COLUMN;
COLUMN FILE_NAME FORMAT A35 TRUNC;
COLUMN TABLESPACE_NAME FORMAT A15 TRUNC;
BREAK ON TABLESPACE_NAME skip 1 on report skip 1;
COMPUTE SUM AVG of blocks on tablespace_name report;
COMPUTE SUM AVG of bytes on tablespace_name report;

TTITLE 'TABLESPACE FRAGMENTATION OF FREE SPACES';
SELECT *
FROM DBA_FREE_SPACE
ORDER BY TABLESPACE_NAME,BYTES;
spool off
```

Script 3

```
SQL> select tablespace_name,sum(bytes),count(*) fragments from dba_free_space
2* group by tablespace_name
TABLESPACE_NAME SUM(BYTES) FRAGMENTS
_______________ __________ _________
ATMNDX          955097088     16
ATMTAB          2628902912    72 (—— Not good , it can be critical
SUMNDX          214212608     10
SUMTAB          180510720     5
HISTNDX         154902528     1
HISTTAB         113360896     3
ROLLBACK        2511241216    46 (—— Not good
SYSTEM          68837376      5
TEMP            4194287616    2
TOOLS           45727744      1
USERS           38043648      1
INTMNDX         1778843648    19 (—- Not good
INTMTAB         5221883904    3
13 rows selected.
```

Note: In some table spaces , the overall free space is divided into many extents (groups of contiguous blocks). Therefore the available free space gets fragmented. This can cause problems when objects have to extend. As a minimum it makes it harder to find contiguous blocks for large "NEXT EXTENT." More internal processing (overhead) is needed to locate the extent that is large enough to be appropriate for a larger "NEXT EXTENT." In cases like this a number of preventive and enhancement measures can be done:

- Redistribute tables and indexes into more dedicated tablespaces,(small tables, large tables, highly updateable tables,etc.).
- Size the "NEXT EXTENT" of tables and indexes such that they follow certain patterns, that is, 1 M, 5 M, 10 M, 50 M, 100 M, 500 M.
- Objects that are very large and grow very fast must be placed in dedicated table spaces.
- Monitor the smallest free space fragment size and compare it with the smallest "next extent;" if they don't match, it is likely that those small free space fragments never get used and cause so-called "bubbles" in the disk space. By using standard next extent sizes, this problem can be kept under control.
- Re-create the work table spaces (INTMNDX, INTMTAB) that are used for intermediate processing periodically. If TRUNCATE TABLE is used, keep the allocated space using "REUSE STORAGE" clause.

Script 4

```
SQL>
SQL> SET PAGES 60;
SQL> CLEAR COLUMN;
columns cleared
SQL> COLUMN FILE_NAME FORMAT A35 TRUNC;
SQL> COLUMN TABLESPACE_NAME FORMAT A15 TRUNC;
SQL> BREAK ON TABLESPACE_NAME skip 1 on report skip 1;
SQL> COMPUTE SUM AVG of blocks on tablespace_name report;
SQL> COMPUTE SUM AVG of bytes on tablespace_name report;
SQL>
SQL> TTITLE 'TABLESPACE FRAGMENTATION OF FREE SPACES';
SQL> SELECT *
  2 FROM DBA_FREE_SPACE
  3 ORDER BY TABLESPACE_NAME,BYTES;

Mon Sep 1 page 1
TABLESPACE FRAGMENTATION OF FREE SPACES
TABLESPACE_NAME FILE_ID     BLOCK_ID    BYTES        BLOCKS
--------------- ---------- ---------- ---------- -------------- ----------
ATMNDX             19       110957      122880       15
                   19       48207       2211840      270
                   19       49727       3317760      405
                   19       30602       4997120      610
                   8        236946      6103040      745
                   19       51982       17080320     2085
                   19       2           25600000     3125
                   19       25502       38625280     4715
                   8        2           46325760     5655
                   8        247961      61440000     7500
                   19       31342       88514560     10805
                   19       142442      325509120    39735
                   19       215012      335781888    40989
*************** ---------- ----------
avg 73509966.8 8973.38462
sum 955629568 116654

ATMTAB             27       234452      40960        5
                   27       255962      40960        5
                   27       255992      73728        9
```

```
                  26        104627      122880      15
                  27        86517       122880      15
                  14        56077       122880      15
                  14        85747       122880      15
                  26        98187       122880      15
                  26        102667      122880      15
                  14        56197       122880      15
                  26        104692      122880      15
                  26        104772      122880      15
                  26        104732      122880      15
                  32        14267       163840      20
                  26        181692      204800      25
                  27        28087       204800      25
                  27        28037       204800      25
                  26        212892      204800      25
                  26        216952      204800      25
                  26        992         368640      45
                  32        239259      409600      50
                  32        43952       532480      65
                  32        44082       532480      65
                  26        175377      778240      95
                  27        96787       901120      110
                  26        85527       942080      115
                  34        31967       1146880     140
                  26        118407      1310720     160
                  30        255832      1384448     169
                  27        96012       2129920     260
                  26        225542      3031040     370
                  26        68762       3153920     385
                  26        235987      3563520     435
                  26        218392      3686400     450
                  26        219742      3686400     450
                  32        13712       4423680     540
                  26        222737      4628480     565
Mon Sep 1 page 2
TABLESPACE FRAGMENTATION OF FREE SPACES
TABLESPACE_NAME   FILE_ID   BLOCK_ID    BYTES       BLOCKS
---------------   -------   ---------   ---------   ---------   ---------
ATMTAB            32        240129      4792320     585
                  26        93962       4792320     585
                  32        33552       4915200     600
                  26        181037      5160960     630
                  26        228512      5160960     630
```

	26	232662	5160960	630
	27	2	5242880	640
	27	98642	5242880	640
	27	92682	5242880	640
	14	62632	5242880	640
	26	103962	5242880	640
	14	60052	5324800	650
	27	5122	5365760	655
	14	121872	5611520	685
	26	123302	6103040	745
	27	88072	6307840	770
	26	248702	6348800	775
	26	254597	7905280	965
	32	253459	8683520	1060
	27	26712	10485760	1280
	26	240742	10649600	1300
	26	23427	15810560	1930
	26	199897	16056320	1960
	26	210897	16056320	1960
	30	2	18964480	2315
	14	189512	51200000	6250
	14	96807	51200000	6250
	14	2842	73400320	8960
	32	34347	78151680	9540
	14	245407	86786048	10594
	32	133374	92528640	11295
	14	42522	110632960	13505
	32	14352	156753920	19135
	32	44212	203161600	24800
	32	144704	209305600	25550
	30	213587	313548800	38275
	30	33357	1475379200	180100
	34	32732	1829019648	223269
***************	___	___	___	___
avg 66214953 8082.88				
sum 4966121472 606216				
SUMNDX	28	243307	122880	15
	9	185181	385024	47
	28	222975	3047424	372
	31	208481	4677632	571
	31	85975	5898240	720
	29	255230	6316032	771
	9	185639	6840320	835

```
                28      243972    8273920      1010
                9       254778    10018816     1223
                9       172337    11231232     1371
                28      254582    11624448     1419
                29      227972    17383424     2122
                31      146855    17825792     2176
                31      80074     22126592     2701
                9       246084    23805952     2906
                29      221807    24289280     2965
                28      229792    25722880     3140
                29      156028    27615232     3371
                29      80757     42680320     5210
                31      14082     54910976     6703
                31      248127    64503808     7874
                38      10272     2013011968   245729
*************** _______ _______ _______ _______ _______ _______
avg 109196009 13329.5909
sum 2402312192 293251
SUMTAB          15      230952    205201408    25049
                11      230252    210935808    25749
                23      198252    473079808    57749
                22      192002    524279808    63999
                25      129752    1034231808   126249
*************** _______ _______ _______ _______ _______ _______
avg 489545728 59759
sum 2447728640 298795
HISTNDX         4       237092    154902528    18909
*************** _______ _______ _______ _______ _______ _______
avg 154902528 18909
sum 154902528 18909
HISTTAB         33      252162    31449088     3839
                33      136962    31457280     3840
                7       249842    50454528     6159
*************** _______ _______ _______ _______ _______ _______
avg 37786965.3 4612.66667
sum 113360896 13838
ROLLBACK        17      1952      1064960      130
                17      20022     1064960      130
                17      19242     1064960      130
                17      13392     1064960      130
                17      782       1064960      130
                17      15212     1064960      130
                17      15992     1064960      130
```

```
                 17        49662      1064960      130
                 17        17032      1064960      130
                 17        18072      1064960      130
                 17        34972      1064960      130
                 17        35492      1064960      130
                 17        32762      1064960      130
                 17        33152      1064960      130
                 17        31722      1064960      130
                 17        32112      1064960      130
                 17        18852      1064960      130
                 17        112582     1064960      130
                 17        35752      1064960      130
Mon Sep 1 page 4
TABLESPACE FRAGMENTATION OF FREE SPACES
TABLESPACE_NAME FILE_ID BLOCK_ID BYTES BLOCKS
-------------- --------- --------- --------- --------- --------- ------
ROLLBACK         17        36012      1064960      130
                 17        36402      1064960      130
                 17        36662      1064960      130
                 17        36922      1064960      130
                 17        33542      1064960      130
                 17        34062      1064960      130
                 17        34582      1064960      130
                 17        37182      1064960      130
                 17        37572      1064960      130
                 17        37832      1064960      130
                 17        18462      1064960      130
                 17        112842     1064960      130
                 17        2212       1064960      130
                 17        8062       1064960      130
                 17        19632      1064960      130
                 17        1432       1064960      130
                 17        30682      2129920      260
                 13        147332     20971520     2560
                 13        128132     31457280     3840
                 17        121162     41533440     5070
                 17        130132     59637760     7280
                 17        85412      59637760     7280
                 17        54212      162938880    19890
                 13        75652      230686720    28160
                 17        225632     248782848    30369
                 13        194692     502243328    61309
                 17        138192     506593280    61840
```

```
                         13           132            608174080     74240
*************** _________ _________ _________ _________ _________ _________
avg 53448094 6524.42553
sum 2512060416 306648
SYSTEM                   1            3502           98304         12
                         1            3488           98304         12
                         1            2792           409600        50
                         1            3591           75448320      9210
*************** _________ _________ _________ _________ _________ _________
avg 19013632 2321
sum 76054528 9284
TEMP                     5            2              2097143808    255999
                         18           2              2097143808    255999
*************** _________ _________ _________ _________ _________ _________
avg 2097143808 255999
sum 4194287616 511998
TOOLS                    2            6252           53649408      6549
*************** _________ _________ _________ _________ _________ _________
avg 53649408 6549
Mon Sep 1 page 5
TABLESPACE FRAGMENTATION OF FREE SPACES
TABLESPACE_NAME          FILE_ID      BLOCK_ID       BYTES         BLOCKS
_____________- _________ _________ _________ _________
sum 53649408 6549
USERS                    12           2732           82485248      10069
*************** _________ _________ _________ _________ _________ _________
avg 82485248 10069
sum 82485248 10069
INTMNDX                  6            199888         147456        18
                         6            134480         335872        41
                         6            68541          475136        58
                         6            27645          573440        70
                         6            90121          737280        90
                         6            111815         884736        108
                         6            86333          1048576       128
                         6            102648         1048576       128
                         6            219780         1146880       140
                         6            66584          1146880       140
                         6            25696          1179648       144
                         6            70648          1310720       160
                         6            113203         1474560       180
                         6            196421         1761280       215
                         6            53195          2555904       312
```

```
                  6          96556        3825664      467
                  6          94577        4677632      571
                  6          104651       4685824      572
                  6          100191       4767744      582
                  6          15978        5038080      615
                  6          116734       5120000      625
                  6          69849        5120000      625
                  6          98238        5406720      660
                  6          210699       5996544      732
                  6          171839       6168576      753
                  6          43100        9224192      1126
                  6          167120       10100736     1233
                  6          165234       10190848     1244
                  6          196700       10428416     1273
                  6          124725       10649600     1300
                  6          163190       10649600     1300
                  6          126597       10674176     1303
                  6          130344       10698752     1306
                  6          211963       11001856     1343
                  6          132144       11313152     1381
                  6          194681       11608064     1417
                  6          128352       11657216     1423
                  6          39796        11706368     1429
                  6          216076       12148736     1483
                  6          70860        12197888     1489
                  6          161120       12247040     1495
                  6          106278       12525568     1529
                  6          136981       13934592     1701
                  6          192512       14016512     1711
                  6          72441        14606336     1783
                  6          113686       14729216     1798
                  6          206960       15269888     1864
Mon Dec 16 page 6
TABLESPACE FRAGMENTATION OF FREE SPACES
TABLESPACE_NAME   FILE_ID    BLOCK_ID     BYTES        BLOCKS
---------------- ---------- ---------- ---------- ----------
INTMNDX           6          176598       17113088     2089
                  6          134598       18096128     2209
                  6          142682       20709376     2528
                  6          119234       28516352     3481
                  6          46101        42754048     5219
                  6          200996       43638784     5327
                  6          78554        49414144     6032
```

```
                    6       182437      65830912     8036
                    6       29590       79953920     9760
                    6       148960      92381184     11277
                    6       53569       92405760     11280
                    6       2668        98713600     12050
                    6       227388      234397696    28613
*************** _________ _________ _________ _________ _________ _________
avg 20202291.2 2466.1
sum 1212137472 147966
INTMTAB             37      121602      52420608     6399
                    35      249602      52420608     6399
                    3       136962      975167488    119039
*************** _________ _________ _________ _________ _________ _________
avg 360002901 43945.6667
sum 1080008704 131837
_________ _________
avg 93898665.9 11462.2395
sum 2.2348E+10 2728013
SQL>
```

Script 5

```
SQL> select * from v$SGA;
NAME                VALUE
__________________  _________
Fixed Size          49772
Variable Size       71769876
Database Buffers    491520000
Redo Buffers        15728640
```

Script 6

```
CREATE VIEW stats$file_view
AS SELECT
   ts.name table_space , i.name file_name , x.phyrds phys_reads,
   x.phywrts phys_writes, x.readtim phys_rd_time, x.writetim phys_wrt_tim,
   x.phyblkrd phys_blks_rd,
   x.phyblkwrt phys_blks_wr
FROM v$filestat x, ts$ ts, v$datafile I, file$ f
WHERE
   i.file#= f.file# AND ts.ts# = f.ts# AND x.file#=f.file#;
```

Script 7

```
Mon Sep 1 page 1
TABLESPACE FRAGMENTATION OF FREE SPACES
TABLE_SPAC FILE_NAME PHYS_READS PHYS_WRITES PHYS_RD_TIME
PHYS_WRT_TIM PHYS_BLKS_RD BLKS_WR
---------- ---------------------- ---------- ----------- ------------ ----------
SYSTEM /dev/xx/raw/v100-00    227   23   232   -860403405   284   23
TOOLS /dev/xx/raw/v100-05       5    1     6    -37408740     5    1
INTMTAB /dev/xx/raw/v2000-32    0    0     0    0             0    0
HISTNDX /dev/xx/raw/v2000-10    0    0     0    0             0    0
TEMP /dev/xx/raw/v2000-14       0    0     0    0             0    0
INTMNDX /dev/xx/raw/v2000-16    0    0     0    0             0    0
HISTTAB /dev/xx/raw/v2000-33    0    0     0    0             0    0
ATMNDX /dev/xx/raw/v2000-21     0    0     0    0             0    0
SUMNDX /dev/xx/raw/v2000-06     0    0     0    0             0    0
SUMTAB /dev/xx/raw/v2000-23     0    0     0    0             0    0
USERS /dev/xx/raw/v100-06       0    0     0    0             0    0
ROLLBACK/dev/xx/raw/v2000-11    3    2     1    -74819888     3    2
ATMTAB /dev/xx/raw/v2000-01     0    0     0    0             0    0
SUMTAB /dev/xx/raw/v2000-30     0    0     0    0             0    0
SUMTAB /dev/xx/raw/v2000-31     0    0     0    0             0    0
ROLLBACK/dev/xx/raw/v2000-12    9    7     1    -261855147    9    7
TEMP /dev/xx/raw/v2000-15       0    0     0    0             0    0
ATMNDX /dev/xx/raw/v2000-22     0    0     0    0             0    0
```

Note:

- Plan the sizes of raw disk files ahead of time. This can facilitate the gradual expansion of tablespaces.

Script 8

```
SELECT name filename, phyrds phys_reads, phywrts phys_writes
FROM v$datafile df , v$filestat fs
WHERE df.file# =fs.file#;
```

```
FILENAME PHYS_READS PHYS_WRITES
------------------------------ ---------- ----------
/dev/xx/raw/v100-00    241    29      ( Not good - HOT file ( High level of I/O)
/dev/xx/raw/v100-05    5      2
```

```
/dev/xx/raw/v2000-32  0    0
/dev/xx/raw/v2000-10  0    0
/dev/xx/raw/v2000-14  0    0
/dev/xx/raw/v2000-16  0    0
/dev/xx/raw/v2000-33  0    0
/dev/xx/raw/v2000-21  0    0
/dev/xx/raw/v2000-06  0    0
/dev/xx/raw/v2000-13  0    0
/dev/xx/raw/v2000-23  0    0
/dev/xx/raw/v100-06   0    0
/dev/xx/raw/v2000-11  3    3
/dev/xx/raw/v2000-01  0    0
/dev/xx/raw/v2000-30  0    0
/dev/xx/raw/v2000-31  0    0
/dev/xx/raw/v2000-12  9    10
/dev/xx/raw/v2000-15  0    0
/dev/xx/raw/v2000-22  0    0
/dev/xx/raw/v2000-28  0    0
```

Script 9

```
SELECT *
FROM V$SGASTAT
WHERE name = 'free memory';
```

```
NAME                  BYTES
--------------------- ----------
free memory           50972196
```

Script 10

```
SELECT name, bytes
FROM V$SGASTAT
WHERE name IN
('db_block_buffers','log_buffer', 'dictionary cache','sql area','library cache');
```

```
NAME                BYTES
----------------------------- -----------
db_block_buffers    245760000 <--The major portion of SGA is the Block buffer cache
log_buffer          15728640
log_buffer          245760
dictionary cache    292512
library cache       386996
sql area            774800
```

Script 11

```
Monitor :      Library Cache PIN HIT ratio
SELECT         (SUM(reloads)/SUM(pins)) * 100
               'Number of library cache miss %'
FROM           V$LIBRARYCACHE;
```

```
Number of library cache miss %
------------------------------
       .023942674 <- pretty good -
```

```
SELECT         sum(pins) " executions" , sum (reloads)
               "cache misses during executions"
FROM           V$LIBRARYCACHE;
```

```
executions cache misses during executions
----------- ------------------------------
73203                  15
```

Script 12

```
SELECT      namespace, gets,
            round(decode(gethits,0,1,gethits)/
            decode(gets,0,1,gets),3)
            "GET HIT RATIO" ,
            pins,
            round(decode(pinhits,0,1,pinhits)/
            decode(pins,0,1,pins),3)
            "PIN HIT RATIO" ,
            reloads , invalidations
FROM        V$LIBRARYCACHE;
```

```
NAMESPACE   GETS GET HIT RATIO  PINS PIN HIT RATIO    RELOADS
INVALIDATIONS
_____________ _________ ____________ _________ ___________ _________ __
SQL AREA          2127   .885   73990   .993   4    28
TABLE/PROCEDURE   953    .686   1752    .867   12   0
BODY              33     .667   33      .394   0    0
TRIGGER           0      1      0       1      0    0
INDEX             21     .048   21      .048   0    0
CLUSTER           27     .444   15      .333   0    0
OBJECT            0      1      0       1      0    0
PIPE              0      1      0       1      0    0
```

Script 13

```
SELECT      SUM(gets) "Data Dictionary Gets"
            , Sum ( getmisses )
            " Data Dictionary Cache get misses"
FROM        V$ROWCACHE;
```

```
SUM(GETS) SUM(GETMISSES)
_________ _____________
13172        2251
```

Script 14

```
SELECT      ((SUM(gets)-
            SUM(getmisses))/SUM(gets))* 100
FROM        V$ROWCACHE;
```

```
(SUM(GETS)-SUM(GETMISSES))/SUM(GETS) * 100
-------------------------------------------
            83 <— not that bad — can get better
```

Script 15

```
SELECT      parameter "name",
            gets "get requests",
            getmisses, scans "scan requests" ,
            scanmisses, modifications, count,
            usage "Current Usage"
FROM        V$ROWCACHE
WHERE       gets != 0
       OR   scans !=0 OR modifications != 0
ORDER BY GETMISSES DESC , SCANMISSES DESC ;
```

name	get requests	GETMISSES	scan requests	SCANMISSES	MODIFICATIONS	COUNT	Usage	
dc_columns	**4470**	**1065**	**517**	**159**	**197**	**951**	**943**	←
dc_constraint_defs	880	431	109	62	12	377	374	
dc_free_extents	**1902**	**240**	**2**	**0**	**3**	**241**	**238**	←
dc_table_grants	**808**	**226**	**0**	**0**	**0**	**223**	**222**	←
dc_objects	951	173	0	0	64	211	204	
dc_segments	645	130	0	0	3	147	130	
dc_indexes	755	127	498	88	21	126	124	
dc_object_ids	649	114	0	0	0	117	114	
dc_tables	2126	83	0	0	46	114	105	

dc_constraint_defs	145	38	74	45	12	33	32
dc_synonyms	85	36	0	0	0	35	33
dc_users	1440	25	0	0	0	32	25
dc_truncates	24	24	0	0	24	29	24
dc_user_grants	1217	23	0	0	0	48	23
dc_rollback_segments	275	9	0	0	13	17	10
dc_usernames	286	4	0	0	0	20	4
dc_used_extents	3	3	0	0	3	18	2
dc_sequences	22	3	0	0	5	6	3
dc_database_links	24	3	0	0	0	7	1
dc_users	14	3	0	0	0	20	3
dc_tablespaces	2	2	0	0	0	16	2
dc_tablespaces	43	2	0	0	43	24	2
dc_tablespace_quotas	3	2	0	0	3	3	2

Note:

- A data warehouse database application usually includes many columns and indexes. It is likely that not all of them will stay cached.
- Having a high number of free extents, fragments are an indication of unnecessary fragmentation and inconsistent extent sizes used in storage clauses. This can place a performance overhead whenever an object needs to expand.
- The number of table grants can be kept low with the use of database roles.

Part III

Synopsis of Oracle Technology

As students we strove, for scholarship to attain,
While scholars toiled and searched, whatever chance did remain,
After efforts and attempts, we faced complete loss,
Dust had been our origin, to dust we will turn again.

TRUE TRANSLATION OF HAKIM OMAR KHAYYAM'S ROBAIYAT

Chapter 13

INTRODUCTION TO SQL

13.1 BASIC DATABASE CONCEPTS

According to researchers, one effective way to relate to a new concept is to follow a top-down categorization approach. Start from a high level of categorization and go down the path of specialization toward a special topic. Based on this methodology, let's start the discussion on the role of a database server in a data warehouse by briefly covering the basic concepts of a database and its roles and capabilities. If you are already familiar with these concepts, you can skip and go on to the next chapter. Otherwise, this chapter covers what you need to become familiar with, and will direct you to further necessary and useful reference materials.

13.1.1 THE THREE-LAYER ARCHITECTURE—ANSI DATABASE MODEL

When studying database servers in general, it is best to start with the well-known SPARC/ANSI architecture. It was proposed by the ANSI/SPARC standards committee[1] in 1978. The goal of this architec-

[1]D. Tsichritzis, A. Klug, 1978. The ANSI 1x3/SPARC DBMS Framework, AFIPS Press.

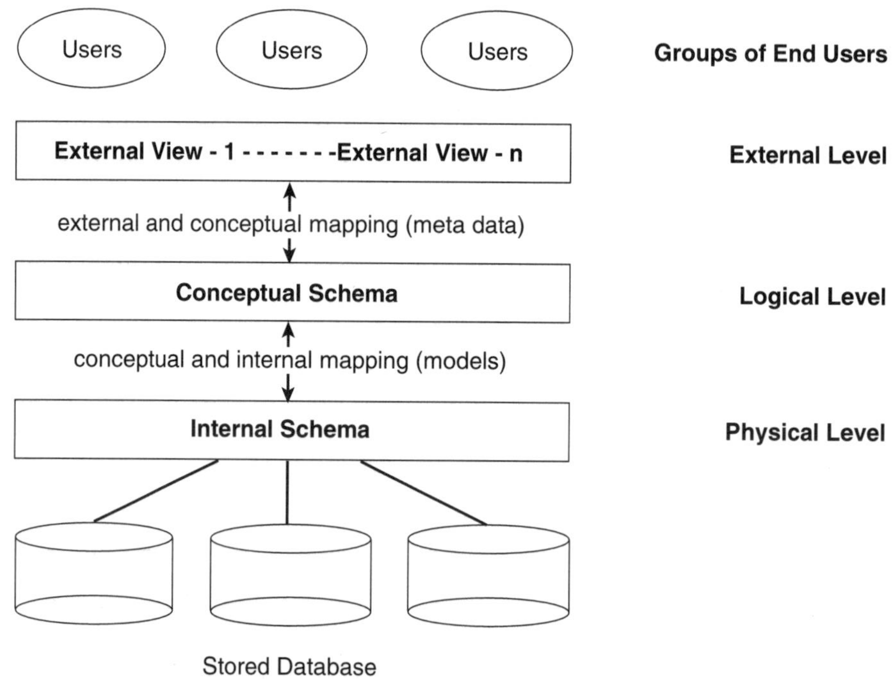

FIGURE 13.1 ANSI Database Model.

ture is to separate the user application models from the physical storage of the data. In other words, it provides logical and physical data independence (see Figure 13.1). This separation provides more system development flexibility and adaptability which, in turn, result in low cost for maintenance and application evolution. SPARC architecture represents the universe of a database application from three separate perspectives, all of which are about the same thing, the data. It is important to know what the expectations are from each user's perspective. This acknowledgement helps produce a well-designed database application. After nearly two decades, this type of architecture is still relevant and flexible. It just needs to be understood and be used as a framework when developing a database application.

External Level → Conceptual Level → Internal level

External Level. End user's description, view, and perception of the data. There could be many user level views and models of the same database.

Conceptual Level. Application developers organize data sets based on their understanding of user requirements. This level is the application developers' description, view, and perception of data. It must include entities, attributes, data types, relationships, user operations, and constraints. It is a single integrated conceptual-level model of a database.

Internal Level. Database Management System (DBMS) is the software that performs the conceptual-to internal-level mapping. Database management systems describe the complete details of how data is physically stored in the database. Database administrators should be familiar with this physical layout and its mapping to the other two levels. Data are actually stored in this level. There is only one single internal level model of a database.

In summary, the principal lesson learned from the ANSI database model is in the logical and physical data independence. Logical independence allows the conceptual model to change without impacting the user's view of the database. Physical independence allows the internal schema to be changed without impacting the conceptual and the external models. To achieve these goals and benefits as stated in the ANSI model, responsibilities resides in the database management system software vendor, the application developer and the development methodology used, and the database administrator. The database administrator should understand and oversee the entire process. These principal benefits cannot be achieved unless they are stated in the definition of each of the three players (see Figure 13.2). Any data warehouse application viewed as major, complex, and strategic that also has a gigantic database application must adhere to the ANSI database model to be successful.

Therefore, a data warehouse overall architecture must first and foremost support the three-layer ANSI/SPARC database model. Due to the nature of a data warehouse application and strategic role of this application, the three-tier approach provides an **open** opportunity and should be considered seriously. The rate with which new tools and techniques are invented and released to the market is much faster than the rate data warehouse projects can afford to be rearchitected. When evaluating a data warehouse application from the standpoint of return on investment, effectiveness, and contribution to the organization's competitive advantage, one must also see how **close** or **open** the application architecture is with respect to the ANSI/SPARC model.

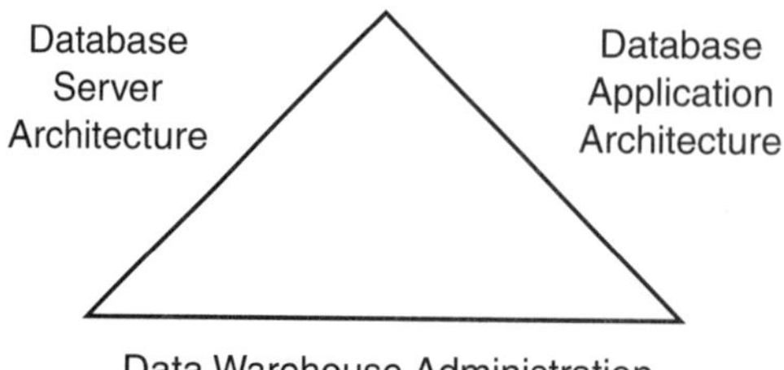

FIGURE 13.2 Three Vital Players of a Data Warehouse Database Application.

13.1.2 INTENDED USE OF A DATABASE MANAGEMENT SYSTEM (DBMS)

When it comes to using an industry-strength DBMS server to produce powerful applications, such as robust, effective, and scalable data warehouse applications, it is vital to be familiar with the classical capabilities of a DBMS server. This familiarity is a necessary foundation for administering the developmental and operational aspects of your data warehouse. The objectives of a DBMS are:

- ❑ Controlling redundancy
- ❑ Restricting unauthorized use
- ❑ Persistence storage
- ❑ Database inference and deduction rules
- ❑ Providing multiple user interface
- ❑ Representing complex relationships among data
- ❑ Enforcing integrity constraint
- ❑ Providing backup and recovery

13.1.3 IMPLICATIONS OF USING DBMS

Once the DBMS is in place, it can provide opportunities to improve the quality of the database application being developed. Some of the most important ones are:

- ❑ Potential for enforcing application development standards
- ❑ Reduce application development time and resources
- ❑ Flexibility as end-user requirements evolve
- ❑ Availability of up-to-date information

- ❑ Economies of scale to permit consolidation of data processing activities

13.1.4 A SCHEMA OR DATA DICTIONARY

As we saw in the ANSI/SPARC model, at every level there is a model or map that describes the view of that particular perspective or player. A schema is a model that is presented using a specific language. The context of a database application when referring to an application schema generally means the application's external level of user requirements and the conceptual level in the ANSI/SPARC model. In the context of a data warehouse, it refers to the schema model representing the end user's view of the data and the external level in the ANSI/SPARC model.

- ❑ The description of a database application is a database schema or metadata
- ❑ Metadata are specified during the database application design phase
- ❑ A displayed schema is called a schema diagram

13.1.5 COMPONENTS OF A TYPICAL DBMS SERVER

Here is a list of the major components of a typical DBMS server as illustrated in Figure 13.3.

1. Stored Data Manager: It controls access to DBMS information stored on a disk storage system.
2. DDL Compiler: Processes schema (metadata) definitions stored in the DDL (Data Definition Language) and stores description of the schema in the DBMS catalog.
3. Run-Time Database Processor: Handles database access by processing the data retrieval and update requests.
4. Query Compiler: Parses and analyzes a query that is entered interactively. It also makes calls to run-time processors to execute these requests.
5. Precompiler: A module which translates DML (Data Manipulation) commands from an application program written in a host language

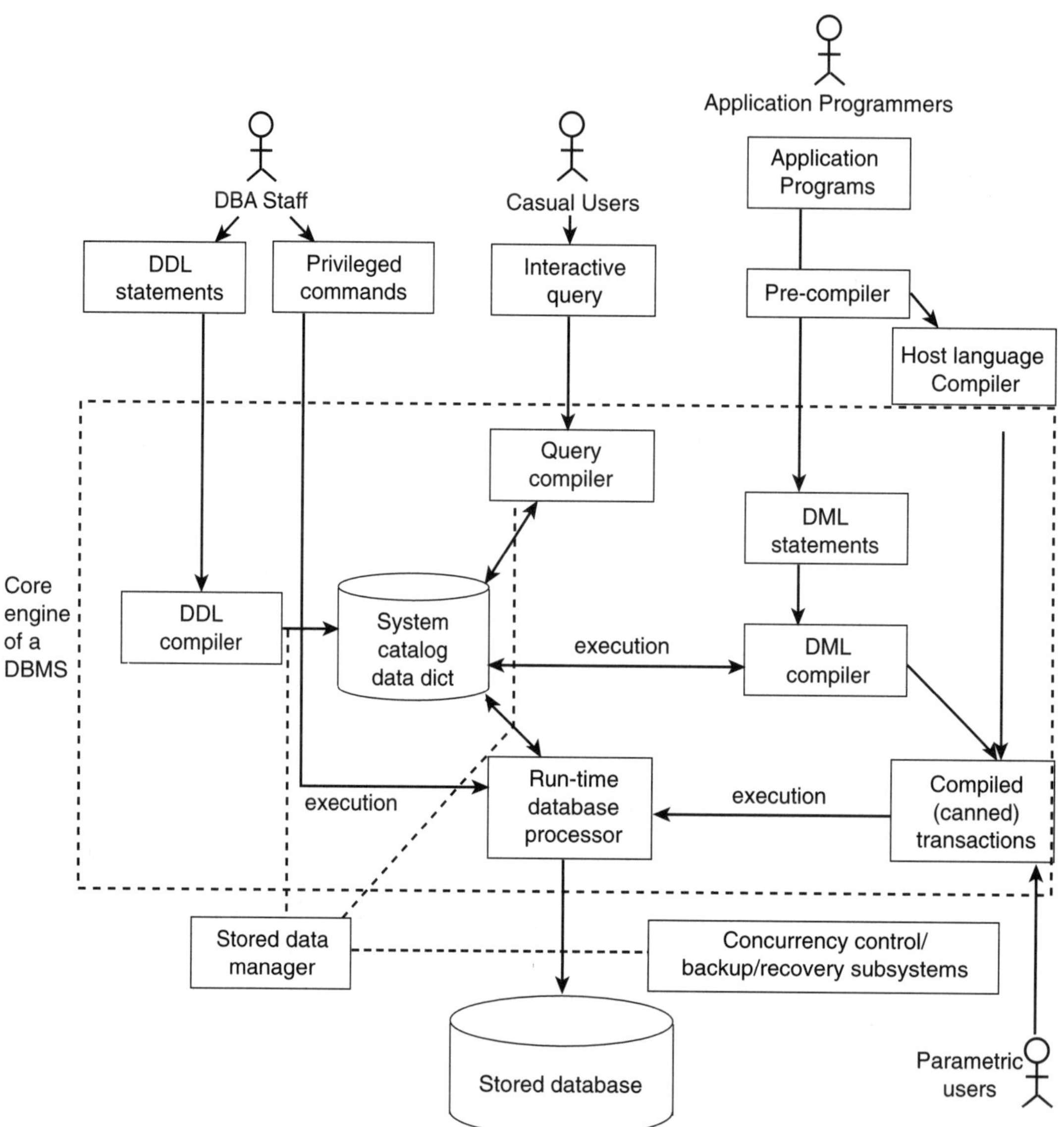

FIGURE 13.3 Major Components of a Typical DBMS Server.
Source: Ramez Elmasri and Shamkant B. Navathe, *Fundamentals of Database Systems,* The Benjamin/Cummings Publishing Company, Inc. Redwood City, 1994, p. 32.

into host language and object code for database access. The output of the precompiler can be compiled into object code using the host language compiler. Once the object code is linked, it turns into a canned application that makes calls to the run-time database processor.

6. DML Compiler: A compiler which translates DML commands into object code for database access.
7. Database Utilities: Components which help the DBA run and administer the system. It usually includes a data loader, backup/recovery module, and performance monitoring system.
8. Data Dictionary System: The system catalog, module definition, schema design decision, usage patterns, and user information are included here. A data dictionary that can also be accessible by end users is sometimes called a data directory.
9. Communication Software: The main function of this software is to provide an interface to databases between remotely located database systems. This software relies on the data communication hardware, phones, networks, and communication devices.

Now that we have reviewed the major components of a typical DBMS server, we will next focus on relational DBMS and its foundation, relational algebra.

13.2 RELATIONAL ALGEBRA AND SET THEORY

Relational algebra and set theory are the mathematical foundations on which data is organized in a relational database. The relational database management system uses a relational-algebra-based language to allow database users to access and manipulate data in the database. Therefore, it is important to know the mathematics behind the database server language and the code embedded in the application components of a data warehouse application. Mathematical language code is a collection of operations that are used to manipulate "set based" structures called relations.

Here are some definitions:

An *element* of a set is a piece of data, like an employee name; for example, Mary or simply, a1.

A *set of elements* is a list of data, like a list of all employee names; for example, Mary, Jane, John, Peter, Paul, . . . or A ={a1, a2,a3,a4,a5,a6, . . . an}.

The order of elements is not important in a list. It doesn't make any difference if the elements are repeated. The set that includes repeated elements is equivalent to the set that lists the elements only once.

A *tuple* or a record is a sequenced group of elements where each element is a member of its own set, that is, information about an employee; for example, (Mary Joe, 9/20/60, IT Engineer, Information Systems, John Doe) or (a1,b1,c1,d1,e1).

The order of elements in a tuple is important. If the order changes, it is not going to be the same tuple or record anymore.

A *relation* is a set of tuples or table of records like the human resource employee information file; for example:

Name	Date of Birth	Job Title	Department	Manager
Mary Joe	9/20/60	IT Engineer	Information Systems	John Doe
Paul Smith	7/7/59	DBA	Information Systems	Jane Jones
Peter Lyons	5/1/65	IT Analyst	Information Systems	Robin White
Sue Smart	4/17/63	Business Analyst	Business Marketing	Rich Lewis

The order of records in a table does not change the integrity of the information. The order in which all the attributes are listed must be the same among all the records in order to ensure the elements of an attribute are all members of the proper domain or set of values.

For example, the information in the following table is incorrect. Although all the employee information of "Paul Smith" and "Peter Lyons" is listed, they are not listed in a consistent order. The value "DBA" is not valid data for the "Date of Birth" attribute.

Name	Date of Birth	Job Title	Department	Manager
Mary Joe	9/20/60	IT Engineer	Information Systems	John Doe
Paul Smith	**DBA**	**7/7/59**	Information Systems	Jane Jones
Peter Lyons	5/1/65	IT Analyst	**Robin White**	**Info System**
Sue Smart	4/17/63	Business Analyst	Business Marketing	Rich Lewis

The original set theory operations are **UNION**, **INTERSECTION**, **DIFFERENCE**, and **CARTESIAN PRODUCT**.

According to C.J. Date's *Introduction to Relational Databases*,[2] relational algebra is the basis of a high-level data sublanguage. Structured Query Language (SQL) is one of those sublanguages that has become the industry standard. To better understand the semantics of SQL statements, we will discuss some of the principle definitions and operations in relational algebra.

13.2.1 RELATIONAL ALGEBRA OPERATORS

- Operations that use sets or relations as the operands
- Relational expressions can be formed using a number of operations and sets nested to any depth
- Relational operations are divided into two categories: Set operators and special operators.

Set Operators: UNION, INTERSECTION, DIFFERENCES, CARTESIAN PRODUCT

Special Operators: SELECTION, PROJECTION, JOIN

Degree of a set: The number of domains whose values are used in a set

Example 1 Set A1={1,3,4} is of degree 3, set A2={11,44,55,66} is of degree 4.

[2]Chris J. Date, *An Introduction to Database Systems,* Volume 1, Fifth Edition, Addison Wesley, 1990.

SET OPERATORS:

Union Compatibility: Two sets are union compatible if they have the same degree and the *n*th attribute of the two relations, for example, relation *A* and relation *B* must be from the same domain. The three operations of union, intersect, difference require this characteristic between the two sets, or relation, or table!

***A*1 union *B*1:** The set of all tuples (records or rows) belonging to either sets *A*1 or *B*1 or both.

***A*1 intersect *B*1:** The set of all tuples belonging to both sets *A*1 and *B*1.

***A*1 difference (or MINUS) *B*1:** The set of all tuples belonging to *A*1 and not *B*1.

Example 2

Relation A

*A*1	*A*2
1	11
3	44
4	55

Relation B

*B*1	*B*2
2	22
1	11
3	55

A Union B

*A*1Union *B*1	*A*2 Union *B*2
1	11
3	44
4	55
2	22
3	55

A Intersect B

*A*1 Int. *B*1	*A*2 Int. *B*2
1	11

A Minus B

*A*1 - *B*1	*A*2 - *B*2
3	44
4	55

13.2.2 EXTENDED CARTESIAN PRODUCT OR TIMES

A Times B. The multiplication or product of two sets *A* and *B* is also a set. The resulting set is a collection of all possible combinations of tuples "t" such that "t" is the concatenation of a tuple. "a" belonging to *A*1 and a tuple "b" belonging to *B*1.

The concatenation of a tuple *A* = (*a*1, . . . , *am*) and a tuple *B* = (*bm*+1, . . . , *bm*+*n*) is the tuple *T* = (*a*1, . . . , *am*, *bm* + 1, . . . , *bm*+*n*).

A	**Times**	***B***	**(Times or Cartesian products)**	
(*A*1,	***A*2)**	**(*B*1,**	***B*2)**	
1	11	2	22	
3	44	2	22	
4	55	2	22	Concatenation of (*a*1, *a*2)
1	11	1	11	from (*A*1, *A*2) with a tuple.
3	44	1	11	(*b*1, *b*2) from (*B*1, *B*2)
4	55	1	11	results into a new 55 tuple
1	11	3	55	(*a*1, *a*2, *b*1, *b*2)
3	44	3	55	
4	55	3	55	

Note: All possible tuples are listed in a Cartesian Product.

Example 3

Let *A* be the set of all books, and *B* the set of all authors. The Cartesian product of these two sets is a set that covers all the possible cases of (books, author) pairs.

Note: All of the set operators have "associative" characteristics except minus.

SPECIAL OPERATORS:

Selection: the algebraic selection operator on a relation results in a horizontal subset of that relation.

Example 4

In common English: Select subset of *A* where *A*2 = "1."

The following keywords are used with this operation: Where boolean expression (logical expression) using and, or, >, =, . . . can be true or false.

Projection: It results in a "vertical" subset of a given relation by selecting a specified attribute.

Example 5

In common English: Project a subset *A*1 of *A* or *A*1 projection of *A* is a subset of *A* that contains only attribute *A1*.

Join: It results into a subset of the Cartesian product of 2 or more relations.

Example 6

A join *B* where *A*1 = *B*1, is a subset of Cartesian product of *A* and *B* when *A*1 = *B*1.

A1	*A2*	*B1*	*B2*
1	11	1	11
3	44	3	55

Natural join is when the column duplication *A*1 and *B*1 is removed and only one is stated.

13.2.3 A RELATIONAL DATABASE

According to C.J. Date,[3] the relational database model consists of two principal components:

1. The relational data structure (relations, keys, domains, two integrity rules)
2. The relational algebra

Additionally, a database system is called **FULLY RELATIONAL** if it supports:

[3]Chris J. Date, *An Introduction to Database Systems,* Volume1, Fifth Edition, Addison Wesley, 1990.

1. A relational database model
2. A query language that is at least as powerful as the relational algebra

Now that we have reviewed the mathematical foundation of relational database systems, let's see how we can use it to model the universe of a particular information need.

13.3 RELATIONAL DATABASE MODELING

Domain: A superset of all the possible values for a specific attribute.

Attribute: An attribute is a subset of domain; it represents the use of a domain within a relation.

Primary Key: The attribute(s) whose values are used to uniquely distinguish a tuple in a relation can be the primary key of the relation. It must be unique. There can be only one primary key in a relation.

Unique Key: If there are other attribute(s) whose values uniquely distinguish a tuple in a relation, they are called unique keys. Sometimes they are also called candidate key or alternate key. It must be unique.

Foreign Key: The attribute(s) whose values are used as primary key in another relation. It may or may not be unique.

Integrity Rules:

Rule 1—entity integrity: No component of a primary key value may be null. All entities must be distinguishable, so they must have a unique identification of some kind.

Rule 2—referential integrity: Foreign keys selected in a foreign relation must already exist as primary keys in the primary relation.

Normalization: It is the iterative process of applying the above rule and eliminating redundancy. Let's suppose all the interesting information about suppliers and their product deliveries are maintained in the same model in the following entity.

Suppliers and Products

Supplier Name	Address	Item	Price	Date
John	920 Rocket	desk	100	1/1/90
John	920 Rocket	table	150	2/2/86
Jane	200 Maple	chair	50	5/9/95
Jane	200 Maple	lamp	20	7/10/96
Frank	100 Maple	desk	120	1/1/96

The above list represents a simple one-dimensional look at the suppliers' information. Now let's consider different usage scenarios.

1. Change of address: John has moved to a new location.
2. Removing a transaction: Frank's product delivery is cancelled.
3. New product delivery: Jane is going to deliver "desks."
4. List of all suppliers in alphabetical order of street names.

A closer look at the above scenarios illustrate the following inefficiencies and inconsistencies in the design of the supplier entity.

1. Update anomalies: Every time a supplier relocates, all its associated transactions have to be updated to reflect the new address.
2. Delete anomalies: If a particular supplier has delivered a product only once. The instant that record is removed, the supplier is not represented any more.
3. Insert anomalies: Every time a supplier delivers, all the information about the supplier name and address has to be repeated.
4. Nonatomic attribute: In order to list the supplier by street name, it requires a string function to be used to extract the street name from the address.

Supplier

Supplier code	Supplier name	Address
1	JOHN	920 ROCKET
2	JANE	200 MAPLE
3	FRANK	200 KING DR

Items

Item code	Item	Price
1	Desk	100.00
1	Chair	50.00
2	Lamp	25.00
3	Desk	80.00

The solution therefore is to provide more categorization and continuous normalization. The goal of normalization is to:

- ❑ Increase update flexibility
- ❑ Reduce data redundancy
- ❑ Promote data sharing

Normalization can be done at different levels depending upon the nature of data usage. As the level increases, the number of entities increases and more joins are required to present a comprehensive picture.

First Normal Form (1NF). All relations in a relational database are required to have ATOMIC attribute values in each record (row or tuple). An ATOMIC data value is a piece of data that is used as a whole. It is preferable to represent attributes of an entity in the appropriate level of detail.

Second Normal Form (2NF). A relation R is in Second Normal Form if and only if it is in 1NF and every non-key attribute is fully dependent on the Primary Key.

Third Normal Form (3NF). A relation *R* is in third normal form if and only if it is in 2NF and every nonkey attribute is nontransitively dependent on the primary key.

Physical Resolution of Logical Models. Give each real-world set of things their own entity and represent it by a database table. If each item *A* can own several *B*s, but each *B* belongs to only one *A*, a one-to-many relationship exists. This relationship can be implemented using foreign key references. If each item *A* can own several *B*s, and each *B* belongs to several *A*s, a many-to-many relationship exists. To implement this scenario, create an intersection table *C*, in which case there will be a one-to-many relationship between *B* and *C* and *A* and *C*, which is equivalent to a many-to-many relationship of *A* and *B*. To avoid many joins, keep the level of normalization low. This is a very common practice in data warehouse database design.

13.4 SQL—STRUCTURED QUERY LANGUAGE

To access data in a relational database, a number of access languages were developed. Structured Query language (SQL) was one of the simplest and most elegant ones that soon became popular. It was established as the industry standard database access language. Like any other programming language, SQL has specific grammar and syntax (see Figure 13.4).

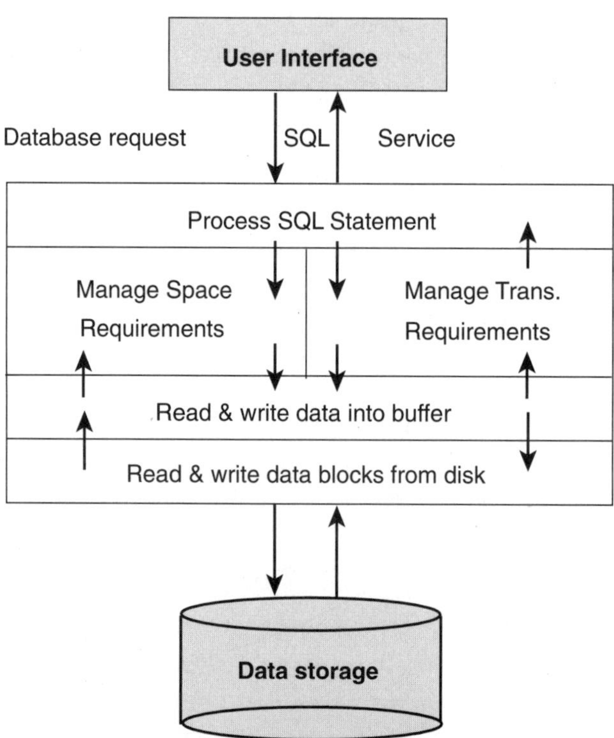

FIGURE 13.4 Subsystems of SQL execution module of a typical Database Management System.

The SQL language was originally developed by Dr. E.F. Codd at IBM in the early 1970s as part of a relational database management system prototype project called System R.[4] In 1976, INGRES was built as a relational database management system and became available. Later in 1979, prior to IBM's releasing its own commercial version of SQL, Oracle Corporation, then known as Relational Software, produced the first commercially available SQL for its **decision support system** called Oracle. This product in the beginning lacked some of the features defined for a relational database model. Oracle has since gone through seven major releases which have taken it beyond the relational model. The revolutionary process is still continuing and Oracle 8 will be based on the object relational model.

SQL is a collection of English-like commands that process a set of records unlike the previous record-based database languages that process one record at a time. The result of a SQL command is again a set of values that can be used in another SQL command. Also, based on the declarative relationships among entities using SQL, the user can navigate through the database model on an ad hoc basis. The physical storage of the data sets can change without requiring any change in the syntax of the SQL commands that access them. As such, it is not dependent on the access method. The physical address and position of the data blocks in the relational database are not required in a SQL command. Of course, this is not to say that the physical location of the data blocks have no impact on the performance of a SQL transaction. In later chapters we will study the internal structure of an Oracle database and will review ways to optimize a SQL statement. It is based on these characteristics that SQL is known as a nonprocedural language.

The American National Standards Institute (ANSI) published a set of minimum specifications in a standards document, ANSI X3.135-1986, which was superceded by ANSI X3.135-1989, **Database Language SQL with Integrity Enhancements** or ANSI SQL89. The latest standardization effort is SQL92.

Despite the standardization effort, different RDBMS vendors do not always comply with all the requirements of the ANSI committee. There is always some slight level of differences in SQL implementation across different vendors. Oracle 7.3, which is being considered in this book, complies with the entry level of SQL92. Oracle's implementation of SQL has additional extensions that add to a range of

[4]*IBM Journal of R & D*, November, 1976.

functionalities and performance characteristics of their product. For the benefit of consistency, when we discuss the features of SQL, Oracle's specific lexical conventions are used. For further discussion in this area, please refer to *Oracle 7 Server SQL Language Reference Manual*.[5]

As SQL is only a language based on the relational model, it does not necessarily use exact generic terms in all cases. The following table provides a cross-reference of the equivalent terms used for the same concepts.

Relational Model	SQL terms
Relation	Table or View
Attribute	Column
Primary Key	Primary Key
Foreign Key	Foreign Key
Integrity Rule I	Primary Key constraint
Integrity Rule II	Referential Integrity constraint

Query languages are divided into two general categories:

DDL: Data Definition Language
DML: Data Manipulation Language

DDL (Data Definition Language). DDL is the set of all those SQL commands that define the creation, modification, or elimination of database objects that contain or refer to data values. Table, as the physical representation of a relation, is the central structural object in a relational model. According to the relational algebra mentioned in the chapter, the result of an operation on relations is a relation. Similarly, the result of a query from a table (or more than one table) can be treated like a table. Other than tables, there are other structural objects that are defined and maintained using DDL. The schema of the database is the set of all these structural objects that are defined using a set of DDLs. For example:

[5] *Oracle 7 Server SQL Language Reference Manual*, Oracle Corporation, 1992, p. 2-1.

Creation	Modification	Elimination
CREATE TABLE	ALTER TABLE	DROP TABLE
CREATE VIEW	ALTER VIEW	DROP VIEW
CREATE CLUSTER	ALTER CLUSTER	DROP CLUSTER
CREATE INDEX	ALTER INDEX	DROP INDEX

The set of all those SQL commands that define the data, object, execution privileges, and security boundaries are sometimes included in the category of DDL.

In the context of a programming language, there is a fundamental difference between a TABLE object as defined in SQL and a STRUCT defined in 3GL (Third Generation Language) like C. A TABLE is a physical structure in the database that will continue to persist after the end of the program whereas a "STRUCT" in C is a user-defined data type that is only defined in memory and will automatically be invalidated and unaccessible once the program is terminated.

DML (Data Manipulation Language). DML is the set of all those SQL commands that allow creation, access, and modification of data values. The data stored in the database can only be manipulated using one of the following four commands. This seeming limitation is actually the basis of the simplicity and popularity of this language.

Creation	Access	Modification	Elimination
INSERT	SELECT	UPDATE	DELETE

13.4.1 ENFORCING THE INTEGRITY RULES

As part of the documentation of the analysis and design phase of an Oracle-based application, it is important to include the following:

1. List all the business and operational rules.
2. Define the entities and attributes and their domains.
3. Identify the relationships among the entities. Identify the primary and foreign keys.

4. Show the association by using verbs and adjectives and place them on the arrows in the ER diagrams.
5. Normalize the relations and name the corresponding tables and columns.
6. Prepare the DDL statements such as CREATE TABLE and save them in SQL script files.
7. Determine the initial values and status codes and create corresponding INSERT statements.

It was mentioned earlier that Oracle server provides referential integrities through the primary key and foreign keys. It also provides entity and attribute integrities through NOT NULL, UNIQUE indexes, check option, and default values.

Syntax of CREATE TABLE:

```
CREATE TABLE [user.]table
 ( column_name data_type,
 column_name data type,
 [
    [UNIQUE] | PRIMARY KEY (column_name [,column_name]...)
    [CONSTRAINT constraint]
 ]
 [
    FOREIGN KEY (column_name [,column_name]...)
    REFERENCES [user.]table(column[,column]...)
    [CONSTRAINT constraint];
```

Syntax of CREATE VIEW:

```
  [CHECK (condition) [CONSTRAINT constraint]]
  [WITH CHECK OPTION [CONSTRAINT constraint]])

  CREATE VIEW [user.]view_name [(alias[,alias]..)]
   AS SELECT .....
    [WITH CHECK OPTION [CONSTRAINT constraint]]
```

13.4.2 INSURING ENTITY INTEGRITY

According to relational model theory, the entity integrity is maintained through the use of primary keys and column constrains. Primary keys in Oracle 7 are implemented using unique indexes. Once the primary key or unique keys are explicitly declared at the database level, Oracle Server automatically creates unique index objects on the targeted attributes. Here are a few reminders when implementing an entity_relationship model:

Theory. The primary keys must not be null and they must have unique values.

Practice

1. Use NOT NULL constraint when defining the column(s) that composes the primary and unique keys in the table.
2. Create a unique index on the column(s) that composes the primary or unique key.
3. Oracle's Implementations. CREATE UNIQUE INDEX index_name ON table_name(column1, . . .)

   [TABLESPACE space_name [STORAGE (...)]].
4. Explicitly name your CONSTRAINT rules based on some naming convention and document them so that later at the application development level, you can locate them easier to write the necessary codes to enforce them
5. Oracle 7 automatic enforcement of the primary and unique keys is due to an automatic generation of UNIQUE indexes on those attributes
6. Oracle 7 provides more complex procedural and transaction integrity and security through the use of database triggers and procedures

13.4.3 SQL DML STATEMENTS

- ❑ SELECT and joins
- ❑ INSERT
- ❑ UPDATE
- ❑ DELETE

SELECT

Example: Who are the employees?

```
-SELECT EMP_NAME FROM EMP;
```

```
-SELECT * FROM DEPT ORDER BY DEPT_NO;
Syntax:
SELECT [ALL I DISTINCT]
{* I table.* I expr [c_alias]} [, {table.* I expr [c_alias]} ]...
FROM [user.]table [t_alias] [,user.]table [t_alias]]....
[WHERE condition]
[CONNECT BY condition
     [START WITH condition ]];
[GROUP BY expr [,expr]...
[HAVING condition]]
[{UNION I INTERSECT I MINUS}
SELECT...]
[ORDER BY {expr I position} [ASC I DESC]
[,{expr I position} [ASC I DESC]]]...
[FOR UPDATE OF column [, column]...[NO WAIT]];
```

INSERT

Example: Define the accounting department based in Sunnyvale.

```
INSERT INTO
Dept (deptno,dept_name,location)
VALUES(1,'ACCOUNTING','SUNNYVALE');
Syntax:
INSERT INTO [user.]table [(column [,column]..)]
{VALUES (value [,value]...)
I
query }
```

UPDATE

Example 1: Modify the name of department No. 1 to "ENGINEERING."

```
UPDATE dept
SET dept_name='ENGINEERING' where dept_no =1;
```

Example 2: No commission should be given to the employees who are trainees.

```
UPDATE Emp SET comm = NULL
WHERE job ='TRAINEE';
```

Example 3: Jones is promoted to a manager in Dept. 20, with a $1000 raise.

```
UPDATE Emp
SET job ='MANAGER',sal =sal+1000,deptno=20
WHERE ename='JONES';
```

Syntax:

```
UPDATE [user.]table [alias]
SET column =expr [,column =expr]...
[WHERE condition]
or
SET (column [,column]...) = (query) .....
```

DELETE

Example 1: Remove all employee records.

```
DELETE FROM emp;
```

Example 2: Remove those salesmen whose commission rate is less than 100%

```
DELETE FROM emp
    WHERE JOB = 'SALESMAN'
      AND comm < 100;
```

Syntax:

```
DELETE [FROM] [user.]table [alias] [WHERE condition]
```

Chapter 14

Oracle RDBMS Overall Architecture

14.1 ORACLE 7 SERVER CAPABILITIES

Oracle Server is a system software that provides data management services to the users of an application system. It consists of a set of cooperative complex computer programs that manage a database by interfacing between users and the data itself (see Figure 14.1). Its data access methodology is based on a relational database model. Oracle provides the mapping between the conceptual level and internal level of the ANSI/SPARC database model. Oracle Server is designed to meet information management needs on a medium- to large-enterprise scale. One of Oracle Server's strongest properties which stems from the relational model foundation is that it provides program-data independence.

Program-data independence is based on ANSI/SPARC three-tier architecture that does not require navigation through the data model to be based on physical storage and pointers among data blocks in the database. It is the logical relationship among data collections that is used to navigate through the data and aid users of the database to come up with correct correlated data. As a result, if the mapping between the logical model and the physical model gets changed,

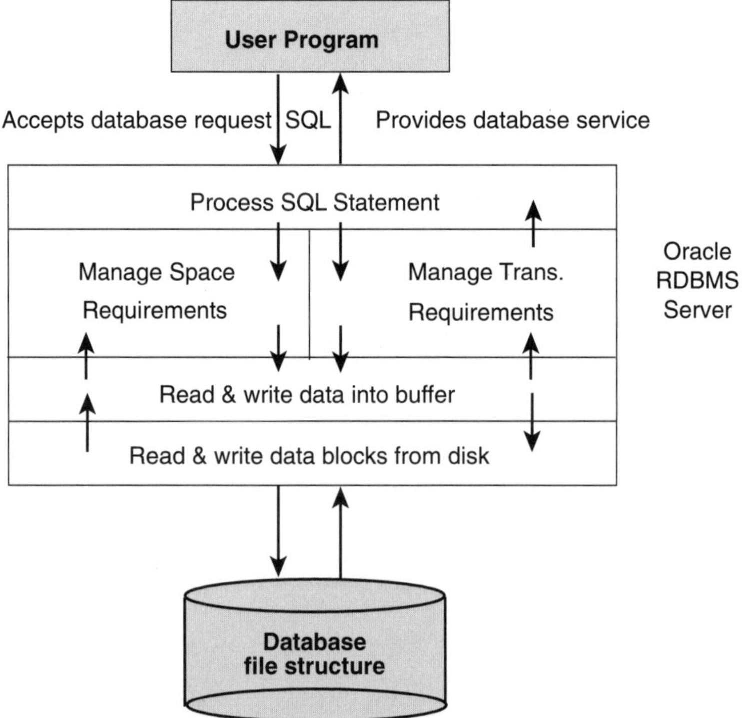

FIGURE 14.1 SQL Subsystems of Oracle RDBMS Server.

which can happen through data reorganization, platform change, and data relocation, the logic of programs written to access data will not be impacted. Realistically speaking, we will see when focusing on database performance, the physical layout of the data is important in reaching optimization goals. Since we are considering Oracle's architecture in the context of a data warehouse application, which that is by nature data intensive and involves large transactions, this area will later be explored in greater detail.

Oracle Server architecture has been implemented so that it supports the prominent capabilities of database management systems. The discussion of these capabilities prepares us for the specific analysis of Oracle internal architecture. Oracle Server has features that support the following capabilities.

14.1.1 PERSISTENCE

Data created or manipulated throughout the execution of database transactions and programs once committed (or finalized by the user) are permanently stored in the database after the termination of the transaction and programs. A piece of data persists regardless of the number of concurrent transactions, intentional or unintentional termination of programs, such as system crashes, network and media failures. The implementation of data persistence in Oracle 7 has been such that once data are committed, even if a crash occurs, data are not lost and in the worst case, they are recoverable.

14.1.2 TRANSACTION

A database transaction is a unit of work performed by the Oracle engine. By definition, it transforms the database from one consistent state to another. A user request requires one or more database transactions, each of which can consist of one or more SQL statements. Once all these transactions are completed, Oracle Server returns a response back to the user. The impact of a transaction on the data is not visible to other concurrent transactions unless the transaction is completed. In case a crash occurs in the middle of processing a transaction, that transaction will automatically be reverted or rolled back. In summary, changes made by a SQL statement included in one transaction only become visible to other transactions that start after the first transaction is committed. Oracle uniquely labels each transaction with a System Change Number (SCN). It is a decimal number and it grows as time extends into the future. For instance, if T1 is one transaction and T2 is another concurrent transaction that commits after T1, then SCN for T2 > SCN for T1.

14.1.3 CONCURRENCY CONTROL AND READ CONSISTENCY

To facilitate the concurrent access to the data, Oracle uses a special lock mechanism which follows the data versioning or time-stamp ordering strategy. In general, three main strategies exist when it comes to implementing concurrency control. They are pessimistic, optimistic and versioning algorithms.[1] Versioning, or the time-stamping algorithm, attempts to provide a highly concurrent environment in which readers of data do not have to wait for writers of data. They can read a previously committed consistent view of data while the same rows of data are being changed. The only time a writer has to wait is when the same rows are undergoing change. According to this model, for every update a new version of the data block is created and the old version is maintained for other read-only transactions. If another transaction tries to change the same data, it has to wait in line to acquire an appropriate lock until the original update transaction is completed. Oracle provides statement-level read consistency automatically, whereas transaction-level read consistency has to be explicitly requested by the user by declaring the transaction as a "read-only transaction."[2]

Here is an example of a regular set of transactions issued in a session:

```
REM Assuming a booked order can be either a "REVENUE"
REM generating or non "REVENUE" generating.
REM Beginning of a session
REM stmt1
SELECT SUM(QUANTITY)
    FROM ORDER_LINES WHERE ORDER_TYPE='REVENUE';
REM stmt2
SELECT SUM(QUANTITY)
    FROM ORDER_LINES WHERE ORDER_TYPE !=
'REVENUE';
REM stmt3
SELECT SUM(QUANTITY)
    FROM ORDER_LINES;

REM End of a session
```

Observation. Assume that the above queries are submitted to a database system that is also busy processing other user requests related to data in the ORDER_LINES table. There is always the possibility that

[1]Dr. Setrag Khoshafian, *Object Oriented Database*, p. 257.

[2]*Oracle 7 Server Concepts Manual*, p. 10-7. Oracle Corporation, 1992.

other user transactions are changing data in the ORDER_LINES table. Some of these changes can include value changes, like change in the QUANTITY ordered. In such a multiuser and concurrent environment, the statements listed in the above session will produce an interesting result. The sum of QUANTITY in stmt1 and stmt2 is not always equal to the sum of QUANTITY in stmt3. It is always possible that the value for QUANTITY changes during the execution of the first two SELECT statements, stm1 and stmt2. In order to assure the same start of execution time, SCN is used to retrieve the right version of the data, and Oracle provides the "READ-ONLY Transaction" facility.

Here is an example of a Read-Only Transaction issued for a session:

```
REM Beginning of a session

    ALTER SESSION SET TRANSACITON READ_ONLY;

    REM stmt1
    SELECT SUM(QUANTITY)
        FROM ORDER_LINES WHERE ORDER_TYPE='REVENUE;
    REM stmt2
    SELECT SUM(QUANTITY)
        FROM ORDER_LINES WHERE ORDER_TYPE !=
    'REVENUE';
    REM stmt3
    SELECT SUM(QUANTITY)
        FROM ORDER_LINES;

    ALTER SESSION SET TRANSACTION READ_WRITE;
    REM End of a session
```

Observation. By defining the three consistent SQL statements as READ_ONLY, the Oracle RDBMS ensures that the same consistent view of data is used in resolving all three SQL statements. Therefore, one can always be confident that the sum of QUANTITY in stmt1 and stmt2 is going to be always equal to the sum of QUANTITY in stmt3.

Figure 14.2 illustrates how Oracle data blocks change at a certain point in time. Rows stored in a database table that are changed at that point in time are highlighted in bold type.

Block 1	Block 2	Block 3	Block 4	Block 5	Block 6	etc...
SCN 2	SCN 2	SCN 3	SCN 2	SCN 4	SCN 2	etc...
row 1	row 1	**row 1**	**row 1**	row 1	**row 1**	
row 2	**row 2**	row 2	row 2	**row 2**		
row 3		row 3				

Transaction scans representing progress in time (t)

t1	t2	t3	t4	t5	t6	t7	etc...
SCN 1	SCN 2	SCN 3	SCN 4	SCN 5	SCN 6	SCN 7	etc...

FIGURE 14.2 Data Blocks Changed as a Result of Different Database Transactions.

14.1.4 BACKUP AND RECOVERY

Oracle Server architecture guarantees that in case of a user, transaction, media, or system failure, the partial and pending changes to the database will be completely discarded and not made permanent once the database is backed up. The committed changes will not be lost and will be at best restorable. These goals are achieved through specially designed internal structures and algorithms. The structures used during recovery are redo log files, rollback segments, control files, and database backup files. Each of these files will be discussed in detail in the next section. The algorithms used for database recovery are based on the **rolling forward** and **rolling backward** state of the data. The objective in rolling forward is to locate those data that have gone through committed changes just before the failure and the process of applying the changes at the database file level. In the same context, rolling backward is to identify the changes not yet committed to data and replace them with the previously committed values for the data at the database file level. Oracle also provides a comprehensive list of backup methods, such as logical, physical, on-line, and off-line. These methods will be described in more detail in later chapters.

14.1.5 DATABASE QUERY

Oracle provides SQL, Structured Query Language, which is a powerful yet simple data access language. All operations and access to both user and system information is done through SQL statements. Oracle's implementation of SQL includes extensions that add to flexibility, control, and optimization of its transactions. The intuitive data dictionary which provides information on database objects can also be navigated using SQL queries. Using Oracle's distributed processing and distributed database options, the physical location of data is transparent to SQL statements. SQL is essentially a nonprocedural language that operates on sets of records rather than one data element at a time. Data that is accessed or changed on multiple nodes in one transaction is kept consistent using one unique SCN. Oracle divides SQL statements into the following five categories:

1. Data Definition Language (DDL)
2. Transaction control statements
3. Session control statements
4. System control statements
5. Embedded SQL statements

Oracle has extended the scope of its database query language SQL as a set-based nonprocedural language to PL/SQL which is a more procedural and block-structured programming language. The advantages of PL/SQL are fourfold:

1. Provides an easy way to declare user-defined transactions
2. Provides an optimized method to do calculations and loop-based and conditional steps
3. Provides an optimized method to use explicit SQL cursors
4. Provides a mechanism to get prepared for object-oriented development paradigm

14.1.6 MULTIPLE VERSIONS OF DATA BLOCKS

As stated earlier, Oracle achieves read consistency by maintaining multiple versions of the same data block. These multiple versions of permanent data are maintained in a structure called rollback segments. Although these older versions of data blocks are placed in these rollback structures, there is no guarantee that they will continue to stay there for a long period of time. Realistically, depending on the space available to the rollback area, the large number of concurrent updates, and the length of time large query transactions are submitted to the same data blocks, the older versions may or may not be found. Therefore, by design Oracle 7 does not guarantee that the older versions of data blocks will be preserved in the rollback area (see Figure 14.3). With proactive planning and extensive sizing during the testing phase, DBAs can identify a set of good sizing and configuration parameters that can increase the possibility of finding the older versions of data blocks. This sizing consideration should be remembered during the physical database design, build, and test phases.

Sample of data blocks changed as of a certain point in time.

Block 1	Block 2	Block 3	Block 4	Block 5	Block 6	etc...
SCN 2	SCN 2	SCN 3	SCN 2	SCN 4	SCN 2	etc...

Multiple versions of data in rollback area

t1	t2	t3	t4	t5	t6	t7	......
SCN 1	SCN 2	SCN 3	SCN 4	SCN 5	SCN 6	SCN 7	......

SCN values increase with time. They can be used to determine how recen has been applied to a block.

Block 1	Block 2	Block 3	Block 3	Block 5	Block 5	Block 6
SCN 1	SCN 1	SCN 1	SCN 2	SCN 1	SCN 3	SCN 1

Note that the rollback version of Block 5 with a higher SCN value (SCN 3 recent than Block 5 with a lower SCN value (SCN1).

FIGURE 14.3 Maintaining Multiple Older Version of a Data Block in Oracle 7.

It is important to understand the impact of the RDBMS design approach that Oracle has used in the context of data warehousing. Oracle Server is a general-purpose RDBMS designed originally for OLTP-type small transactions, not OLAP and large transactions. In recent years, Oracle has done some strategic planning in regard to providing data warehouse friendly features. Nevertheless, one should consider the overhead involved in maintaining multiple versions during query optimization. Other relational database management systems designed for OLAP, such as Red Brick, completely avoid providing this feature which is considered overhead for a data warehousing application. They base their assumptions on a data warehouse not being volatile or changed very often and used for read-only purposes.

To avoid this overhead, the level of changes applied to the data while they are being read must be kept to a minimum. This can be built into the design to ensure that the batch subject areas functional changes are isolated from the data sets accessed by on-line ad hoc query users.

14.1.7 DATA INTEGRITY

Oracle maintains database integrity through detailed and comprehensive management of database transactions. It is based on the principle definition that a transaction should take the database from one consistent state to another consistent state. To support the integrity, Oracle provides a facility called **integrity constraints** to define the rules which state the scope based on some user-defined rule. Once defined, Oracle enforces integrity constraints at the database level. Enforcing the integrity constraint at the database level means, in addition to whatever level of integrity constraint's programmed in the user interface, compliance to the integrity rules are guaranteed at the Oracle RDBMS level. This is the most dependable integrity constraint that allows the centralization of user-defined rules. Specifically, in the case of client/server architecture, it provides more program and integrity rule independence. Once the object is created, the constraint defined for that object will determine if a particular operation is valid or not. These constraints are all stored along with the object definition itself in the data dictionary area similar to the database system card catalog. Therefore, integrity at the database level provides uniform data and access validation at a lower level, not at the application level which is costly and more error prone.

Predefined attribute-based integrity constraints are divided into five categories:

NOT NULL	Does not allow a missing value in a column
PRIMARY KEY	Does not allow missing or duplicate values in a column
UNIQUE	Does not allow duplicate values in a column
FOREIGN KEY	Requires that every value used in the column(s) match with a single value in the corresponding reference table's primary key column(s). In case of deletion of the corresponding primary key value, a DELETE CASCADE can be defined on the foreign key. If activated, a DELETE CASCADE action can automatically remove the foreign key references once the primary key is removed.
CHECK	Does not allow values for the columns restricted in a condition stated

In addition to the above predefined integrity rules, Oracle provides a facility to define more complex nondeclarative constraints that do not get addressed with the standard integrity constraints. Constraints, such as when a record is changed, keep the history of changes in another audit table. To implement such complex constraints, a procedural language is required to identify the steps and actions and is achieved through database triggers and PL/SQL blocks. A database trigger can only be defined for a table and consists of a set of PL/SQL statements that are grouped together in a PL/SQL block. It is implicitly executed or **fired** whenever a specific INSERT, DELETE, or UPDATE operation, depending on the type of trigger, is issued against the same table.

14.1.8 SECURITY CONTROL

Oracle provides a fail-safe mechanism to control and monitor data and system security. System security addresses the system-level resources and privileges available to a user. The data security addresses the data content and the operations allowed on the system. Security is controlled and managed through a set of properties that define the scope of a user's security. Mechanisms that Oracle provides to facilitate the security management are as follows:

Security mechanism	Purpose
Database user name and password	Basic access control to the database
Disk space quota per user	Defines the limit as to the storage space available in a particular table space area.
User resource usage profile	Defines the range of system resources available to a member of a user profile
Database-level user groups (ROLE)	Provide a means to form a logical grouping for a set of database and system privileges available to a user or role
Auditing user activity facility	Monitors and records a set of session activities
Assigning (GRANT) and removing (REVOKE) data and system rights	Define the range of system and object privileges to a user or role.
Assigning specific storage space (DEFAULT TABLESPACE) and sorting area (TEMPORARY TABLESPACE)	Default table space area for object creation, expansion, and temporary sorting activities.

The support of all these functionalities does not come free. They almost always will cause transaction overhead and can have performance impact. Therefore, the best approach is to use only those features that are absolutely necessary for the data warehouse. For instance, the auditing facility provides a full range of options. Once configured, every SQL command, success, failure, and so on, can be tracked and audited. Of course, that will create a large number of records and can generate space problems if not handled properly. A close analysis of the security requirements may reveal that it is more important to know who reads what data through what tool and when, rather than who changed the data. In a data warehousing application, most data changes occur through batch processing. The security requirements should focus more on the usage of the data and tools rather than data manipulation. Often the data security requirements are finer than what a RDBMS can provide at the object and operation levels. It may require a slice of data be made available to a group of users. For instance, not all users of a data warehouse are allowed to see all **cost of goods** or **revenue** numbers. Moreover, finance users who are allowed to see the numbers may only be allowed to see the numbers associated with their business area. As you can see, this becomes interesting and complex. In such cases, database-level object, operation, and system security mechanisms will not be good enough and a special application-level data security layer may need to be designed and built.

14.1.9 PERFORMANCE OPTIMIZATION

The SQL optimizer is one of the most interesting components of any RDBMS architecture. The challenge is that a SQL statement may be completely correct **logically**, but from a **practical** viewpoint it may not execute in any useful manner. That is when the optimizer's role becomes important. Its main role is to enhance the execution of a database transaction automatically and transparently to the user. Going back to the ANSI/SPARC model and the three-tier database architecture, it does make sense to have the user focus on the correctness of the logic based on the requirements and have the database engine in the physical layer focus on the "best way to get to the data." Over the years, Oracle optimizer has really come a long way. From the days when it was based on certain specific no-secret rules (RULE-based optimizer) to the present, Oracle 7.3, which is based on some statistical information, number of CPUs and disks, and maybe some heuristics (COST-based optimizer), the optimizer "tries" to find the most optimized route to the data. Conceptually, Oracle Optimizer follows the following process:

- ❑ It evaluates the type of SQL expressions
- ❑ It transforms the SQL statement into a simpler logical equivalent
- ❑ It chooses COST- or RULE-based optimization algorithms
- ❑ It identifies the best path to access each table referenced
- ❑ It decides on the order of table joins
- ❑ It decides on the join operation for each join statement

Although theoretically in a relational database the physical location of data should not impact the access time, realistically it does. Like most other RDBMS, Oracle provides a set of mechanisms to enhance the query performance. The scope of this set has increased in Oracle 7.3 which is actually very useful and needed in data warehousing applications.

Performance feature	Description
Performance index	To reduce the time spent in accessing the selected data, an index structured on the column is used to directly point to the possible resulting rows.
Clustering tables and indexes	When tables and indexes are accessed together, they can be stored together at the physical level. This expedites the access time. The clustering technique is beneficial when there are very few UPDATES and INSERTS compared to the SELECTS.
Analyzing distribution of data	Using the ANALYZE command, data in tables and indexes can be statistically analyzed and recorded in the data dictionary for Optimizer to use.
Optimizer hints	Optimizer can be directed to explicitly take a specific approach and operation when planning the query path. Based on table size, memory CPU, disk, indexes, and number of records expected to be returned, one approach may produce a better query plan than another. Optimizer hints are placed right after the SELECT keyword enclosed with '/*' &'*/'.
Shares SQL and PL/SQL parsed form	Saves the significant time spent to parse a statement if it has been parsed once as part of another transaction.

Performance feature	Description
Cost-based query optimizer	Identifying the best access path to data based on the distribution and selectivity statistics obtained from analyzing the data content of tables.
Cache buffer management	Database blocks, redo log blocks, and temporary sort blocks are cached in memory as much as possible.
Fast commit	Committed transactions are grouped and recorded in the redo logs as a group, thus increasing I/O throughput.
Optimized block storage definition	Detailed and explicit data-block, object-level, and table-space-level storage definition can reduce fragmentation and chaining.
Cached data dictionary	Information on database objects and privileges are readily available in memory.
Parallel query processing	Takes advantage of SMP and MPP by partitioning and distributing the sort, table scan, and join operations to more than one CPU.
Direct memory to disk access	Avoids the cache buffer management layer and reads and writes directly between disk and memory.
Fine-grain tuning configuration parameters	Based on the specifics of the server environment and type of usage decide on how best to utilize and tune over 150 configuration parameters to reach performance and throughput goals.
Recognizes star query style multitable joins	Identify the star query model among the tables that are being joined and use Cartesian products among the dimensions and the fact table.

14.1.10 RULE-BASED OPTIMIZER

The rule-based optimizer is the default mode unless it is changed through a configuration parameter called OPTIMIZER_MODE before the startup of the instance. It evaluates the syntax and decides which data set to start from and how to match it with the remaining criteria.

The important concept here is to "word" the SQL statement so that it is not only logically correct but it also requires a smaller set of data to be retrieved first. The idea here is, starting the search in a smaller area can always involve less search and match activity and can lead to the desired result much quicker. Of course, this is easy as long as the SQL statements are **worded** by an experienced Oracle 7 SQL literate user. For instance, data warehouse parameterized reports or front-end tools developed using Oracle's tools provide the opportunity of submitting an **optimized** SQL statement that has followed the rules. The *Oracle 7 Developers' Guide*[3] provides the list of all the rules. The important ones to remember are:

- ❑ Specifying the physical address of a row, ROWID, is the fastest way to retrieve data
- ❑ Reading the entire table, FULL TABLE SCAN, is the slowest way to retrieve data
- ❑ Specify the value of a column that has unique values and is indexed
- ❑ Specify the CLUSTER KEY values
- ❑ Data sets area is selected by evaluating:
    - bottom clause first and then the next one up
    - right-most table in FROM clause and then move to left
    - right predicates in WHERE clause and then move to left
    - left predicates in OR clause and then move to right
- ❑ Optimizer ignores the index if the column(s) are involved in a function or expression
- ❑ Use NOT EXISTS instead of NOT IN
- ❑ If possible, use JOIN to cross-reference tables rather than EXISTS
- ❑ If possible, avoid sort/merge of data sets

[3]*Oracle 7 Application Developer's Guide*, Oracle Corporation, 1992, p.5-1.

As you can see, the rule based algorithm is driven by the syntax, order of tables, indexes, WHERE clause predicate, column positions in indexes, and expressions in the SQL statement. Fortunately or should we say unfortunately, not all SQL statements submitted to the Oracle Optimizer are "custom-made." That is where the cost optimizer role becomes very important.

14.1.11 COST BASED OPTIMIZER

The cost-based optimizer algorithm is driven by a comparative analysis of a number of different possible access paths to data. Whichever produces the less "costly" access path will be the path used to access the desired data. The important concept to note here is that the cost-based optimizer is on an average and ultimately the preferred approach. This does not mean that cost based always leads to the fastest path for desired data when compared to rule based algorithm. It is important to perform adequate benchmarking analysis before choosing one versus the other. The cost-based optimizer looks promising in Oracle 7.3 but it still has a lot of room for improvement.

The cost-based optimizer (CBO) requires some level of statistics on the tables and indexes involved in order to work properly. The following two asynchronous commands collect statistics of the physical data distribution at the row and block level and record them in the system data dictionary for the cost optimizer to make a reference.

```
ANALYZE TABLE table_name ESTIMATE STATISTICS;
ANALYZE INDEX index_name ESTIMATE STATISTICS;
```

As the distribution of data changes, the statistics collected using the above commands become obsolete and may not produce optimized results. Therefore, periodically after every considerable level of changes, the table and indexes involved must be analyzed again.

Oracle 7 collects a vast amount of information in the systems data dictionary area regarding the performance of all transactions processed from the start of the database instance. Once these statistics are understood and trended they can be an effective performance tuning tool for the DBA. The challenge is to understand their logical role and the resource they are monitoring.[4]

[4]Ibid. Chap. 13.

In summary, these capabilities make Oracle 7 a good candidate for the role of the back-end data repository in a data warehouse architecture.

- The relational foundation provides a familiar environment to model and create a normalized view of detailed data in the data warehouse.
- Compliance with ANSI SQL provides many choices in regard to front-end ad hoc query tools and application development tools.
- Oracle's robust architecture supports all the principal DBMS capabilities.
- The consistent read approach allows high-volume concurrent read and write access which facilitates incremental data refresh.
- Very large database sizes on large selection of advance I/O subsystems are supported.
- Runs on a wide range of hardware servers.
- Takes advantage of 64-bit Very Large Memory (VLM) architecture.
- Provides performance scalability through its client/server distributed processing architecture that utilizes SMP and MPP servers.
- Data file I/O activity and data block space usage can be monitored and optimized as data volume and usage level vary.
- Provides a comprehensive and flexible data and object security model.
- Supports cost-based optimizer.
- Provides an in-depth data dictionary and database performance statistics which can be analyzed and used as a basis for capacity planning and throughput.
- Oracle Server is highly tunable and can be adapted for long query performance.
- Provides high availability through the use of on-line hot backup and Oracle Parallel Server technology.
- Allows user activity monitoring and control of database access and resources.
- Provides basic and complex database level data integrity enforcement.
- Supports homogeneous and nonhomogeneous distributed database transactions which facilitates data replication and transportation.

- Applications developed using Oracle are portable to most other platforms.
- Over 80 percent of the internal code for Oracle is the same across may platforms.
- Strong player in advance database technology with a strategy to address data warehousing needs.
- Provides a full range of tools to support the entire database application life cycle.
- Committed to providing a full range of indexing scheme appropriate for OLAP.
- Has an object-oriented strategy and is going to be supported in Oracle 8.

As shown in Figure 14.1 Oracle 7 Server's architecture consists of a number of layers, partitions, subsystems and modules. We will briefly focus on each of the major components. Let us start with the file structure that provides the persistent storage capabilities.

14.2 FILE STRUCTURE

The file structure of an Oracle 7 database (see Figure 14.4) can be analyzed from two different perspectives:

- Internal
- External

14.2.1 INTERNAL VS. EXTERNAL VIEW OF THE FILE STRUCTURE

The internal (logical view) of the file structure consists of database objects such as:

- Blocks
- Extents
- Segments
- Tables
- Keys

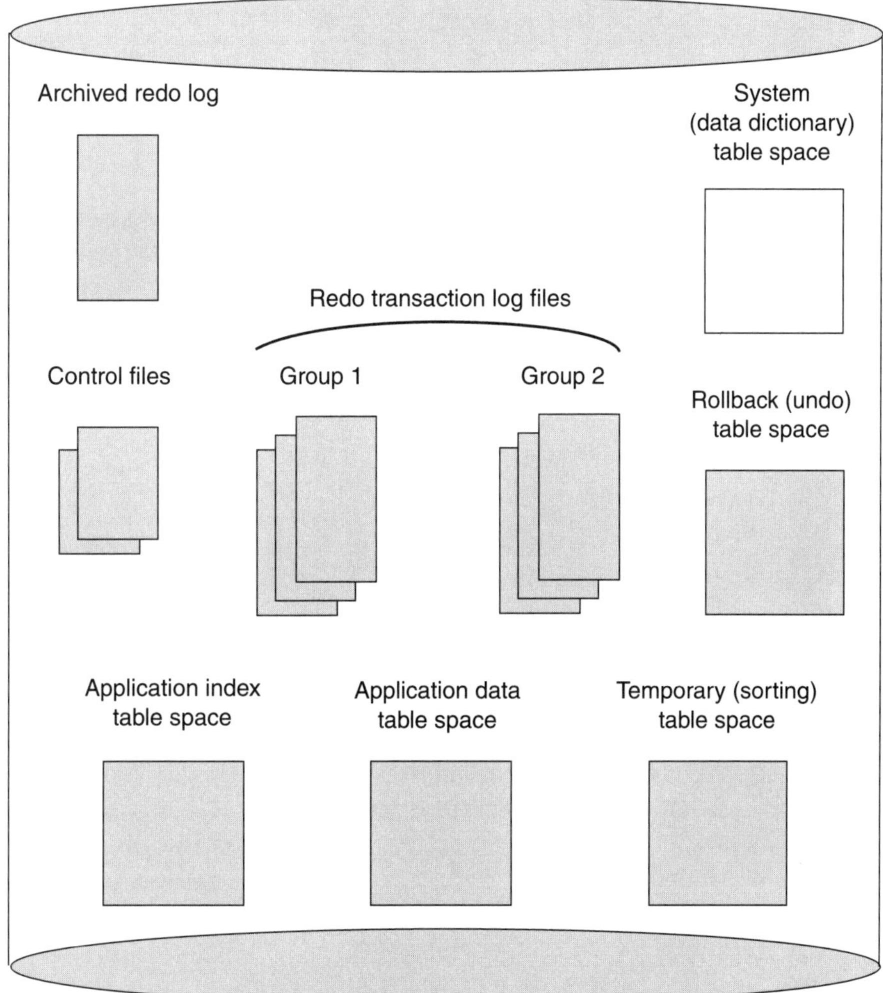

FIGURE 14.4 Conceptual View of the Oracle File Structure.

- Indexes
- Views
- Sequences
- Users
- Database links
- Roles

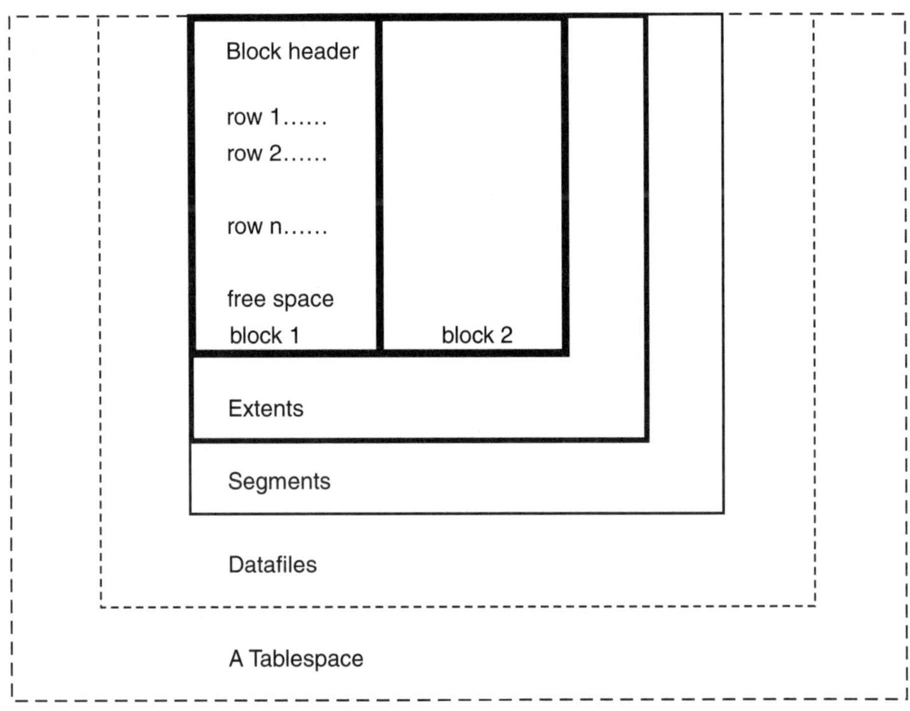

FIGURE 14.5 Conceptual View of an Oracle Database Block Structure.

A database block is the lowest level of detail in the hierarchy of file structure. As a result, ROWID which is the physical address of a row has reference to the block, file, and the offset location of the row in the block (see Figure 14.5). An ASCII representation of ROWID, the unique physical address of a row, is formed by concatenating all three concepts. Accessing a row through its ROWID is the fastest way to read a record. Of course, if for any reason the records are moved to a different location on the disk, the ROWID of the records will change and it will reflect the new file ID, block ID, and its offset in the block.

Format of ROWID: Block ID. *N*th row file ID. in the block. For instance, ROWID = 00004. 00005. 0005 is the address of the 5th row in the 5th block in file no. 5. Block id 0000 is not used for data.

A set of contiguous block forms an extent. A set of extents used in conjunction with a single database object is a segment. A tablespace consists of a number of segments. A table space is the logical umbrella that includes at least one or more data files. It is important to plan the physical layout of the database so it is flexible for expansion, optimization and balanced across the I/O subsystem. The planning effort is called the database physical layout design. There is no doubt that the physical layout of an Oracle database, specifically a large and data intensive one like a data warehouse, plays an important role in the transaction performance. In other words, the goal of a physical layout design planning should be to:

- Minimize I/O contention based on a sampling of end-user queries and batch processing
- Minimize dynamic database expansion
- Facilitate fine-grain backup and recovery

14.2.2 EXTERNAL (PHYSICAL VIEW)

The external view consists of storage components that are visible to the operating system with a number of differently formatted files which have a specific role in the architecture that supports one or more of the DBMS capabilities. The differentiating factor is their role and their file format in the architecture.

- Data files and table spaces
- Redo log file
- Archived redo log
- Control file
- Configuration file

Data Files and Tablespaces. Data files are always defined in the context of a specific tablespace. They cannot be created without specifying a tablespace with a storage definition. The minimum functional specific data files are as follows:

System Tablespace: Holds the information that maps the logical view to the internal structure of the Oracle RDBMS. It is also sometimes called the catalog or data dictionary. This table space is not very large, generally about 50 megabytes. It is important to keep it only for system objects, otherwise it can create a roadblock to performance optimization. It must be protected from high transaction files.

Temporary Tablespace: Holds temporary storages and table-like objects that are optimized for temporary segment-type work. The segments that are not in use will be dropped by system monitor (SMON) background process separately. In Oracle 7.3 the block level mapping of this type of table space is specialized and optimized for sorting activities. Once a table space is declared to be of type "TEMPORARY," it should only be used for that purpose and not as a general object storage area.

Rollback Tablespace: We recommend a dedicated regular tablespace to store only segments used for rollback activities. Each segment is used for a number of in-process transactions and stores a version of the data. The segments are called ROLLBACK SEGMENTs and are different from TABLE and INDEX. It is formatted to be more optimized for rollback and read consistent activity. It is vital to make sure that the information in a rollback tablespace is not lost during a less than perfect SHUTDOWN process, that is, a SHUTDOWN ABORT or a crash. It is the information in the rollback segments that guides SMON as to what transactions need to be cleaned up.

Index Tablespace: We recommend a dedicated regular tablespace to store index segments. These indexes provide fast access to actual data stored in database tables.

Data Tablespace: We recommend a dedicated regular tablespace be used to store different types of object segments. For instance, objects like table, cluster, and snapshot must be stored in separate tablespaces.

Redo log and archived redo log files. Redo transaction logs provide two major benefits in different ways:

1. Instance recovery
2. Group commit

The first benefit, instance recovery, is the more important of the two. It acts like an insurance policy for every database transaction. It allows instant recovery in case of sudden shutdown. It provides the minimum information about those transactions that change data or structure the data in a compact form called a redo transaction log entry. This log entry is adequate for SMON to play back in case of database recovery, thus reproducing the impact of the original transaction. This way a committed transaction is not lost once it is completed. The space requirement of this recording strategy is not small. The default is that there must be at least two redo log transaction files. The redo log entries are written in a sequential way for simplicity and low overhead impact. Once a file is completed, a log switch occurs and all the entries are converted into redo log files that get transferred into the appropriate database files. When that task is completed, the redo background process starts writing into the second redo log file, and so on. As a result the important but compact transaction information gets overwritten. To avoid this and to have more recovery protection, the optional ARCH process can help in this area. If this option is turned on, it backs up the content of a redo log automatically once it is completed and log switch has occurred. The location of the backup and archived redo logs is determined through the ARCH_LOG_DEST parameter in the INIT.ORA file with the archiving capabilities turned on.

The important thing to remember here is that a data warehouse application goes through major data and structural changes during the batch load and processing in addition to servicing ad hoc queries. End users' ad hoc query performance is more important and so it is not worth compromising the performance for an instant recovery feature.

Control file. Control files play the role of identification cards to an Oracle database. They are created at the time of database creation. From that point on, the system automatically keeps them updated. They are configured using the initialization parameter CONTROL_FILE. Every database has its own set of control files. It is important to keep them in a separate location and name them differently. At the database startup time these files are located and read. The information recorded in the control files reflects pertinent configuration and integrity information about the database. Unless all this information is verified, the database files cannot be opened. As a result, the content of the control files is of utmost importance. It is required to have at least two separate copies of this file. The following information is maintained:

- Database name
- The integrity of each data file
- Data file names and table spaces
- The maximum number of data files
- The character set domain

Init.ora—The Configuration File

Parameter name	Parameter Value	Purpose
db_name	dw	database name
open_cursors	300	
optimizer_mode	choose	optimizer algorithm
Processes	300	maximum no. of processes
sessions	335	maximum no. of sessions
timed_statistics	TRUE	collect performance statistics
resource_limit	FALSE	
single_process	FALSE	
cpu_count	6	SMP—6 CPU available
shared_pool_size	73400320	SQL library+data dictionary
shared_pool_reserved_size	0	
shared_pool_reserved_min_alloc	0	
pre_page_sga	FALSE	
enqueue_resources	1500	
control_files	/dev/vol1/control_dw_1.dbf /dev/vol2/control_dw_2.dbf /oracle/dw/control_dw_3.dbf	
db_block_buffers	40000	data block cached
db_block_size	8192	8K data block size
db_block_checkpoint_batch	8	
db_block_lru_statistics	FALSE	
db_block_lru_extended_statistics	0	
log_checkpoint_interval	40000	checkpoint infrequent

Parameter name	Parameter Value	Purpose
log_checkpoint_timeout	0	
log_small_entry_max_size	800	redo log latch contention
log_simultaneous_copies	16	redo log latch contention
db_files	255	
db_file_simultaneous_writes	4	
db_file_multiblock_read_count	64	by default get 64 block
log_buffer	15728640	Redo log buffer cache
checkpoint_process	TRUE	Separate checkpoints
temporary_table_locks	50	
dml_locks	700	
row_locking	always	
max_rollback_segments	40	
transactions	368	
transactions_per_rollback_segment	7	
rollback_segments	roll01,roll02,roll03,roll04	
sequence_cache_entries	100	
sequence_cache_hash_buckets	10	
mts_service	dw	
mts_servers	0	
mts_max_servers	0	
mts_max_dispatchers	0	
open_links	20	
audit_trail	DB	Automatic db auditing
sort_area_size	104857600	sorting area in bytes
sort_area_retained_size	1024000	shrink sort area
cache_size_threshold	8000	default size to cache a table
parallel_max_servers	60	
background_dump_dest	/dump/dw/bdump	
user_dump_dest	/dump/dw/udump	
core_dump_dest	/dump/dw/cdump	
spin_count	8000	CPU cycle algorithm
use_readv	TRUE	
db_writers	1	one database writer process

In summary, Oracle space management and administration requires continuous monitoring and trending of the following statistics over time:

- Knowledge of the goals and services of the application
- Frequency and level of access
- Growth pattern

14.3 PROCESS ARCHITECTURE

Lets study the programs that are responsible for accomplishing the tasks of providing the database capabilities mentioned earlier.

Interface Name	Role in the Architecture
USER interface	User initiates a session with Oracle.
CLIENT interface	Data is provided to user through a client program.
SERVER interface	Every database request coming from a client program is handled by a server program.
System global area	The shared memory segment that provides buffer cache management and maintains the database integrity.
Background processes	They perform the standard functions and services of the database server.
INIT.ORA configuration parameter file	This file contains the database server startup values for over 150 configurations or tuning parameters.
Database files	Where data is physically stored. Only database background processes can read and write into these files. The files are formatted in a proprietary fashion, that is, optimized for better performance.

The server background process communicates with Oracle instance and is responsible for the resolution of the requests. It communicates with instance processes through a shared memory structure called the System Global Area (SGA). The processes run in the background as separate processes.

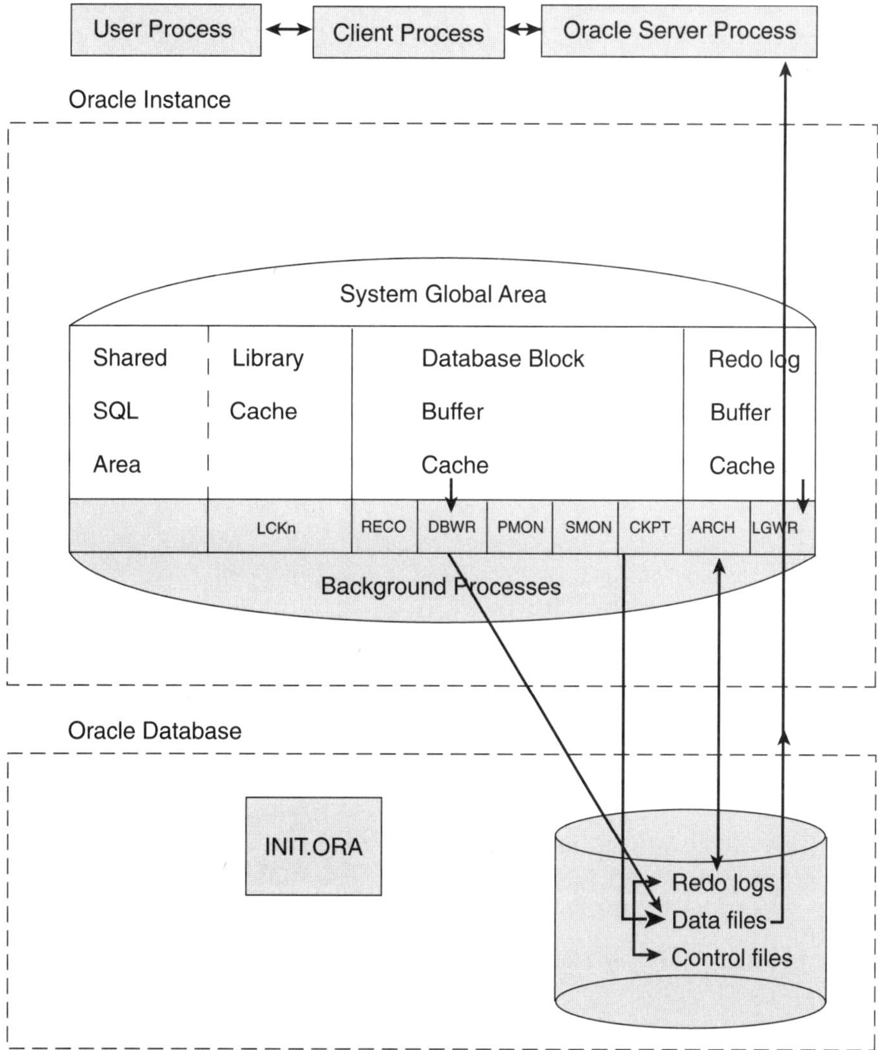

FIGURE 14.6 Conceptual View of Oracle Client/Server Architecture.

Let's briefly look at the processing components of an Oracle database instance and their individual roles. (See Figure 14.6.) The background processes can be divided into two categories, mandatory and optional.

Mandatory Background Processes	Optional Background Processes
DBWR	ARCH
LGWR	RECO
SMON	CKPT
PMON	LCKn
	Dnnn
	Snnn
	SNPn

We are going to briefly look at their roles one by one. This discussion is going to set the foundation for discussions on configuring and tuning Oracle Server for a data warehouse application.

14.3.1 DATABASE WRITER (DBWR)

Database Writer (DBWR) manages the content of the database block buffer cache area (controlled by the DB_BLOCK_BUFFER parameter) and the library dictionary cache (controlled by the SHARED_POOL_AREA parameter) in SGA. It writes the used buffers back to the data files in batch. Improving the efficiency of DBWR and its throughput has significant tuning impact. Depending on how many processors and physical disks are available, it is possible to have more than one DBWR to maximize parallelism and reduce waiting in the disk or CPU queue. The DB_WRITER parameter determines how many DBWRs will be started upon database startup.

14.3.2 LOG WRITER (LGWR)

Log Writer (LGWR) manages the redo (repeatable transaction) information in the redo log buffer cache area (controlled by the LOG_BUFFER parameter). It writes the redo log entries from buffer to the redo log files sequentially in batch. As it completes one redo log file it "switches" and starts writing over the other redo log file. Therefore, as part of the minimum configuration, there must be at least two redo log files per database instance. It is preferable to have more than two to avoid contention between the DBWR and LGWR processes. In the context of a data warehouse application, during refresh cycle large numbers of redo entries are entered. To maximize throughput, fewer checkpoints should take place. This can be achieved by having large redo log files and specially tuned init.ora parameters to minimize checkpoint processes as much as possible.

14.3.3 SYSTEM MONITOR (SMON)

The System Monitor (SMON) performs three major tasks during the instance startup:

1. Transaction recovery
2. Cleaning up temporary segments
3. Coalescing free spaces

The primary function of transaction recovery is done whenever the system is going through the process of coming up on-line and it is in the so called "startup" mode. During that time, SMON identifies the skipped transactions that are in process when they got disrupted by a database instance failure. Before any data file is brought on-line, SMON applies all the corresponding skipped transactions. In the case of Oracle Multiple Instance or Oracle Parallel Server, if one server instance fails and crashes, SMON of one other instance does the transaction recovery for the failed server.

The secondary function of SMON is the cleaning up of the temporary sort segments that are no longer in use in the database files. These segments are automatically dropped at startup and later while the database is on-line and the freed space is returned back to the database.

The ternary function of SMON is the coalescing of adjacent free spaces that are marked as different extents into one single and larger extent in the database files. This also happens periodically and improves the chance of finding larger free contiguous space for the next transaction. The frequency of this action can be different in different versions of Oracle 7.

14.3.4 PROCESS MONITOR (PMON)

The Process Monitor (PMON) performs process recovery when a user process fails and is no longer active. In such a case, PMON, which is otherwise dormant, wakes up and assumes the role of the failed process and automatically cleans up objects in buffer cache used by the failed process. This cleaning up also includes removing the failed process ID from the list of active processes, updating the status of the transaction table in the rollback segment in use, and releasing the locks and latches held by the failed process. In the case of an Oracle multi-threaded server configuration, PMON also monitors dispatcher and server background processes and restarts them in case they have failed. For a client/server setup, it is possible to have a slight network failure that in turn causes user process failure. PMON in such cases rolls back the uncommitted transactions of the failed process.

14.3.5 ARCHIVER (ARCH)

The Archiver (ARCH) automatically makes a backup copy of the completed redo transaction log file to an archive destination which is generally on disk.

14.3.6 RECOVERER (RECO)

The Recoverer (RECO) background process appears only when the distributed server optional configuration is chosen. In such a configuration multiple Oracle Servers can participate in a database transaction. Users issuing a transaction may be on one server, whereas data may reside in a number of remotely located databases. The processing of this kind of transaction requires the collaboration of all the database servers involved. The integrity of this tranaction is dependent on the availability and timely acknowledgment of all the database servers. If any kind of failure occurs, some level of cleanup work should take place. The role of RECO is to automatically resolve such failures and distribute transactions automatically when a network/node fails.

14.3.7 LOCK (LCK0)

Lock (LCK0) controls the interinstance locking of resources used by the Oracle Parallel Server (OPS) kernel.

14.4 MEMORY STRUCTURE

14.4.1 SHARED SQL AREA

- The portion of shared memory in SGA that contains parsed and optimized forms of SQL or PL/SQL blocks and a list of objects referenced in them
- INIT.ORA Parameter: SHARED_POOL_SIZE

14.4.2 SGA (SHARED SYSTEM GLOBAL AREA)

- SGA should be sized appropriately according to the contiguous shared memory segment limitation of the operating system level configuration
- An SGA that is too small for the level of database activity causes unnecessary recursive calls and parsing which impact the transaction performance
- An SGA that is too large for the operating-system-level configuration can get paged or swapped out of memory which have crippling effects on all transaction performances

14.4.3 DATABASE BLOCK BUFFER AREA

- Init.ora parameters: db_block_buffer (number of buffers) and db_block_size (bytes)
- Caches logical data blocks read from data files
- Blocks are purged based on LRU algorithm
- Log buffer area
- Init.ora parameter: log_buffer (bytes)
- After every database block buffer activity, redo information is generated and held here before it goes to redo log files
- Control area
- Maintains the integrity of SGA

14.4.4 SHARED POOL AREA

- Init.ora parameter: shared_pool_size (number in bytes)
- Dictionary cache purges using a LRU algorithm
- Monitor statistics in V$ROWCACHE for tuning
- Increase shared_pool_area if sum GETS > 10%

14.4.5 LIBRARY CACHE: SHARED AND PRIVATE SQL AND PL/SQL

- The parsed and text form of SQL and PL/SQL statements
- Execution plan
- List of referenced objects
- It gets purged using LRU algorithm
- Parsing is expensive. If two equivalent SQL statements are worded differently they are considered different
- Using generic and shared code helps avoid overpopulating the shared SQL area (develop shared code using triggers, procedures, etc.)

14.4.6 PRIVATE SQL AND PL/SQL AREA

- PGA: Process Global Area
- Each Server process has a Process Global Area (PGA)
- SGA holds SQL statements and more sharing can take place
- PGA can be much smaller. It holds enough information in cursor state to execute a SQL statement
- Use CURSOR_SPACE_FOR_TIME = TRUE. It de-allocates a shared SQL area when all cursors are closed. The use of this parameter has less performance overhead than checking the Shared SQL area for identical SQL statement

Tips:

1. Use shared code
2. Develop coding conventions

14.4.7 DATABASE VS. INSTANCE

The layer that stores the persistent state of the data in an Oracle Server X is called the Oracle Database X (more static). The layer that is responsible for changing content database X and maintains it (more dynamic) from one state to another and is a function of time is called an Oracle Instance X (see Figure 14.7). An Oracle instance is composed of the System Global Area (SGA) and the set of background processes communicating and sharing data through a shared memory structure (SGA). Every time an Oracle database is brought on-line, the instance has to complete the "startup" process. Every time the database is brought off-line, the instance has to complete the "shutdown" process.

A database can be maintained by more than one instance, in which case it is called a multi-instance database or in Oracle's terminology, an Oracle Parallel Server configuration. In this configuration every instance can continue to access the database while other instance(s) are failing or are down. It provides high availability and system redundancy. The instances involved in a multi-instance configuration stay in close communication through a fast network line. They continue to process transactions using individual CPU and main memory resources.

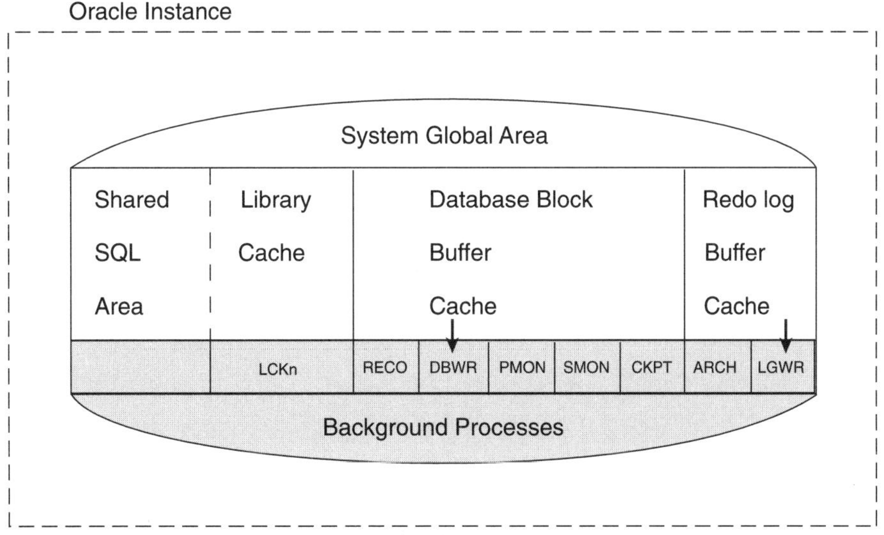

FIGURE 14.7 An Oracle Instance.

14.5 THE STORY OF AN ORACLE TRANSACTION

Every SQL transaction that is submitted by a user process to Oracle is actually processed through an Oracle Server background process (depending on the server configuration, it can be either a shared server or a dedicated server process). This background process is responsible for the transaction. The server process has access to the structures in SGA and can communicate to the server through SGA. It will acquire a transaction ID for the statement and run it through a series of steps. Once the result is achieved the server process will return the result back to the user process. These steps are explained below.

14.5.1 SQL STATEMENT PROCESSING

1. Statement is parsed:
   - Check syntax, table existence, column existence, and security
   - Check to see if the statement exists in SGA
     - If yes, it checks to see if the referenced objects are the same
     - Check to see if user has access to the referenced objects
     - If yes, the execution plan is reused
     - Store the text and parsed format in the **Shared SQL Area**
   - Acquires a **parse** lock on the particular data dictionary items
   - The execution plan (the parse tree) is determined
   - If distributed, sends the statement to the appropriate nodes
2. Statement is binded:
   - Values are bound to the variables
3. Statement is executed:
   - If data blocks are not in SGA, bring data blocks to SGA
   - Perform DML operation
   - Record pointers are placed in the first rows for SELECT statements
4. In case of SELECT, data is fetched:
   - Records are fetched and record pointers are advanced down the list of records

5. Processing results are placed in the **response queue**
6. Dispatcher detects results in the response queue. It picks them up and passes them to the user process across SQL*Net
7. User process receives the data or message. The results are placed in the user process buffer area

14.6 CONFIGURATION OPTIONS

An Oracle installation can be customized based on the nature of the application. As new versions of Oracle get released, the range of configuration options expands. Oracle's newest release, Oracle 7.3 Universal Server, provides a rich set of options. Not all of these options are needed for a data warehouse back-end repository. The options considered here have been available since the original release of Oracle 7 and are more likely to be used in the context of a data warehouse.

- Dedicated Server
- Multithreaded Server
- Parallel Server

Each of these configurations requires its own set of initialization configuration systems and Oracle RDBMS parameters. At this level we limit the discussion to the general concept and requirements that call for one option versus the other.

14.6.1 ORACLE DEDICATED SERVER

Oracle Dedicated Server is the most commonly used configuration option. It is based on the client/server model and is appropriate for a data warehouse repository. Its main strengths are:

- A client request does not have to wait for service provider. A dedicated server process is always available to handle the request.
- It is much easier to administer compared to the other two options.

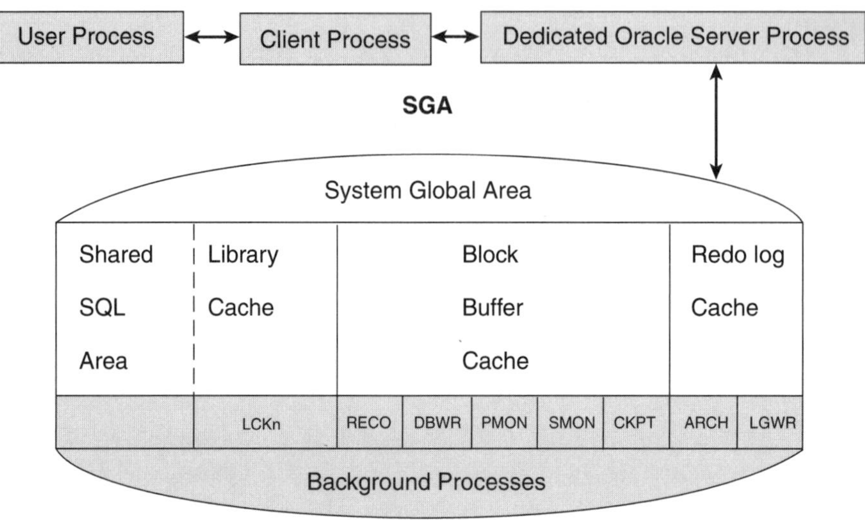

14.6.2 ORACLE MULTITHREADED SERVER (MTS)

Oracle's Multithreaded Server configuration is specially beneficial when the host server cannot support too many user processes and database transaction scalability is needed. Oracle's Multithreaded Server option provides this short-term scalability solution through shared server processes as opposed to dedicated server processes (see Figure 14.8). It's main strengths are:

- ❏ scalability to support growth in transaction volume
- ❏ requirement for less memory

The main cost of these added benefits is higher administrative resources and planning requirements.

The internal processing of a database transaction by multithreaded servers can be broken down into the following **seven** steps:

1. User/client process passes the call information to the Oracle Server process to be resolved. If the client is across the network, the user process startup procedure establishes a connection across the network via UPI (**User Program Interface** layer—SQL*NET).

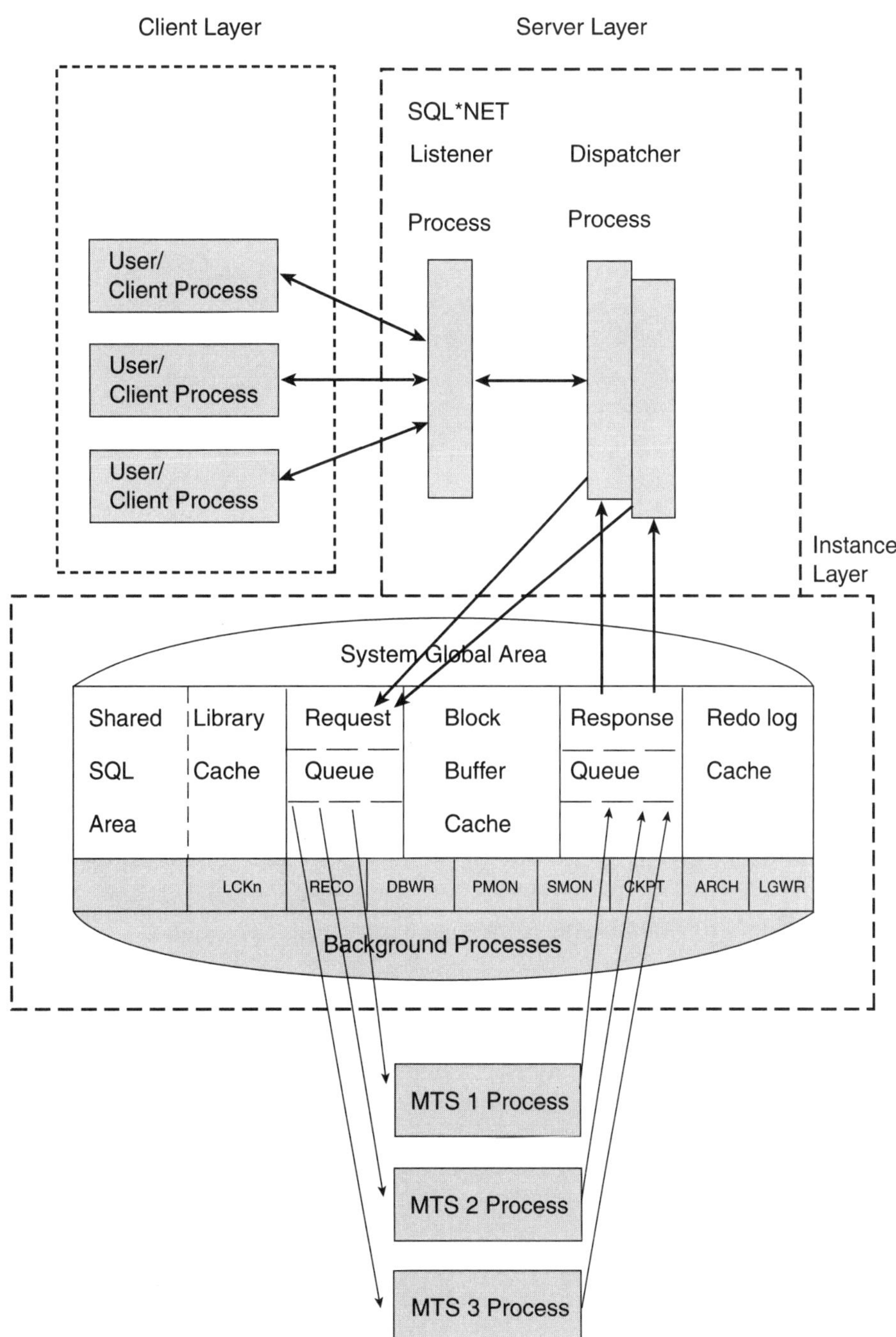

FIGURE 14.8 Multithreaded Server.

2. The SQL*NET **listener** process on the server receives the incoming **request**, determines its protocol, port, and server ID requirements. Then it passes the request to the correct Oracle instance's **dispatcher**. As a result, the user process connects to the dispatcher.
3. The SQL statement is sent by the user application.
4. The dispatcher places the request in the **request queue** in the SGA.
5. A **shared server** process picks up the process request from the request queue and starts to **service** it.
6. The shared server process creates a **cursor cache entry** area for the user statement in PGA.
7. Multiple user processes can use the same shared SQL area for the identical statements.

14.6.3 ORACLE PARALLEL SERVER

The Oracle Parallel Server is modeled after loosely coupled cluster systems where host systems have control of their own memory and CPUs but share the control over a set of disk systems. It is most appropriate when high on-line availability of the database and transaction scalability are of great importance. In such a scenario, more than one instance of a database connects to a single shared database and use their own memory and CPU resources to handle user requests. The main strengths are:

- Provides host redundancy and high accessibility of the database
- Scalability to support growth in transaction volume
- Separates RDBMS user processes from operating system maintenance processes

This configuration demands the highest level of administrative resources and is appropriate only when the database module accesses are mostly done through one of the hosts. It is not appropriate for applications that are not partitioned and database update activities on the same set of data cannot be limited to one of the hosts. In such scenarios, the network link among the hosts get over burdened with the large volume of cross server traffic and resource locks. (See Figure 14.9).

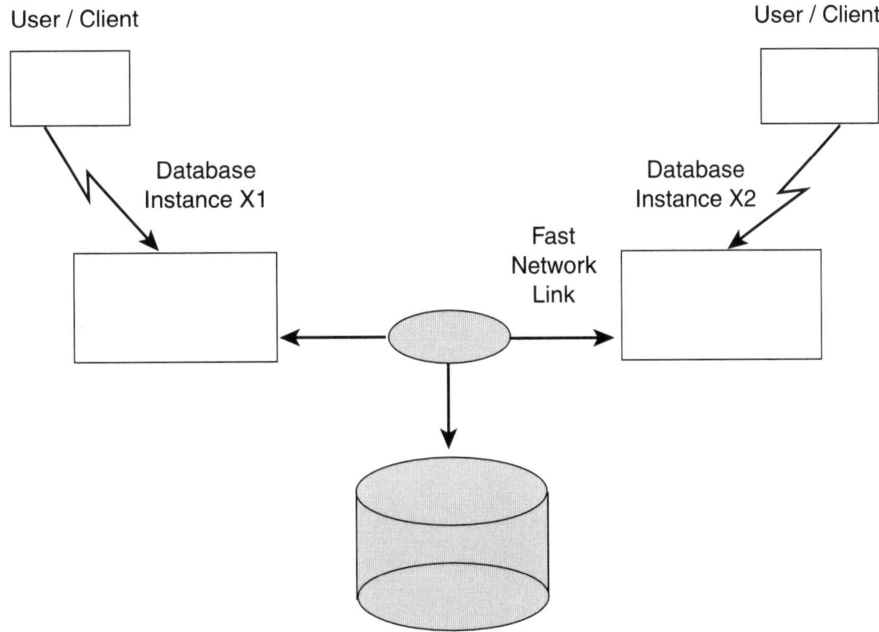

FIGURE 14.9 Multiple Instance of a Database.

Chapter 15

ORACLE DATABASE LANGUAGES: SQL AND PL/SQL

15.1 ORACLE'S IMPLEMENTATION OF SQL

In Chapter 4 we discussed the conceptual aspects of the relational model as the foundation for relational databases. We presented an overview of some of the important features of SQL as the industry standard database query language. We will now focus on the extensions that Oracle has added to the ANSI SQL syntax. The objective is to see how we can utilize this customization to implement a more optimized and scalable data warehouse application. As explained in the previous chapters it is very common for data warehouse repositories to grow rapidly in terms of subject variety, data volume, and number of user queries. It is very important to seriously consider scalability at the design and implementation stages. As part of the application release, every program module must be code reviewed for the following characteristics:

- Efficient use of system resources
- Optimized performance of both batch-processing and on-line access

- ❑ Support for data slice security

Let's see what construct types can be used in the physical implementation of the database design model.

15.1.1 ORACLE 7 OBJECT CONSTRUCT TYPES

Database objects in Oracle 7 are divided into several types. An overview of these types is presented below. Each database user account is called a "schema" which is like a user's virtual space in the database. A user's schema defines all the objects a user owns or has access to. For ease of manageability, all database objects specific to an application can also belong to a schema named after that application. In such a case, the application schema becomes the owner of all its objects and can grant access to other database users. The content of all these schema can be analyzed and managed through a set of system tables called a database catalog or data dictionary. The tables are automatically maintained as objects go through structural changes. Once the schema is created, we can use SQL and simply query this system data dictionary to inquire about its status and structure. In other words, any object creation or alteration is verifiable or reportable through the data dictionary.

Oracle 7 database construct types are:

- ❑ DATABASE
- ❑ TABLESPACE
- ❑ USER
- ❑ ROLE
- ❑ PROFILE
- ❑ TABLE
- ❑ VIEW
- ❑ INDEX
- ❑ SEQUENCE
- ❑ SYNONYM
- ❑ CLUSTER
- ❑ LOCK
- ❑ PROCEDURE
- ❑ TRIGGER

- FUNCTION
- PACKAGE
- DATABASE LINK
- SNAPSHOT
- SNAPSHOT LOG

The definition, modification, and elimination of these objects which serve either as **containers** or **processors** of data are all done through a set of DDL statements. These DDL statements have a simple and intuitive syntax:

General format of a DDL	Usage
CREATE object_type, object_name, object_attributes	Defines a particular object by specifying its type and its attributes
ALTER object_type, object_name	Modifies the structure of a particular object
DROP object_type, object_name	Eliminates a particular object

The *Oracle 7 Server SQL Language Reference*[1] provides comprehensive grammar for the implementation of SQL. The following examples illustrate creating and modifying database objects using SQL.

Example 1

```
CREATE TABLE orders (
order_no                NUMBER NOT NULL
                        CONSTRAINT orders_pk Primary key
                        USING INDEX
                        TABLESPACE booking_index
                        STORAGE (INITIAL 1M NEXT 1M
                        PCTINCREASE 0),
po_customer             NUMBER NOT NULL
                        CONSTRAINT po_customer_fk
                        REFERENCES customers (po_customer),

order_date              DATE NOT NULL,
order_status            VARCHAR2(10) NOT NULL
```

[1]*Oracle 7 Server SQL Language Reference Manual*, 1992, p. 2-2.

```
                                 CHECK (order_status IN
                                 ('ENTERED','CHECKED','BOOKED',
                                 'CLOSED','HOLD'),
create_user                      VARCHAR2(30) DEFAULT USER,
creation_date                    DATE DEFAULT SYSDATE,
update_user                      VARCHAR2(30) DEFAULT USER,
update_date                      DATE DEFAULT SYSDATE)

                                 PCTFREE 30
                                 PCTUSED 70
                                 STORAGE (INITIAL 100M NEXT 100M
                                 PCTINCREASE 0)
                                 TABLESPACE booking_data;
```

Example 2

```
ALTER TABLE orders ADD (Sales_agt_id
NUMBER);
ALTER TABLE orders ADD
CONSTRAINT sales_agt_fk FOREIGN KEY
(sales_org)
REFERENCES sales_org;
```

Example 3

```
CREATE INDEX orders_n1 ON orders
(po_customer)
TABLESPACE booking_index
STORAGE (INITIAL 1M NEXT 1M
PCTINCREASE 0)
PCTFREE 0;
```

SYSDATE and USER are two-system defined functions that can be used to provide system-level information such as current date and time stamp and user login account.

Declarative integrity is done through the use of the PRIMARY KEY, FOREIGN KEY, DEFAULT, CHECK, and NOT NULL options. These integrity options, once enabled, are enforced at the database level.

To avoid dynamic space allocation and segment fragmentation, a customized storage allocation pattern can be supplied through the use of PCTFREE, PCTUSED, and STORAGE clauses.

Objects related to a specific subject area are grouped together in a subject-specific logical space boundary using a TABLESPACE clause. This will ease the data recovery, physical layout, and capacity planning.

Data constructs are stored in a data-only tablespace and index constructs are stored in an index-only tablespace. This will help avoid I/O resource contention.

15.1.2 THE POWER OF DATA DICTIONARY

At any given point in time an Oracle user can retrieve the details of each object definition and status from the data dictionary views. For instance, using a simple SQL query from USER_OBJECTS we can find out about the type and number of different object types in our application schema.

Example 1

```
SELECT        object_type , count(*) object_count
FROM          USER_OBJECTS
GROUP BY      object_type
ORDER BY      object_type;
```

The result may look like this:

OBJECT_TYPE	OBJECT_COUNT
DATABASE LINK	16
INDEX	502
PACKAGE	82
PACKAGE BODY	82
SEQUENCE	18
SYNONYM	128
TABLE	356
TRIGGER	8
VIEW	20

The extensions that Oracle has added to SQL are generally optional features that can be omitted if SQL code portability is a criterion. The data dictionary objects can be utilized from four different perspectives:

1. A user's schema
2. All other visible schema
3. System's schema (persistent state)
4. System's schema (dynamic state)

The following table provides a starter's list of data dictionary objects for each perspective.

It summarizes the DDL SQL statements along with the corresponding data dictionary views that can provide information on the impact of the DDL statements.

Category	Used by	View Name
A user 's schema • Prefix: USER_	Any Oracle user who would like to retrieve information about his/her objects (owned by user login name) by default has access to this group of views.	USER_OBJECTS USER_TABLES USER_INDEXES USER_IND_COLUMNS USER_CONSTRAINTS USER_TAB_PRIVS USER_TS_QUOTAS USER_CONS_COLUMNS USER_SEGMENTS USER_EXTENTS USER_USERS
All other visible schema • Prefix: • ALL_	Any end user who would like to retrieve information on objects owned by themselves and others to which they have access to can use this group of views. User should have explicit authorization on those objects before they can become visible.	ALL_OBJECTS ALL_TABLES ALL_INDEXES ALL_IND_COLUMNS ALL_CONSTRAINTS ALL_TAB_PRIVS ALL_TS_QUOTAS ALL_CONS_COLUMNS ALL_SEGMENTS ALL_EXTENTS ALL_USERS
System's schema (persistent state) • Prefix:	At the system level, a database administrator who is a privileged user (DBA accounts) can	DBA_OBJECTS DBA_TABLES DBA_INDEXES DBA_IND_COLUMNS

Category	Used by	View Name
DBA_	retrieve information about all objects in the database regardless of its owners. No explicit grant is required. These groups of views provide a comprehensive view of the system.	DBA_CONSTRAINTS DBA_TAB_PRIVS DBA_TS_QUOTAS DBA_CONS_COLUMNS DBA_SEGMENTS DBA_EXTENTS DBA_TABLESPACES DBA_DATAFILES; DBA_USERS
System's schema (dynamic state) • Prefix: • V$ or X$	By default, it is available only to DBA accounts but it can also be made available to other user accounts.	V$PROCESS V$SESSION V$LOCK V$ROLLSTAT V$PARAMETERS V$ACCESS V$FILESTAT V$RESOURCE V$LOG V$LOG_HISTORY V$LIBRARYCACHE

Example 2. To find out about the status or details of an object specification, one can query USER_OBJECTS as the first step. The assumption is made that the Oracle account "APPL_ADMIN" is the login user name that owns the application schema.

```
SELECT     object_name, object_type, creation_date
FROM       DBA_OBJECTS
WHERE      owner = 'APPL_ADMIN';
```

Example 3. List those database objects that contain data such as table, index, and so on, and are scattered into nonconsecutive storage segments (fragments). List those that consists more than 25 fragments in order of severity :

```
SELECT     segment_name, segment_type, extents, bytes
FROM       USER_SEGMENTS
WHERE      extents > 25
ORDER BY   extents desc, segment_type ;
```

SEGMENT_NAME	SEGMENT_TYPE	EXTENTS	BYTES
SOL_PRODUCT_ID	INDEX	90	104,079,360
BMLCT_N2	INDEX	53	95,846,400
PL_PK	INDEX	50	15,769,600
BMLCT_N3	INDEX	49	86,261,760
DSS1_FISC_PRD_ID	INDEX	47	92,651,520
DW_EXPENSE_COLLN_FY96	TABLE	47	67,297,280
CC_N3	INDEX	39	26,296,320
CC_N1	INDEX	38	23,797,760
CC_N2	INDEX	38	23,797,760
BMLCT_N1	INDEX	36	76,677,120
IJM_BAD_CSM_100896	TABLE	33	8,151,040
PSCT_N1	INDEX	29	44,359,680
DSS1_PO_CUST_CHANNEL_NAME	INDEX	26	256,081,920
NCB_I_N4	INDEX	26	325,091,328

The information in USER_SEGMENTS can be joined with information in DBA_TABLESPACES which can help determine the scale of the problem. Should it be addressed on a smaller scale, isolate tables and indexes, and if on a larger scale, at a tablespace or schema level? The Oracle data dictionary provides useful detailed information and dynamic statistics about objects, sessions, transactions, users, throughput, and so on. With a little planning and research, a new DBA can put in place a number of effective DBA SQL reports that can aid in monitoring the system status. In case of a data warehouse application, it is a good investment to use one of many database system monitoring tools to aid in proactive administration of the database system in the long run.

We conclude this topic by providing you with some direction in regards to DDL statements and the use of data dictionary objects that reflects the results of corresponding DDLs.

Object Name	Available DDLs	Data Dictionary	Contains
Database	CREATE DATABASE ALTER DATABASE	V$DATABASE V$VERSION V$LICENSE V$LOG V$LOGFILE V$OPTION	Database information/configuration as stated in control file.
Table space	CREATE TABLESPACE ALTER TABLESPACE DROP TABLESPACE	DBA_TABLESPACES DBA_DATA_FILES DBA_TS_QUOTAS V$DATAFILE	Table space characteristics including the underlining data files and usage quotas.
User	CREATE USER ALTER USER DROP USER	USER_USERS USER_TS_QUOTAS USER_OBJECTS	User.
Role	CREATE ROLE ALTER ROLE DROP ROLE	DBA_ROLES DBA_ROLE_PRIVS DBA_TAB_PRIVS	Role is a logical representation of a group of privileges and accessibility.
Profile	CREATE PROFILE	USER_PROFILES	Profile of users in terms of system resource limitations and quotas.
Table	CREATE TABLE ALTER TABLE DROP TABLE TRUNCATE TABLE ANALYZE TABLE	USER_TABLES USER_TAB_PRIVS USER_CONSTRAINTS USER_CONS_COLUMNS	Table definition.
View	CREATE VIEW DROP VIEW	USER_VIEWS	Views provide a logical table of results that is based on a query.
Index	CREATE INDEX ALTER INDEX ANALYZE INDEX	USER_INDEXES USER_IND_COLUMNS	List of all indexes and indexed columns.

Object Name	Available DDLs	Data Dictionary	Contains
Sequence	CREATE SEQUENCE ALTER SEQUENCE DROP SEQUENCE	USER_SEQUENCES	List of all sequences created by the user.
Synonym	CREATE SYNONYM DROP SYNONYM	USER_SYNONYMS	Hides the details of an object name by referencing an equivalent name.
Clusters	CREATE CLUSTER	USER_CLUSTERS	Hash clusters can be used to improve the join performance of at least two tables that are often accessed together.
Lock	LOCK TABLE IN	USER_LOCKS V$ACCESS V$LOCK	To ensure integrity and manage the data concurrency Oracle uses.
Procedures	CREATE PROCEDURE REPLACE PROCEDURE ALTER PROCEDURE DROP PROCEDURE	USER_SOURCES USER_DEPENDENCIES USER_ERRORS USER_DEPENDENCIES	Lists the content of a PL/SQL procedure.
Triggers	CREATE TRIGGER DROP TRIGGER	USER_TRIGGERS USER_TRIGGER_COLS USER_DEPENDENCIES	Triggers and column usage and dependency.
Functions	CREATE FUNCTION DROP FUNCTION	USER_SOURCE USER_OBJECTS USER_DEPENDENCIES	Lists the content of a PL/SQL procedure that also returns a value result.
Packages	CREATE PACKAGE ALTER PACKAGE DROP PACKAGE	USER_OBJECTS V$DB_OBJECT_CACHE USER_DEPENDENCIES	A number of related procedures can be joined and packed together as one package.

Object Name	Available DDLs	Data Dictionary	Contains
Database Link	CREATE DATABASE LINK DROP DATABASE LINK	DBA_DB_LINKS V$DBLINK DBA_SYNONYMS	Database link provides a transparent link between two database nodes.
Snapshots	CREATE SNAPSHOT DROP SNAPSHOT	USER_SNAPSHOTS USER_VIEWS USER_TABLES	Snapshots provide a mechanism to asynchronously replicate an Oracle 7 table or tables.
Snapshot logs	CREATE SNAPSHOT LOG ON DROP SNAPSHOT LOG	USER_SNAPSHOT_LOGS	Snapshot logs keep track of every row ID that gets changed in the master table.
Rollback segment	CREATE ROLLBACK SEGMENT DROP ROLLBACK SEGMENT	DBA_ROLLBACK_SEGS	Rollback segments are used to support every transaction and provide read consistency.

15.2 PROCEDURAL PL/SQL (ORACLE 7'S "COMPLETE" DATABASE LANGUAGE)

15.2.1 DESIGN WITH EFFICIENCY AND PERFORMANCE IN MIND

Bruce MacLennan compiled an interesting list of principles of programming languages that are quite appropriate to be mentioned here since we are discussing the features of the SQL and PL/SQL languages. These principles will help us keep in mind what usually is very easy to miss when designing and implementing systems. An adaptation of his principles are listed in the following table.

Programming Principles	Definitions
Abstraction	Avoid requiring something to be stated more than once; factor out the recurring pattern.
Automation	Automate mechanical, tedious, or error-prone activities.
Defense in Depth	If an error gets through one line of defense, syntactic checking, then it should be caught by the next line of defense (type checking, in this case).
Information Hiding	Module should be designed so that 1. The user has all the information they need to use the module correctly. 2. The implementor has all the information needed to implement the module correctly and nothing more.
Labeling	We should not require the user to know the absolute position of an item in a list. Instead, we should associate labels with any position that must be referenced elsewhere.
Localized Cost	A user should only pay for what he uses; avoid distributed costs.
Manifest Interface	All interfaces should be apparent in the syntax.
Portability	Portable codes across different platforms.
Preservation of Information	The language should allow the representation of information that the user knows and the compiler needs.
Regularity	Regular rules without exceptions are easier to learn, use, describe, and implement.
Security	No program that violates the definition of the language or its own intended structure should escape detection.
Simplicity	Simplicity of the components and functions.
Structure	The static structure of the program should correspond in a simple way to the dynamic structure of the corresponding computations.
Syntactic Consistency	Things which look similar should be similar and things which look different should be different.
Zero-One-Infinity	The only reasonable numbers in a programming language design are zero, one, and infinity.

15.2.2 SQL IS NOT A "COMPLETE" LANGUAGE

Until now the flexibility and simplicity of SQL have been emphasized in this book. In reality, SQL is flexible as long as data manipulation can be expressed using set algebra which includes sets and set operation. SQL is not a very flexible language when the essense of data manipulation calls for procedural programming, conditional process flow, computations, loop processing, and exception handling. To complete the database language picture, Oracle has designed PL/SQL to address the shortcomings of SQL. PL/SQL is not ANSI standard. If portability of your data warehouse application code is a major criterion, then you need to be aware that any module that uses PL/SQL will not necessarily be portable to another RDBMS. PL/SQL is simple and easy to learn and it is similar to ADA programming language.

One of the major benefits of PL/SQL is that it provides the foundation for a more enhanced application development process. It allows application rules, referred to here as **application transactions** to be implemented. An application transaction is generally composed of more than one database transaction.

15.2.3 COMPARING AN APPLICATION TRANSACTION TO A DATABASE TRANSACTION

In general, a database transaction can be thought of as a program that has the following properties:

Atomic: A transaction is completed and visible to other transactions only after all the steps are completed successfully.

Consistent: The integrity constraints are observed and followed during the execution of a transaction.

Isolated: Concurrent transactions do not interfere with each other's process flow and produce data quality issue.

Durable: The impact of a completed transaction should last. If the transaction is aborted, the impact of changes performed should be reverted.

Every SQL statement can be a single database transaction from an Oracle RDBMS perspective. By the same token but on a larger scope, an application transaction is a logical unit of work that consists of steps and actions planned by the application designer. The designer decides how the application functions and which complex integrity rules should be modularized and implemented. A PL/SQL program unit provides the means to build this user-defined logical unit of work. It may very well include one or more SQL statements. These statements are all executed by a single user in a single session. A transaction begins with the first executable statement. A transaction ends when it is explicitly committed or rolled back.

For instance, an order entry transaction consists of several logical steps:

Transaction: Order entered

- Create the order
- Identify the customer
- Enter the order lines

Transaction: Order booked

- Check the configuration
- Check the inventory
- Check customer's credit
- Book the order

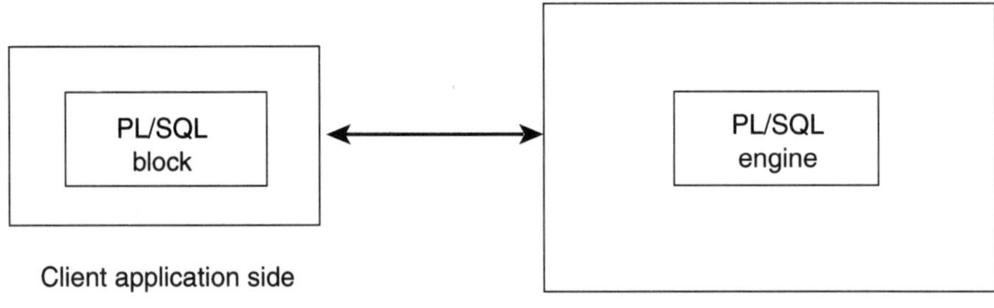

The PL/SQL code can be executed either on the side of the application (embedded in the Oracle Tools), or it is executed by the RDBMS, like SQL*Plus. PL/SQL is intended to provide an increase in performance, data encapsulation, and program extensibility by providing a procedural style of coding. A developer can control the process flow using:

- IF..THEN...ELSE
- LOOPS...
- EXCEPTION....
- COMMENTS /*...*/
- DECLARE objects...
- Controlled scope

15.2.4 PL/SQL 2.0 CONSTRUCTS

There are a number of different types of PL/SQL program units such as:

- Anonymous block
- Stored procedure
- Stored function
- Package specification and package body
- Database trigger

In general, a PL/SQL block (code segment) consists of:

```
BEGIN
    DECLARE       /* Declaration section*/
    ..........
    BEGIN         /* Executable subprogram section */
    ..........
    EXCEPTION     /* Exception handling section*/
    ..........
    END;
END;
```

A PL/SQL block can be considered a PL/SQL statement and therefore lead into nested blocks.

The definition of a PL/SQL block and the execution plan can be stored in the database like other objects such as views. These stored PL/SQL blocks are called **stored procedures**. If the procedure returns a value, it is further defined to be a stored function. If the PL/SQL block is to be executed upon a specific change to records of a table, it is called a **trigger**. A group of related procedures sharing the same set of global environment is called a **stored package**. A stored procedure can help centralize the application rule and help create an application library which is easily shared and utilized by other tools and applications. It is more efficient to execute a PL/SQL block that is parsed and stored in the database versus one that resides outside the database in a SQL script or embedded in a program.

A SQL statement or a PL/SQL block goes through a parsing stage before getting executed. This parsing stage constitutes a significant time portion of the total elapsed time. Any attempt to reduce that time will improve the performance of a transaction. Oracle 7 RDBMS architecture shares the parse format of both SQL and PL/SQL blocks by placing them in the library cache of SGA for a period of time. With proper configuration, this improves database throughput by avoiding the parsing step. Once the parse format is found in SGA, only the results are used and repeated parsing is avoided. This parsed information is eventually flushed out of SGA to make room for newer statements. In case of a stored procedure, trigger (Oracle 7.3), or function, the parsed format is stored in the database which is permanent compared to the content of SGA.

15.3 SECTIONS OF A PL/SQL BLOCK

A Declaration section. The declaration section is used for declaring user-defined variables, constants, and exceptions flags (scenarios). This section is optional. Variables can be defined explicitly in the declaration section or implicitly in the body of PL/SQL.

- ❑ Constant
- ❑ Variable
- ❑ Exception

Example 1

```
DECLARE
        V_fiscal_period NUMBER := 1; — numerical variable initialized
        ...........
BEGIN
        ...........
END;
```

An Executable section. The executable section includes the SQL executable statements. The complex integrity rules or data manipulation are handled through a number of executable statements. Examples of statements follow.

Executable Statement	Example
Database access	SELECT fiscal_period_id INTO V_fiscal_period FROM .....; INSERT ......; UPDATE ......; DELETE .....;
Assignments	V_fiscal_period := C_first_period
Conditional	IF ...THEN...ELSEIF
Jump and Loop	• WHILE... • DO.... • FOR • GOTO
Transaction Control	SAVEPOINT • COMMIT WORK • ROLLBACK WORK
Comment	Precede the comment with — or enclose the statement in /* and */.

An Exception (Error or Condition) Handling Section. The exception handling section is used for trapping and managing errors, warnings, special cases, and exceptions in the PL/SQL block. It includes statements that are executed when certain conditions or exceptions are raised in the executable section of the PL/SQL block.

Syntax for defining an exception:

```
:
WHEN exception_name [ OR exception_name..] THEN
      — sequence of statements
WHEN OTHERS THEN
      — sequence of statements
      — Predefined Errors (Implicitly declared EXCEPTION flags):
WHEN TOO_MANY_ROWS
WHEN NO_DATA_FOUND
WHEN DUP_VALUE_ON_INDEX
```

Example 2. In this example the predefined EXCEPTION flag "NO_DATA_FOUND" is used. It gets raised when a SELECT or UPDATE statement does not find any result records.

```
DECLARE
        V_fiscal_period_num              NUMBER;
        V_quantity                       NUMBER;
        V_quantity_fct                   NUMBER;
        V_market_index                   NUMBER := 0.078;

BEGIN
        V_fiscal_period_num := 1;
SELECT sum( quantity_booked) INTO V_quantity FROM SALES_ORDERS
        WHERE fiscal_period = V_fiscal_period_num;

        V_quantity_fct := V_quantity * 1.20 * V_market_index;
        UPDATE booking_fct SET quantity_fct = V_quantity_fct
        WHERE fiscal_period = V_fiscal_period;

EXCEPTION
        WHEN NO_DATA_FOUND THEN
        /* we assume there is a table called MESSAGES that is used a log table.*/
        INSERT INTO messages(message, time_stamp) VALUES
                ('no_data_found, sysdate);
END;
```

Example 3. In the following example, a SELECT statement has returned more than one record. In PL/SQL version 1, a regular SELECT statement populates only a one-dimensional variable. It is considered an erroneous condition if more than one record is qualified to be selected. Therefore, in the following example, the predefined (implicitly defined) EXCEPTION flag, TOO_MANY_ROWS, is raised. The table "PRODUCT" stores the list of all the product IDs in the column called "product_id." The product ID is provided to this PL/SQL block through a substitution variable "&V_product_id" checks the integrity of a product ID by checking its existance in the database. If it does not exist or if more than one record has the same ID, an erroneous condition has occurred and it should be reported properly

```
DECLARE
                V_record_id NUMBER ;
BEGIN
                SELECT product_id INTO record_id FROM product
                WHERE product.product_id = &product_id;
```

```
EXCEPTION
            WHEN TOO_MANY_ROWS THEN
                  INSERT INTO messages VALUES
                  ('More than one record have the same ID',sysdate);
            WHEN NO_DATA_FOUND THEN
                  INSERT INTO messages VALUES
                  ('No product is found with this ID',sysdate);
END;
```

EXCEPTION flags can also be user-defined. These user-defined EXCEPTIONs must be named differently than the predefined (implicitly defined) EXCEPTIONs. They are declared and called by the developer.

Example 4. In the following example, the balance of a bank account is checked using a given account number. Depending on the balance, a special flag is raised.

```
DECLARE
      special_case            EXCEPTION;
      negative_balance        EXCEPTION;
      Account                 number = &account_no;
      act_balance             number;

BEGIN
      SELECT balance INTO act_balance FROM accounts WHERE account_no =
account;
      IF balance < 0 THEN
            RAISE negative_balance;
      ELSEIF balance = 0 THEN
            RAISE special_case;
      END IF;
EXCEPTION
      WHEN special_case THEN
            INSERT INTO messages (time_stamp,message)
            VALUES(sysdate,'No funds available');
      WHEN negative_balance THEN
            INSERT INTO messages (time_stamp,message)
            VALUES(sysdate, 'Negative balance');
      commit;
END;
```

Note:

1. Only one exception handler is allowed per block.
2. Oracle 7 provides more information about the last error through the two predefined functions, namely, SQLCODE and SQLERRM. SQLCODE provides the unique error number defined and generated by Oracle 7, whereas SQLERRM provides the error message associated with the error number which is also generated by Oracle.

The following are default values:

SQLCODE = 0
SQLERRM = "normal, successful completion"

The following example shows how the default values are used, although they cannot be used directly in some cases. Using some temporary variables we can work around this issue.

Example 5. Scenario: Report any Oracle error that occurs before exiting the routine.

```
DECLARE
    Tsqlcode number;
    Tsqlerrm char(70);
    /* temporary variables should be used in queries, instead of the actual
    system variables(functions)
            SQLCODE and SQLERRM*/
    BEGIN
            .....
    EXCEPTION
            WHEN OTHERS THEN
              Tsqlcode :=SQLCODE;
              Tsqlerrm :=SQLERRM;
              INSERT INTO messages
              VALUES(' Error Code :'|| Tsqlcode || 'Tsqlerrm', sysdate);
END;
```

15.4 DATA TYPE AND FUNCTION SUPPORT

Variables can also be declared dynamically using %TYPE and %ROWTYPE. In other words, they can be declared to have the same data type as an existing column or record in a table in the database.

CHAR
DATE
BOOLEAN
user.table.column%TYPE
user.table%ROWTYPE

Example 6. Scenario: Consider a row in "DEPT" table: "deptno," "location," and "dname," and the column "job" in "EMP" table. Relocate department 100 to DALLAS and call it "PURCHASING." Also reflect the name of this department in the title of those working in the department.

```
DECLARE
        title               emp.job%TYPE;
        depart_rec          dept%ROWTYPE;
BEGIN
        SELECT deptno, location, deptname INTO depart_rec FROM DEPT
        WHERE deptno = 100;
        depart_rec.location := 'DALLAS';
        depart_rec.dname := 'PURCHASING';
        UPDATE DEPT SET location = depart_rec.location , dname =
depart_rec.dname
                WHERE deptno = depart_rec.deptno;
        title := ' IN PURCHASING';
        UPDATE EMP set job= job || title WHERE deptno = depart_rec.deptno;
END;
```

15.5 TRANSACTION TRACING AND MONITORING FACILITIES

The Oracle 7 data dictionary not only captures the static state of the database but also collects the dynamic statistics about every transaction and the resources used during the processing.

Here is a list of some of those views:

V$TRANSACTION
V$SYSSTAT

V$SESSION
V$SESSION_WAIT
V$SESS_IO
V$SGA
V$SGA_STAT
V$SQLAREA
V$SQLTEXT
V$WAITSTAT

15.5.1 TRANSACTION CONTROL

In a PL/SQL block one can have control over the "saving" of the changes using two statements, savepoint and rollback. They allow more flexibility and establish more user control over a specific group of DML statements.

Syntax:

```
SAVEPOINT pointer_name;
ROLLBACK [WORK] TO [SAVEPOINT ] pointer_name;
```

Example 7. You can be more selective and save all the changes when an error occurs by doing the following:

```
BEGIN
....
 SAVEPOINT A;
....
 SAVEPOINT B;
....
 ROLLBACK TO SAVEPOINT B;
 COMMIT;
END;
```

15.5.2 PROCESS FLOW IN A PL/SQL BLOCK

Loops provide a means of repeating a statement or sequence of events. The following types of loop in PL/SQL can provide process flow control.

- ❑ Simple loops
- ❑ Numeric FOR loops
- ❑ WHILE loops

Simple Loop Syntax:

```
LOOP
            sequence of statements
EXIT [WHEN condition] ;
END LOOP — can cause infinite loop
```

EXIT is used to prevent infinite loop

Example 8. Add the word "DEPARTMENT" to all the department names. Assume department numbers start from 100 and increase by 10. The last department number is 300.

```
BEGIN
            counter := 100;
            LOOP
                UPDATE dept
                SET dname = 'DEPARTMENT 'll dname
                WHERE deptno = counter;
                counter := counter +10;
                EXIT WHEN counter = 300;
                END LOOP;
END;
```

15.5.3 NUMERIC FOR LOOP SYNTAX

```
FOR         index in [REVERSE] integer .. integer LOOP
            /* executable statements */
END LOOP;
```

Example 9. Compute and store the factorial values from 1 to 500.

```
DECLARE
        series_ number
BEGIN
```

```
        series_value ;=1;
        FOR i in 1..500 LOOP
                series_value:=series_value*i;
                INSERT INTO TEMP1(series)  VALUES(series_value;
        END LOOP;
END;
```

Notes on loop index:

1. Type of the index must be NUMBER
2. It is implicitly defined to be referenced in the loop.
3. Its value cannot be changed in the loop example:

Example 10. Renumber the employee numbers from 1001 to 2000. Assume they currently run from 1 to 1000.

```
DECLARE
Loop_index char(20) := 'CALCULATING';
BEGIN
        FOR Loop_index IN 1001..2000 LOOP
        /*Loop_index gets implicitly declared again*/

        UPDATE EMP SET empno = Loop_index
                WHERE empno = loop_index -1000;
        END LOOP;
END;
```

15.5.4 NUMERIC WHILE LOOP SYNTAX

```
WHILE condition LOOP
      sequence of statements
END LOOP;
```

Example 11. Scenario: Modify the series values less than 10 in the factorial series table TEMP.

```
DECLARE
        Loop_counter NUMBER(5) := 1;
BEGIN
        WHILE Loop_counter < 10
        LOOP
                UPDATE TEMP set series = series + Loop_counter
                        WHERE series = Loop_counter;
                Loop_counter := Loop_counter +1;
        END LOOP;
END;
```

References

[1] Codd, E.F. 1970. *A Relational Model for Large Shared Data Banks*. Communications of the ACM 13.

[2] Codd, E.F. 1990. *A Relational Model for Data Management*, Version 2. Reading, MA: Addison-Wesley.

[3] Codd, E.F. 1993. *Providing OLAP(On-Line Analytical Processing) to User-Analysts: An IT mandate*. E.F. Codd and Associates.

[4] Date, C.J. 1990. *An Introduction to Database Systems*, Vol.1, 5th ed. Reading, MA: Addison-Wesley.

[5] Loney, Kevin. 1994. *Oracle 7 DBA Handbook 7*, 3rd ed. Oracle Press: Osborn- McGrawHill.

[6] Owen, Kevin T. 1996. *Building Intelligent Databases with Oracle 7 PL/SQL Triggers & Stored Procedures*. Prentice Hall.

[7] *Oracle 7 Server Application Developer's Guide 1992*. Oracle Corporation.

[8] Fayyad U., Piatetsky-Shapiro G., Smyth P., and Uthurusamy, R. 1996. *Advances in Knowledge Discovery and Data Mining*. AAAI Press/The MIT Press.

[9] Khoshafian, S. 1996. *MultiMedia and Imaging Databases*. Morgan Kaufmann.

[10] Tanenbaum, A. 1992. *Modern Operating Systems*. Prentice Hall.

[11] Poe, V. 1996. *Building a Data Warehouse for Decision Support*. Prentice Hall.

[12] Mattison, Rob. 1996. *Data Warehousing*. McGraw-Hill.

[13] Kimball, Ralph. 1996. *The Data Warehouse Toolkit*. Wiley.

[14] Barquin, Ramon, and Edelstein, Herb.1997. *Planning and Desiging The Data Warehouse*. Prentice Hall.

[15] Klots, B. 1996. *Cache Coherency in Oracle Parallel Server*. In Proceedings of the 22nd VLDB Conference 1996.

[16] Dyreson, C., and Cook, James. 1996. *Informational Retrieval from an Incomplete Data Cube*. In Proceedings of the 22nd VLDB Conference 1996.

[17] Gupta, A., Harinarayan, V., and Quass, D. 1995. *Aggregate-Query Processing in Data Warehousing Environments*. In Proceedings of the 22nd VLDB Conference 1996.

[18] Shukla, A., Naughton, J., Deshpande, P., and Ramasamy, K. 1996. *Storage Estimation for Multidimensional Aggregates in the Presence of Hierarchies*. In Proceedings of the 22nd VLDB Conference 1996.

[19] Agrawal, S., Agrawal, R., Deshpande, P., Gupta, A., Naughton, J., Ramakrishnan, R., and Sarawagi, S. 1996. *On the Computation of Multidimensional Aggregates*. In Proceedings of the 22nd VLDB Conference 1996.

[20] Srivastava, D., Dar, S., Jagadish, H.V., and Levy A. 1996. *Answering Queries with Aggregation Using Views*. In Proceedings of the 22nd VLDB Conference 1996.

[21] Zargham, M. R. 1996. *Computer Architecture Single and Parallel Systems*. Prentice Hall.

[22] Scheuermann P., Shim, Junho, and Vingralek R. 1996. *Watchman: A Data Warehouse Intelligent Cache Manager*. In Proceedings of the 22nd VLDB Conference 1996.

[23] *Oracle Server Concepts Manual 1992*. Oracle Corporation.

[24] Inmon, W., Hackathorn, R. 1994. *Using the Data Warehouse*. Wiley.

[25] McDermid, John. 1991. *Software Engineer's Reference Book*. ComputerWeekly.

[26] Browning, Tim. 1995. *Capacity Planning for Computer Systems*. AP Professional.

[27] Barker, R., and Longman, C. 1992. *CASE*METHOD Function and Process Modeling*. Oracle Corporation. Addison Wesley.

[28] Elmasri, R., and Navathe, S. 1994. *Fundamentals of Database Systems*, 2nd ed. The Benjamin/Cummings Publishing Company, Inc.

[29] Scheer, A.W. 1989. *Enterprise-Wide Data Modeling: Information Systems in Industry*. Springer-Verlag Berlin Heidelberg.

[30] Chen, P.P.1981. *Entity-Relationship Approach to Information Modeling and Analysis*. Proceeding of the 2nd International Conference on Entity-Relationship Approach (1981), Amsterdam-NewYork-Oxford 1983.

[31] Cattell, R.G.G. 1991. *Object Data Management: Object-Oriented and Extended Relational Database Systems*. Addison Wesley 1991.

[32] Seibert, G. *Oracle Data Processing: A Manager's Handbook*. Windcrest/McGraw-Hill 1993.

[33] Cattell, R.G.G. 1996. *The Object Database Standard: ODMG-93 Release 1.2*. Morgan Kaufmann.

[34] Khoshafian, S. 1993. *Object-Oriented Databases*. Wiley.

[35] Koch, G., and Loney, K. 1995. *Oracle—The Complete Reference*, 3rd ed. Oracle Press. Osborne-McGraw-Hill.

[36] Velpuri, Rama. 1995. *Oracle Backup and Recovery Handbook*. Oracle Press. Osborne-McGraw-Hill.

[37] Booch, G. 1994. *Object-Oriented Analysis and Design with Applications*, 2nd ed. Rational, The Benjamin/Cummings Publishing Company, Inc.

[38] Hugo, Toledo, Jr. 1996. *Oracle Networking*. Oracle Press. Osborne-McGraw-Hill.

[39] Corey, M.J., Abbey, M., and Dechichio D. Jr. *Tuning Oracle*. Oracle Press. Osborne-McGraw-Hill.

Glossary

Alternate Key Alternate key in the context of relational database model refers to any unique key(s) of an Entity that can be selected as the primary key of that entity.

API In the context of application development, API refers to the Application Programming Interface layer of a software architecture that facilitates the communication and messaging between modules. An API of a module provides an interface that includes functions and routines that can be called by external objects to request services independent of the internal configuration of that module.

Application Domain Application domain is a set of modules and objects that can belong to one or several classes. Each object can be responsible for specific services related to a subset of attributes and data elements represented in the data warehouse subject areas.

Application Problem Domain Application problem domain is a set of high level user descriptions of their specific information need.

Architecture Architecture is the big picture perception of the technical solution that needs to be implemented to meet the requirements of user application problem domain.

Association Association is the relevant relationship that can exist between different attributes of subject area. For instance there is an association between the sales order transaction, the sales order type and the end-user bookings definition.

Atomic data Atomic data in the context of data warehousing is the granular level detail transaction that is transported and transformed in the data warehouse.

Attribute Attribute in the context of data warehousing is a relevant and descriptive data element in a subject area.

Back-end Back-end in the context of data warehousing is the database server and the application modules responsible for the storage, transportation and transformation of data in the data warehouse.

Backup Backup in the context of a database server is the process of creating a redundant set of database files that can be used in restoring the database at a later time (if needed).

Batch Batch in the context of software execution is referred to processes that do not require interactive input and once invoked, can progress independently in a multi processing environment.

Business Intelligence Business Intelligence in the context of data warehousing refers to the core and sometimes hidden business know-how, success and failure criteria, strategies and plans that are mission critical.

Business Knowledge Business knowledge in the context of data warehousing refers to the set of parameters, processes , interactions, workflow , cause and effect that are relevant to the business mission, goals, products and services.

CASE CASE in the context of application development refers to the Computer Assisted System Engineering techniques that are used to model software systems or components of a system.

Categorization Categorization in the context of data warehousing is to identify the grouping and classes of a detail transaction based on some relevant attributes. For instance, some sales order records are "revenue generating" bookings and some are "non-revenue" bookings depending on who was the customer, and what was the product.

Client Client in the context of data warehousing is the requester of services, from the provider of the services, which is referred to as the server.

Clustering Clustering in the context of computer architecture refers to the configuration that consists of more than one closely networked but independent servers that share only a set of external disks.

Collection Data Collection data in the context of data warehousing refers to the set of tables that store the summarized, aggregated and sometimes de-normalized version of data. It is the collection of records containing many dimensions

COMMIT COMMIT in the context of Oracle Server refers to the transaction control command that results in the permanent record of the pending changes to the data.

Composite Key Composite key in the context of the relational model; refers to the keys (unique, primary or foreign)

Consolidation When data belonging to a subject area has to come from more than one system of records, (database application or manual record keeping), data sets have to go through a consolidation process and made homogeneous in the eyes of the data warehouse end-user.

Context Retrieval Retrieving more information from many documents as it relates to specific term or concept.

Coupling Directly inter dependency among entities (e.g. coupled systems.)

Data Aggregation Creating a profile of data over some period of time. For instance, weekly transactions are gathered and summarized into one record representing the weekly activities.

Data Cleansing Removing multiple, overlapping and sometimes confusing definition or representation of the same concept at the data value level. For instance, removing multiple names of the same customer and using only one of them.

Data Definition Formal representation of a business concept in terms of database fields, data sets, conditional search criteria, and calculation.

Data Dictionary A catalogue of database objects and data instances and their definitions.

Data Extraction The process of copying and replicating the data sets from the source systems to the data warehouse staging environment.

Data Integration Merging semantically homogeneous data sets coming from different application systems into a unified database entity.

Data Mart Subset of data from data warehouse as it relates to special needs of an operating environment.

Data Mining The techniques used in the process of knowledge discovery in databases.

Data Quality The measure of the integrity and correctness of data compared to its source. Data integrity validation is the process of verifying the data extracted is accurate and usable.

Data Metrics A measure of how much data in the data warehouse is being managed , accessed, by who and when.

Data Refreshment Every time new data records are loaded into the data warehouse and integrated with the existing records.

Data Scrubbing Also referred to as data cleansing, it refers to the removal of any anomalies and inconsistancies in the data values. The process of standardizing the reference data.

Data Transformation It is the process of extracting, cleaning, loading and storing in the data warehouse. Data transformation mapping provides information on the identity, usability and business definition and assumptions as it travels from one end of the data warehouse to the other.

Data Design Figuring out how the data will be arranged in the data warehouse based on the data architecture.

Data Source The process of identifying where the interesting data exists and validating that the data, as defined by users, is actually there.

Database Administration A collection of day to day and strategic plans and tasks necessary to insure database services integrity, availability, security, reliability, S/W installation and upgrades.

Database Instance In context of an Oracle architecture, a database instance is the database state point in time as described by the content of SGA and state of the background processes.

Database Transaction Logging In context of Oracle architecture, the transaction logging is done through the Redo log buffers, Redo log background process and the Redo log files.

Database Server In the context of Oracle Client/Server, the database application and database server is separated into front-end client application and back-end database server. It consists of the Oracle software that handles the requests coming from the client applications.

DATAFILE In context of Oracle architecture. The database files dedicated to data blocks.

Transaction Control Statement In the context of Oracle architecture, these statements manage the changes made by DML statements. The COMMIT, ROLLBACK, and SET TRANSACTION are examples of Transaction Control Statements. They also group DML statements into a single transaction.

DDL It refers to Database Definition Language. The database language that is used to define and modify database objects structure. CREATE, ALTER, DROP are examples of Data Definition Language.

Decision Support Applications Special database applications specially built to facilitate the information based analysis and research processes.

De-fragmentation The process of reallocating data in non-contiguous blocks and extents into consecutive blocks while maintaining the data integrity. On context of Oracle Server, this can be done through Export/Import utilities and re-creating the table.

De-normalization It is the reverse process of normalization in a relational model. Denormalization of a few related entities is achieved through creating a new entity by joining the other entities through their foreign keys.

Dimensional Modeling It is the process of identifying and describing the entities, attributes and relationships (association and hierarchical) among data elements, using the star schema modeling techniques.

Direct Load In context of Oracle server, it is the process of storing data into the database using a path (utility, option) that bypasses the Oracle buffer cache.

Direct Read In context of Oracle server, it is the process of reading data from I/O subsystems through bypassing the data blocks in SGA.

Vertical Applications Vertical applications refers to specialized and customized applications that represent a single line of business.

Virtual Data Warehouse Virtual data warehouse refers to a layer of OLTP operational systems that performs the selection, cleansing, aggregation and publishing of the subject areas intended for the data warehouse. It is not a separate and independent system or database.

Visual Data Warehouse Visual data warehouse refers to IBM's version of a data warehousing solution.

VLDB VLDB in the context of database technologies refers to Very Large Database servers that are capable of managing over 1 terabyte of data.

VLM VLM in the context of the computer architecture is refers to Very Large Memory feature of a server that is capable of providing over 32 Gig of main memory.

Warehouse Server Warehouse server in the context of data warehousing is refers to the platform that house the back-end database serves of the data warehouse architecture.

Index

A

B

C

E

P

Q

R

S

T

U

V

W

Z

meta

1) Funding — STRATEGY — Final goal; user objectives; discuss data (historical) depth + breadth

Funding IS business

2) understand — ANALYSIS — modeling; business rules

subject, attributes, ranges, security, audit

CHARACTERIZE info

3) Design — CHARACTERIZE taxonomies; multidimen; concept of outline; explain how to organize the data

PAUSE

model business process, user the data — model (Desk) Document Develop

Build

integration Jobs + events — Testing — security data, so much time to test as to model

Rollout

Support

---

* Do these 3 steps best · to do a demo to ensure the $$

- impact analysis